Susan Stebbing

OXFORD NEW HISTORIES OF PHILOSOPHY

Series Editors

Christia Mercer, Melvin Rogers, and Eileen O'Neill (1953–2017)

*

Advisory Board

Lawrie Balfour, Jacqueline Broad, Marguerite Deslauriers, Karen Detlefsen, Bachir Diagne, Don Garrett, Robert Gooding-Williams, Andrew Janiak, Marcy Lascano, Lisa Shapiro, Tommie Shelby

*

Oxford New Histories of Philosophy provides essential resources for those aiming to diversify the content of their philosophy courses, revisit traditional narratives about the history of philosophy, or better understand the richness of philosophy's past. Examining previously neglected or understudied philosophical figures, movements, and traditions, the series includes both innovative new scholarship and new primary sources.

*

Published in the series

Mexican Philosophy in the 20th Century: Essential Readings
Edited by Carlos Alberto Sánchez and Robert Eli Sanchez Jr.

Sophie de Grouchy's Letters on Sympathy: *A Critical Engagement with Adam Smith's* The Theory of Moral Sentiments
Edited by Sandrine Bergès and Eric Schliesser. Translated by Sandrine Bergès.

Margaret Cavendish: Essential Writings
Edited by David Cunning

Women Philosophers of Seventeenth-Century England: Selected Correspondence
Edited by Jacqueline Broad

The Correspondence of Catharine Macaulay
Edited by Karen Green

Mary Shepherd's Essays on the Perception of an External Universe
Edited by Antonia Lolordo

Women Philosophers of Eighteenth-Century England: Selected Correspondence
Edited by Jacqueline Broad

Frances Power Cobbe: Essential Writings of a Nineteenth-Century Feminist Philosopher
Edited by Alison Stone

Korean Women Philosophers and the Ideal of a Female Sage: Essential Writings of Im Yungjidang and Gang Jeongildang
Edited and Translated by Philip J. Ivanhoe and Hwa Yeong Wang

Louise Dupin's Work on Women: *Selections*
Edited and Translated by Angela Hunter and Rebecca Wilkin

Edith Landmann-Kalischer: Essays on Art, Aesthetics, and Value
Edited by Samantha Matherne. Translated by Daniel O. Dahlstrom

Mary Ann Shadd Cary: Essential Writings of a Nineteenth-Century Black Radical Feminist
Edited by Nneka D. Dennie

Slavery and Race: Philosophical Debates in the Eighteenth-Century
Julia Jorati

Maria W. Stewart: Essential Writings of a Nineteenth-Century Black Abolitionist
Edited by Douglas A. Jones Jr.

Slavery and Race: Philosophical Debates in the Sixteenth and Seventeenth Centuries
Julia Jorati

The Emotions of Nonviolence: Revisiting Martin Luther King Jr.'s
"Letter from Birmingham Jail"
Meena Krishnamurthy

Susan Stebbing: Analysis, Common Sense, and Public Philosophy
Edited by Annalisa Coliva and Louis Doulas

Susan Stebbing

Analysis, Common Sense, and Public Philosophy

Edited by
ANNALISA COLIVA AND LOUIS DOULAS

OXFORD
UNIVERSITY PRESS

Oxford University Press is a department of the University of Oxford.
It furthers the University's objective of excellence in research, scholarship,
and education by publishing worldwide. Oxford is a registered trade mark of
Oxford University Press in the UK and in certain other countries.

Published in the United States of America by Oxford University Press
198 Madison Avenue, New York, NY 10016, United States of America.

© Oxford University Press 2025

All rights reserved. No part of this publication may be reproduced, stored in a retrieval system, transmitted, used for text and data mining, or used for training artificial intelligence, in any form or by any means, without the prior permission in writing of Oxford University Press, or as expressly permitted by law, by license or under terms agreed with the appropriate reprographics rights organization. Inquiries concerning reproduction outside the scope of the above should be sent to the Rights Department, Oxford University Press, at the address above.

You must not circulate this work in any other form
and you must impose this same condition on any acquirer.

CIP data is on file at the Library of Congress

ISBN 9780197682340 (pbk.)
ISBN 9780197682333 (hbk.)

DOI: 10.1093/9780197682371.001.0001

Paperback printed by Marquis Book Printing, Canada
Hardback printed by Lightning Source, Inc., United States of America

The manufacturer's authorized representative in the EU for product safety is
Oxford University Press España S.A., Parque Empresarial San Fernando de Henares,
Avenida de Castilla, 2 – 28830 Madrid (www.oup.es/en).

Contents

Detailed Contents	ix
Series Editors' Foreword	xiii
Acknowledgments	xv
List of Abbreviations	xvii
List of Contributors	xix

Introduction: Susan Stebbing: Analysis, Common Sense, and Public Philosophy   1
Annalisa Coliva and Louis Doulas

SECTION I. THE SIGNIFICANCE OF SUSAN STEBBING'S WORK ON ANALYSIS

The Significance of Susan Stebbing's Work on Analysis   31
Annalisa Coliva

Stebbing on Clarity   52
Eric Schliesser

SECTION II. PUBLIC PHILOSOPHY, SCIENCE, AND COMMON SENSE

Susan Stebbing's Anti-Idealist Philosophy of Physics: Her Rebuttal of Eddington's Argument from Intrinsic Nature   81
Frederique Janssen-Lauret

Making Sense of Stebbing and Moore on Common Sense   101
Louis Doulas

Susan Stebbing's Critique of Popular Science: Guiding or Gatekeeping?   128
Karl Egerton

viii CONTENTS

Stebbing's Pelicans: Public Philosophy in *Philosophy and the Physicists* and *Thinking to Some Purpose*   151
   Peter West

SECTION III. THE LOGIC AND POLITICS OF EVERYDAY LANGUAGE

Susan Stebbing and Some Poorly Explored Venues of Analytic Philosophy   173
   Nikolay Milkov

Susan Stebbing and the Politics of Symbolic Logic   193
   David E. Dunning

SECTION IV. NATURAL LANGUAGE, DEFINITIONS, AND VERBAL DISPUTES

Susan Stebbing: Philosophy, Pragmatics, and Critical Discourse Analysis   211
   Siobhan Chapman

Stebbing on Linguistic Convention: Understanding, Definition, and Verbal Disputes   230
   Bryan Pickel

Stebbing, Translations, and Verbal Disputes   252
   Teresa Kouri Kissel

Name Index   267
Subject Index   269

Detailed Contents

Series Editors' Foreword	xiii
Acknowledgments	xv
List of Abbreviations	xvii
List of Contributors	xix

Introduction: Susan Stebbing: Analysis, Common Sense,
and Public Philosophy   1
  Annalisa Coliva and Louis Doulas
  1   Susan Stebbing: A Biographical Sketch   3
  2   Reception, Marginalization, and Rediscovery   8
  3   The Structure and Content of the Volume   12
    3.1   The Significance of Susan Stebbing's Work on Analysis   12
    3.2   Public Philosophy, Science, and Common Sense   15
    3.3   The Logic and Politics of Everyday Language   20
    3.4   Natural Language, Definitions, and Verbal Disputes   22

SECTION I. THE SIGNIFICANCE OF SUSAN STEBBING'S WORK ON ANALYSIS

The Significance of Susan Stebbing's Work on Analysis   31
  Annalisa Coliva
  1   Introduction   31
  2   Stebbing on Metaphysical Analysis   32
  3   The Epistemological Significance of "The Method of Analysis in
    Metaphysics"   34
  4   The Significance of Metaphysical Analysis, Its Aims and Limitations   39
  5   Conclusions   49

Stebbing on Clarity   52
  Eric Schliesser
  1   Prelude: From the Way of Ideas to How to Make Our Ideas Clear   53
  2   The Standard Conception of Clarity in Early Analytic Philosophy   55
  3   Stebbing on Analytic Clarification   58
  4   Nagel and Carnap   64
  5   Stebbing on Democratic Clarity   67

X DETAILED CONTENTS

SECTION II. PUBLIC PHILOSOPHY, SCIENCE, AND COMMON SENSE

Susan Stebbing's Anti-Idealist Philosophy of Physics:
Her Rebuttal of Eddington's Argument from Intrinsic Nature   81
Frederique Janssen-Lauret
  1 Introduction: Stebbing's Anti-Idealist Philosophy of Physics
     and Her Differences from Moore   81
  2 Analytic Philosophy and the Interpretation of Modern Physics:
     Stebbing's Views   83
  3 Eddington's Argument from Intrinsic Nature   94
  4 Stebbing's Objections   97
  5 Conclusion   98

Making Sense of Stebbing and Moore on Common Sense   101
Louis Doulas
  1 Introduction   101
  2 The Basics of Common Sense   103
  3 Between Ecumenical and Sectarian Readings   107
  4 Common-Sense Knowledge as Scientific Knowledge   115
  5 Stebbing's Unity Thesis   120

Susan Stebbing's Critique of Popular Science: Guiding or
Gatekeeping?   128
Karl Egerton
  1 Introduction   128
  2 The Fear of Gatekeeping   129
  3 The Strategies of *Philosophy and the Physicists*   131
    3.1 The Work at a Glance   131
    3.2 Misled by Metaphor   132
    3.3 Evasive Equivocation   138
    3.4 Haziness on History   140
    3.5 Bringing the Strands of Critique Together   143
  4 *Philosophy and the Physicists* in Context   144
  5 Guiding Without Gatekeeping Today   146

Stebbing's Pelicans: Public Philosophy in *Philosophy and
the Physicists* and *Thinking to Some Purpose*   151
Peter West
Introduction   151
  1 The Audience, Targets, and Aims of Stebbing's Pelicans   153
    1.1 *Philosophy and the Physicists*   153
    1.2 Thinking to Some Purpose   156
  2 A Unified Project   159

DETAILED CONTENTS   xi

3 Stebbing's Public Philosophy	163
3.1 Public Philosophy and Thinking Clearly	163
3.2 A "Skills and Training" Approach to Public Philosophy	165
Conclusion	169

SECTION III. THE LOGIC AND POLITICS OF EVERYDAY LANGUAGE

Susan Stebbing and Some Poorly Explored Venues of Analytic Philosophy	173
Nikolay Milkov	
Overview	173
1 Introduction	173
2 Susan Stebbing and Analytic Philosophy	174
2.1 Stebbing's Progress Toward Analytic Philosophy	174
2.2 Stebbing as Analytic Philosopher	175
3 Susan Stebbing on Thinking and Politics	177
3.1 Logic and Thinking	177
3.2 Ethics and Political Philosophy	179
4 Early English Analytic Philosophy vis-à-vis Social and Political Problems	182
4.1 Russell on Rationality and Thinking	185
4.2 Stebbing's Project after the Second World War	188
5 Stebbing's Project and Late Analytic Philosophy	189
6 Epilogue	190

Susan Stebbing and the Politics of Symbolic Logic	193
David E. Dunning	
1 Introduction	193
2 Logical Pedagogy: Two Divisions of Labor	195
3 Between Normativity and Expertise	200
4 Finding Politics, Finding *Purpose*	202
5 What Logic Can and Cannot Do	204
6 Conclusion: Logic as a Condition of Freedom	205

SECTION IV. NATURAL LANGUAGE, DEFINITIONS, AND VERBAL DISPUTES

Susan Stebbing: Philosophy, Pragmatics, and Critical Discourse Analysis	211
Siobhan Chapman	
1 Introduction	211

xii DETAILED CONTENTS

2	Stebbing on Natural Language	213
3	Linguistic Approaches to Natural Language	220
	3.1 Pragmatics	220
	3.2 Critical Discourse Analysis	224
4	Conclusions	227

Stebbing on Linguistic Convention: Understanding, Definition, and Verbal Disputes

Bryan Pickel

		230
1	Convention in Language	231
	1.1 Natural and Conventional Signs	231
	1.2 Conventional Use	235
	1.3 Sentence Meaning	235
2	Definition	237
	2.1 What Is a Definition?	238
	2.2 Definition Versus Introduction	239
3	Consequences	242
	3.1 Are Definitions Arbitrary?	242
	3.2 Verbal Disputes	244
4	Analyticity and Logic	246
5	Conclusion	249

Stebbing, Translations, and Verbal Disputes

Teresa Kouri Kissel

		252
1	Overview	252
2	Introduction	252
3	The Translation Test in *Ideals and Illusions*	253
4	Translations and Analyses	255
5	Verbal Disputes	261
6	Stebbing's Solution to Vermeulen's Problem	263
7	Conclusion	264

Name Index	267
Subject Index	269

Series Editors' Foreword

Oxford New Histories of Philosophy (ONHP) speaks to a new climate in philosophy.

There is a growing awareness that philosophy's past is richer and more diverse than previously understood. It has become clear that canonical figures are best studied in a broad context. More exciting still is the recognition that our philosophical heritage contains long-forgotten innovative ideas, movements, and thinkers. Sometimes these thinkers warrant serious study in their own right; sometimes their importance resides in the conversations they helped reframe or problems they devised; often their philosophical proposals force us to rethink long-held assumptions about a period or genre; and frequently they cast well-known philosophical discussions in a fresh light.

There is also a mounting sense among philosophers that our discipline benefits from a diversity of perspectives and a commitment to inclusiveness. In a time when questions about justice, inequality, dignity, education, discrimination, and climate (to name a few) are especially vivid, it is appropriate to mine historical texts for insights that can shift conversations and reframe solutions. Given that philosophy's very long history contains astute discussions of a vast array of topics, the time is right to cast a broad historical net.

Lastly, there is increasing interest among philosophy instructors in speaking to the diversity and concerns of their students. Although historical discussions and texts can serve as a powerful means of doing so, finding the necessary time and tools to excavate long-buried historical materials is challenging.

Oxford New Histories of Philosophy is designed to address all these needs. It contains new editions and translations of significant historical texts. These primary materials make available, often for the first time, ideas and works by women, people of colour, and movements in philosophy's past that were groundbreaking in their day but left out of traditional accounts. Informative introductions help instructors and students navigate the new material. Alongside its primary texts, ONHP also publishes

xiv SERIES EDITORS' FOREWORD

monographs and collections of essays that offer philosophically subtle analyses of understudied topics, movements, and figures. In combining primary materials and astute philosophical analyses, ONHP makes it easier for philosophers, historians, and instructors to include in their courses and research exciting new materials drawn from philosophy's past.

ONHP's range is wide, both historically and culturally. The series includes, for example, the writings of African American philosophers, twentieth-century Mexican philosophers, early modern and late medieval women, Islamic and Jewish authors, and non-western thinkers. It excavates and analyses problems and ideas that were prominent in their day but forgotten by later historians. And it serves as a significant aid to philosophers in teaching and researching this material.

As we expand the range of philosophical voices, it is important to acknowledge one voice responsible for this series. Eileen O'Neill was a series editor until her death, December 1, 2017. She was instrumental in motivating and conceptualizing ONHP. Her brilliant scholarship, advocacy, and generosity made all the difference to the efforts that this series is meant to represent. She will be deeply missed, as a scholar and a friend.

We are proud to contribute to philosophy's present and to a richer understanding of its past.

Christia Mercer and Melvin Rogers
Series Editors

Acknowledgments

The editors would like to thank Christia Mercer and Melvin Rogers for their unfaltering support of the present volume and its inclusion in the *Oxford New Histories of Philosophy* series. They would also like to thank two anonymous referees, and all contributors to the volume for their tremendous work, and Peter Ohlin at Oxford University Press, for making it possible.

Abbreviations

References to the Works of Arthur Eddington
NPW   *The Nature of the Physical World*

References to the Works of G. E. Moore
DCS   "A Defence of Common Sense"
HP   "Hume's Philosophy"
LP   *Lectures on Philosophy*
NROP   "The Nature and Reality of Objects of Perception"
PEW   "Proof of an External World"
RMC   "A Reply to My Critics"
SMPP   *Some Main Problems of Philosophy*

References to the Works of Susan Stebbing
LPA   "Logical Positivism and Analysis"
MAM   "The Method of Analysis in Metaphysics"
MEL   *A Modern Elementary Logic*
MIL   *A Modern Introduction to Logic*
MI   "Moore's Influence"
PP   *Philosophy and the Physicists*
RMP   "Realism and Modern Physics"
SPA   "Some Puzzles About Analysis"
TSP   *Thinking to Some Purpose*

References to the Works of Ludwig Wittgenstein
OC   *On Certainty*
PI   *Philosophical Investigations*

Contributors

Siobhan Chapman is professor of English at the University of Liverpool. She has published widely on pragmatics and the history of analytic philosophy. Her publications include *Susan Stebbing and the Language of Common Sense* (Palgrave 2013) and *The Pragmatics of Revision: George Moore's Acts of Rewriting* (Palgrave 2020).

Annalisa Coliva is Chancellor's Professor in the Department of Philosophy, University of California Irvine. She has published widely on Moore and Wittgenstein, hinge epistemology, and the self and self-knowledge. Her latest books are *Wittgenstein Rehinged: The Relevance of* On Certainty *for Contemporary Epistemology* (Anthem 2022); *Skepticism* (Routledge 2022), with Duncan Pritchard; *Relativism* (Routledge 2020), with Maria Baghramian; and *Wittgenstein and Social Epistemology* (Cambridge University Press 2025). Her *Social and Applied Hinge Epistemology* is forthcoming (Oxford University Press).

Louis Doulas is a Postdoctoral Fellow in the Extending New Narratives in the History of Philosophy project at McGill University. His research is both historical and theoretical, focusing on the history of analytic philosophy—particularly the work of Susan Stebbing and G. E. Moore—and on issues in epistemology and methodology. His articles have appeared in such venues as the *Journal of the History of Philosophy*, *Philosophical Studies*, and *Analysis*.

David E. Dunning is a curator of history of science at the Smithsonian's National Museum of American History, where he works with the museum's mathematics and computer collections. He has published widely in the history of logic. He is currently completing a book manuscript on the emergence of logic as a mathematical discipline and its role in the development of digital computers and AI.

Karl Egerton is assistant professor at the University of Nottingham. Within his research interest in the history of analytic philosophy he has published work on the legacy of W. V. Quine and of Susan Stebbing, and he has also published research in metametaphysics, the philosophy of games, and medical ethics.

Frederique Janssen-Lauret is senior lecturer in philosophy at the University of Manchester. Her work spans philosophical logic and the history of logic and analytic philosophy. She is the author of *Susan Stebbing* (Cambridge University Press 2022), the editor of *Quine, Structure, and Ontology* (Oxford University Press 2020), and joint translator and editor of Quine's *The Significance of the New Logic* (Cambridge

xx CONTRIBUTORS

University Press 2018). She has published numerous articles on logic, Stebbing, W. V. Quine, Ruth Barcan Marcus, and others in major journals such as *Philosophical Quarterly, Synthese*, and the *British Journal for the History of Philosophy*.

Teresa Kouri Kissel is associate professor of philosophy at Old Dominion University in Norfolk, Virginia. Her primary interests are in philosophy of logic, mathematics, and language, with a focus on the relationship between the meanings of the connectives in formal and natural languages. She just finished an NEH Fellowship to complete a book on Stebbing's notion of common sense.

Nikolay Milkov is professor of philosophy at the University of Paderborn. He has published widely on the history of analytic philosophy. His most recent publications include *A Hundred Years of English Philosophy* (Kluwer 2003); *Early Analytic Philosophy and the German Philosophical Tradition* (Bloomsbury 2020); and *Hermann Lotze's Influence on Twentieth Century Philosophy* (De Gruyter 2023).

Bryan Pickel is senior lecturer in philosophy at the University of Glasgow. His main areas of research are metaphysics, the philosophy of language, and the history of analytic philosophy. He is working on a book on *The Structure of the Proposition*.

Eric Schliesser is professor of political science, with a focus on political theory, at the University of Amsterdam. His publications include his monograph, *Adam Smith: Systematic Philosopher and Public Thinker* (2017), and together with Sandrine Berges *Sophie de Grouchy's Letters on Sympathy: A Critical Engagement with Adam Smith's The Theory of Moral Sentiments* (2019). He has edited numerous volumes including *Ten Neglected Classics of Philosophy* (2017), *Neglected Classics of Philosophy: Volume 2* (2022), all with Oxford University Press. He has also co-edited a special issue, "Women in Early Analytic Philosophy," of the *Journal for the History of Analytical Philosophy* (2017) with Maria van der Schaar.

Peter West is assistant professor in philosophy at Northeastern University London. His work focuses on two areas in philosophy's history: early modern philosophy, with special attention to the philosophy of mind in Berkeley, Cavendish, Shepherd, and early analytic philosophy, with a focus on a generation of women in early twentieth century British philosophy, including Susan Stebbing, Dorothy Emmet, and Margaret Macdonald.

Introduction

Susan Stebbing: Analysis, Common Sense, and Public Philosophy

Annalisa Coliva and Louis Doulas

I always wished that she would write a book, or at least a paper, free from the pressure of other duties or any promise to have it done by a certain time. But no—there was always something, if not a committee meeting then a taxi for Ireland, and with a suitcase in her hand and a hat trifle insecure upon her head she would be gone.

— John Wisdom (1948: 2)

Susan Stebbing was busy. From the publication of her MA thesis in 1914[1] to her final writings in the early 1940s, she produced a remarkable body of work: seven books,[2] some 120 articles and reviews, and countless lectures. This work—spanning logic, language, metaphysics, critical thinking, ethics, and the philosophy of science—was written for both academic philosophers and a broader public, a public that she believed had both the right and the need to think clearly in an era of political confusion, the misleading rhetoric of popular science, and the rise of authoritarianism.

Her books were widely read and frequently reprinted. *A Modern Introduction to Logic* (1930) was the first textbook of its time to integrate the "new logic" of Frege and of Whitehead and Russell's *Principia Mathematica* with traditional syllogistic logic, while also relating them to

---

[1] *Pragmatism and French Voluntarism* (1914).
[2] Excluding her published MA thesis mentioned above, these books are: *A Modern Introduction to Logic* (1930); *Logic in Practice* (1934); *Philosophy and the Physicists* (1937); *Thinking to Some Purpose* (1939); *Ideals and Illusions* (1941); and *A Modern Elementary Logic* (1943).

2 SUSAN STEBBING

broader issues in scientific reasoning and methodology.[3] *Thinking to Some Purpose* (1939), written in response to the growing misuse of language and reasoning in public and political discourse, became a Penguin best-seller in Britain. Many of her journal articles were similarly influential and widely discussed. Key interventions, such as "The Method of Analysis in Metaphysics" (1932–33) and her 1933 British Academy Lecture, "Logical Positivism and Analysis," helped advance central methods and debates in early analytic philosophy, bridging conversations between Cambridge and the Continent.

And then, of course, there was everything in between—the meetings, appointments, and taxis to somewhere, alluded to above by her colleague John Wisdom. All of it reflected Stebbing's active role in shaping the institutional life of British philosophy and beyond, assuming roles that were, at the time, rare for a woman and all the more influential for the field. A visiting professorship in 1931 took her to Columbia University, where she lectured on mathematical logic and metaphysics. She served as president of both the Aristotelian Society and the Mind Association. In 1933, she co-founded the journal *Analysis*, which would soon become highly influential.[4] In that same year, she made literal headlines by becoming the first woman in Britain to hold a chair in philosophy.

While Stebbing may not have produced a single work entirely free from the pressures of her career, her output was nothing short of extraordinary. All this was accomplished within a system that, as a woman and a person with disabilities,[5] afforded her few structural advantages. Despite these constraints, Stebbing not only secured a place for herself as a leading figure in British academic philosophy, but also helped grow the analytic tradition at its foundations—a tradition that continues to bear the mark of her influence, even if her name has all too often been absent from its narratives.

Wisdom's image in the epigraph—of Stebbing with her hat slightly askew, already out the door—captures something essential. Even in motion, even under pressure, Stebbing left behind a body of work that remains urgent, relevant, and deeply worth returning to.

---

[3] At the time, "[n]o other book of its kind had then been published," writes Wisdom (1948: 2). Michael Beaney has also suggested that it "might be regarded as the first textbook of analytic philosophy" (2013: 43).
[4] Among the journal's co-founders were Austin Duncan-Jones (who served as its first editor), C. A. Mace, and Gilbert Ryle.
[5] Stebbing suffered from Ménière's disease. See §1 below.

INTRODUCTION 3

1 Susan Stebbing: A Biographical Sketch

"Lizzie Susan" Stebbing was born in 1885 in Finchley, North London, the youngest of six children. She suffered early on from Ménière's disease, a chronic disorder that causes bouts of vertigo and tinnitus and would struggle with its often-debilitating symptoms for the entirety of her life.[6] As a result, the young Stebbing's health was deemed precarious, and she was determined to be unfit for full-time schooling; Stebbing's early education would therefore be the product of homeschooling. Eventually, however, she would go on to study at the recently opened Girton College, Cambridge,[7] the first women's college in the United Kingdom. Initially interested in reading for a science degree,[8] Stebbing's poor and unpredictable health prohibited her from doing so.[9] She studied history instead, taking Part I and II of the History Tripos in 1906 and 1907, respectively.

But in 1907 something happened. Studying in the library for Part II of the History Tripos, Stebbing stumbled upon F. H. Bradley's *Appearance and Reality* and was apparently so gripped that she decided that she would also go for the Moral Sciences Tripos. And so, she did.[10] Receiving training from the logician W. E. Johnson,[11] Stebbing took (and passed) Part I of the Moral Science Tripos in 1908, a year after completing the History Tripos.

Though women were able to take the Tripos and be awarded the requisite classifications, they would not go on to receive degrees; Cambridge and Oxford, among several other British institutions, refused degrees to women at this time. Consequently, despite being educated in two subjects, Stebbing would not receive degrees in either one. Indeed, it would not be possible for

[6] Chapman (2013: 42) notes that Stebbing often refers to her ill health in both her personal correspondence and professional papers.

[7] Girton was founded in 1869 and opened in 1873, only twelve years before Stebbing was born.

[8] There are slightly conflicting reports here, as Chapman (2013: 11) has pointed out. In Stebbing's *Mind* obituary, for example, it's reported that she was initially interested in reading classics. As indicated by Chapman, however, the *Mind* obituary contains a slew of biographical errors. Another obituary in the *Girton Review* claims that Stebbing was originally interested in reading for a science degree, a claim that is apparently based on the testimony of one of her friends.

[9] Janssen-Lauret (2022: 9) suggests that there may have been gendered pressures that pulled Stebbing away from both classics and the sciences given that these were highly "male-coded" fields in nineteenth-century academia.

[10] This story appears in several accounts of Stebbing's early intellectual life, though it may be somewhat apocryphal. The anecdote nevertheless captures something of the decisive shift in Stebbing's intellectual interests during this period.

[11] Another logician active during this period was E. E. Constance Jones, mistress of Girton College and a protégé of Henry Sidgwick. She was also the first woman to speak at the Cambridge Moral Sciences Club. Although Stebbing didn't officially study with her, she did engage with Jones's work on logic.

4 SUSAN STEBBING

a woman to earn a degree from Cambridge in Stebbing's lifetime; the first degree wouldn't be awarded to a Cambridge-educated woman until 1948—five years after Stebbing's death.[12]

Rather than remain at Cambridge to complete Part II of the Moral Tripos, Stebbing decided to leave, heading south to the University of London, to pursue an MA in Moral Science. There, she could earn a degree,[13] doing so in 1912 from King's College with a thesis on American pragmatism and French voluntarism. Some of Stebbing's first published articles emerge around this time, including a paper criticizing Henri Bergson's theory of knowledge in 1913 and a 1915 defense of Aristotelian logic, responding to attacks on its philosophical relevance.[14] Stebbing's masterful study of a logic far more powerful than Aristotle's syllogistic system would appear thirteen years later. It was also around this time, 1917, that Stebbing encountered a philosopher—"not [Bertrand] Russell"—at a meeting of the Aristotelian Society "who began to ask me questions with a vehement insistence that considerably alarmed me" (1942: 530). The questions were directed at Stebbing's paper, "Relation and Coherence" (1916–17), which she had just finished reading to the Society. The questions continued, and by the end, this philosopher had, according to Stebbing, "unraveled [her] muddles and enabled [her] to see more clearly" (1942: 530).

Stebbing would soon discover that this philosopher was none other than G. E. Moore. She would joust with him again at the Society's following meeting, in 1918, where she would criticize some of his ideas in her paper "The Philosophical Importance of the Verb 'To Be'" (1917–18). Both occasions prompted a spirited correspondence that developed into a lifelong friendship, one that also included Moore's wife, Dorothy Moore.[15]

Between her MA graduation in 1912 and 1920, Stebbing struggled to find a permanent academic position. She held several temporary, part-time teaching posts in both London and Cambridge which also included a brief stint as a

---

[12] Oxford began granting degrees to women slightly earlier, in 1920.

[13] The University of London granted degrees to women beginning in 1878.

[14] See Stebbing (1913) and Stebbing (1915), respectively. Stebbing's early work on Bergson remains relatively underexplored, though recent scholarship has begun to shed light on this aspect of her thought. See Vrahimis (2022, chapter 7) and Day (2023). See also Moravec and West (2023) who argue that Bergson may have been one of Stebbing's hidden interlocutors in *Philosophy and the Physicists*.

[15] See, for instance, the twenty extant letters from Stebbing to Moore (and Dorothy), dated between 1918 and 1942, housed in the Cambridge University Library. That Stebbing was influenced by Moore is evident in her writings and has been noted by several commentators (Milkov 2003; Beaney 2003, 2016; Chapman 2013; Beaney and Chapman 2017). This influence, however, is sometimes overstated, leading to a reductive—"Moorean"—reading of her philosophical contributions. See Coliva (this volume), Doulas (this volume), and Janssen-Lauret (this volume) for further discussion.

INTRODUCTION 5

schoolteacher in 1915.[16] She also retained ties with Girton College where, while finishing her degree at the University of London, she had become a Visiting Lecturer in 1911, before becoming director of Moral Science Studies in 1918. Yet, even with these appointments, Stebbing's future remained uncertain. Despite this, she managed to publish seven articles, many of them appearing in *Mind* and the *Proceedings of the Aristotelian Society*, where she criticized pragmatic conceptions of truth. There was also the publication of her first book, *Pragmatism and French Voluntarism* (1914), which was drawn from her MA thesis and published by Cambridge University Press.

Having experienced the atrocities of the Great War, Stebbing found herself compelled to act. Lecturing on behalf of the League of Nations Union, she traveled the country after the World War I to promote pacifism. When those efforts were eventually met in vain twenty-one years later, she helped take in Jewish refugees from Nazi-occupied countries.[17] By 1920, however, Stebbing had secured an appointment as an assistant lecturer in philosophy at Bedford College (now Royal Holloway, University of London), a women's college in London. Things moved quickly from there: she was promoted to lecturer the following year, securing a five-year appointment, and by 1923–24 was offered a full-time lectureship—just shy of turning forty. She would remain at Bedford College for the rest of her life.

By the 1920s, Stebbing's philosophical interests had shifted away from the themes of her MA thesis and turned more decisively toward the philosophy of science—particularly the work of Alfred North Whitehead. Whitehead was, for a time, a figure of deep philosophical admiration for Stebbing. Although she would later find his writings increasingly obscure and metaphysically muddled, many of her publications in the philosophy of science remain deeply informed by his ideas.[18] Stebbing also found herself engaged in debates about realism and materialism with respect to modern physics. Here, however, Stebbing found little to admire. Her stance was unabashedly

---

[16] This was at the Kingsley Lodge School for Girls, a school in which Stebbing and two close friends, Vivian Shepherd and Hilda Gavin, had become joint owners. Though Stebbing would teach there only briefly, she would remain closely involved with the school. During World War II, Stebbing would use Kingsley to house refugee children (Chapman 2013: 37, 159).

[17] Chapman (2013: 38, 126).

[18] This is perhaps most evident in Stebbing's endorsement of Whitehead's rejection of "bifurcation theories"—views that divide nature into what are often called primary and secondary qualities, with the latter (e.g., colors, sounds, and scents) typically excluded from accounts of reality. Stebbing states that she is in "complete agreement" with Whitehead on this point and further affirms that "their extrusion [i.e., the extrusion of secondary qualities] leads to a vicious bifurcation" (1928: 114–15). The philosophical relationship between Stebbing and Whitehead remains an important area of scholarship that has yet to be fully explored.

6 SUSAN STEBBING

critical, particularly toward the confused philosophical thinking she identified in the writings of acclaimed physicists like Arthur Eddington and James Jeans, who, in her view, had too hastily drawn metaphysical conclusions from the latest developments in modern physics. "Both these writers," Stebbing remarks, "approach their task through an emotional fog; they present their views with an amount of personification and metaphor that reduces them to the level of revivalist preachers" (1937: 6). The tone was hardly unusual for Stebbing who rarely veered away from telling it like it is.[19]

The next decade, roughly between 1930 and Stebbing's death in 1943, would bring about a flurry of productivity. After the publication of *A Modern Introduction to Logic* in 1930—a book which "confirmed Stebbing's place as a voice in contemporary British philosophy" (Chapman 2013: 58)—Stebbing would devote much philosophical attention to what came to be known as "Cambridge analysis," a label Stebbing very much disliked but which stuck because of the influence exerted by Cambridge-educated Russell and Moore (as well as Wittgenstein) on several younger generations of philosophers. However, it was by no means clear whether each of these figures meant the same thing by "analysis" or what exactly it meant to say that philosophy is concerned with analysis. Indeed, it was this younger group of philosophers—most notably Stebbing and John Wisdom—who believed it was their task to sort this all out.

Many of Stebbing's publications during this period are focused on just that.[20] In fact, Stebbing was arguably among the first to clearly distinguish two kinds of analysis: *metaphysical* analysis (or what Stebbing called "directional" analysis) and *logical* analysis (or what Wisdom called "same-level" analysis).[21] Several of Stebbing's major philosophical contributions came in the form of distinguishing and decoupling metaphysical analysis from logical analysis.[22] Stebbing not only sought to register a distinction between these two different forms of analysis but to show that this was indeed a distinction *with* a difference. Whereas logical analysis aims to replace ordinary, natural language expressions with their logically perspicuous counterparts,

---

[19] Although Stebbing could be just as critical of herself. Many of her papers begin with the frank admission that her earlier ideas were "hopeless" or "muddled." See Chapman (2013: 87) who also comments on this idiosyncrasy.

[20] See especially "The Method of Analysis in Metaphysics" (1932–33); "Logical Positivism and Analysis" (1933); and "Some Puzzles about Analysis" (1938–39).

[21] See Wisdom (1934).

[22] The latter came to be loosely associated with the Vienna school and accordingly came to be known as the "Vienna school of analysis," whereas the former became closely associated with the Cambridge school. See Beaney (2003) for further discussion.

metaphysical analysis aims to uncover, or identify, the ultimate facts that the constituents of propositions refer to.[23] It's this difference in aim and purpose that Stebbing saw the logical positivists (of both the Vienna and Berlin schools) as failing to appreciate and understand. Hence, she saw their treatment of analysis as incomplete.[24]

Increasingly, however, Stebbing began to place little stock in metaphysical analysis, coming to view it as "a hangover from the days when 'the problem of the external world' was envisaged as primarily a problem of justifying common sense beliefs" (1942: 527). Instead, she began turning her attention to logical analysis and the analysis of language. Two books would emerge out of this shift in direction: *Philosophy and the Physicists* (1937) and *Thinking to Some Purpose* (1939), the latter becoming a Penguin best seller in Britain. Their aims were largely to uncover the various ways that language can obfuscate and mislead in the context of popular science and the media, respectively. Written with the intention of reaching a wider audience, "public philosophy" was a genre Stebbing found herself drawn to. This was, perhaps, not without good reason. The world had plunged itself into war—its second in twenty-one years—with horrors even more unimaginable than the first. Stebbing's two books here, along with the later *Ideals and Illusions* (1941) and her posthumously published Hobhouse Memorial lecture, *Men and Moral Principles* (1944), served as handbooks that endeavored to defend democratic ideals. They remained steadfastly focused on instructing people how to think more clearly by paying attention to how language is used by politicians and journalists.[25] Deconstructing examples culled from various news

---

[23] The difference can be captured in a slightly different way. We might say that the relation involved in logical analysis is a symmetrical relation (one of synonymy) whereas the relation involved in metaphysical analysis is an asymmetrical one. See Stebbing (1932: 311, fn. 4) who glosses the difference in a similar way.

[24] For a detailed discussion of Stebbing's views on this point, see Franco (2024). Though Stebbing was critical of various tenets of logical positivism, it's important to keep in mind that—substantive differences aside—she broadly shared the group's vision of a scientifically oriented philosophy, particularly that of Schlick (see Tuboly 2020: 9). She is often credited with helping to introduce positivism to Cambridge and London—for example, by inviting Carnap to deliver three lectures on logical syntax at Bedford College in 1934. Stebbing was also personally connected with several members of the Vienna Circle, most notably Schlick—who was "a great admirer of Professor Stebbing's work" (quoted in Chapman 2013: 88)—and Neurath, who reported to Carnap that they had become "best friends" (quoted in Tuboly 2020: 9). Stebbing later served as president of Neurath's Isotype Institute at Oxford. See Chapman (2013, ch. 5), Beaney (2016), Richardson (2017: 151–55), Körber (2019, 2025), and Körber and Tuboly (2025) for further discussion of Stebbing's relationship to the positivists.

[25] There is a strong intellectualist bent in many of Stebbing's works here. See Pickel (2022) for a qualified defense of this position. See also Kremer (2017: 31) who suggests that Stebbing stands as an unacknowledged but proximate figure within the scope of Ryle's various attacks on intellectualism.

8   SUSAN STEBBING

clippings, Stebbing would show how language is used to deceive and mislead, leading us to error and "potted thinking."[26] Indeed, it was around this time, in 1938, that Stebbing and a group of other writers established *The Modern Quarterly*, a leftist journal "committed to fighting Fascism."[27] Stebbing, despite proclaiming to be "not politically minded,"[28] would have fooled most.

After 1939, Stebbing was busier than ever. While she would no longer publish any full-length journal articles, she would be invited to numerous talks and symposiums, write *A Modern Elementary Logic* (1943), and contribute to the Schilpp volume *The Philosophy of G. E. Moore*. Stebbing's momentum during this time, however, would be short-lived. In 1941, she would be diagnosed with cancer. She would recover, with treatment and an operation, before falling ill again, undergoing yet another operation in July of 1943. It was to no avail: Stebbing would pass away two months later on September 11 of that year. Her future projects—a detailed comparison of Moore and Russell's philosophical development, a book on convention in science, and more—were simply not to be. And, yet, Stebbing already left us with plenty.

2 Reception, Marginalization, and Rediscovery

The case of Susan Stebbing is not necessarily one of *historical* marginalization. Though, of course, Stebbing was working against the patriarchal structures of the Victorian/Edwardian era, as well as British academia and the male-dominated discipline of philosophy,[29] neither she nor her work was neglected by her peers and colleagues. She held presidencies at two of the most prestigious philosophical societies, published in her field's top journals and helped found another, published books with some of the best popular presses, held a permanent lectureship in philosophy at a university

---

For discussion of the relationship between critical thinking and formal logic in several of Stebbing's works above, see Douglas and Nassim (2021). See Milkov (this volume) and Dunning (this volume) for further discussion.

[26] For Stebbing, "potted thinking" refers to the oversimplification of an idea or expression, such as a slogan or catchword. Not all potted thinking is vicious, however.

[27] Chapman (2013: 122).

[28] Stebbing (1939: 254).

[29] A vivid, unfortunate reminder of the times: With G. E. Moore retiring, Stebbing was thought to be a worthy replacement, except her gender precluded her from being seriously considered. In a letter to two close colleagues, Stebbing reports with frustration, "On Thursday, [Gilbert] Ryle . . . annoyed me by saying (re the appointment) 'Of course everyone thinks you are the right person to succeed Moore, except that you are a woman'. (I don't swear those were his words—but as nearly as I remember!)" (quoted in Chapman 2013: 126).

INTRODUCTION 9

in a major city center, and interfaced and debated with some of philosophy's and science's best minds at the time—the same minds who discussed and responded to her work.

Stebbing's case is better characterized as a case of *historiographical* marginalization.[30] Stebbing simply stopped being discussed. Today, she is not a household name; analytic philosophers don't know her and don't read her; she is not mentioned in the same breath as Russell, Moore, or Wittgenstein. Yet, as Michael Beaney has pointed out, "[Stebbing] did more than anyone else to promote the development of analytic philosophy in Britain" (2017: 78). Stebbing, then, was erased from the very discipline she played a foundational role in shaping and developing.

Stebbing's disappearance from the story of analytic philosophy is borne out by a brief survey of the historiographical record. Ten influential histories of analytic philosophy, published between 1949 and 2012, offer a telling illustration of her absence.

Year	Title	Author	Paratextual Mentions of Stebbing
1949	*Elements of Analytic Philosophy*	Arthur Pap	Index: 0 Bib/Ref: 7
1956	*Philosophical Analysis: Its Development Between the Two World Wars*	J. O. Urmson	Index: 4 Bib/Ref: 3
1957	*A Hundred Years of Philosophy*	John Passmore	Index: 16 Bib/Ref: 4
1958	*English Philosophy since 1900*	G. J. Warnock	Index: 0 Bib/Ref: 1
1993	*Origins of Analytic Philosophy*	Michael Dummett	Index: 0 Bib/Ref: 0
2000	*Twentieth-Century Analytic Philosophy*	Avrum Stroll	Index: 0 Bib/Ref: 1
2003a	*Philosophical Analysis in the Twentieth Century, Vol. 1: The Founding Giants*	Scott Soames	Index: 0 Bib/Ref: 0
2003b	*Philosophical Analysis in the Twentieth Century, Vol. 2: The Age of Meaning*	Scott Soames	Index: 0 Bib/Ref: 0
2008	*What is Analytic Philosophy*	Hans-Johann Glock	Index: 0 Bib/Ref: 0
2012	*A Brief History of Analytic Philosophy*	Stephen P. Schwartz	Index: 0 Bib/Ref: 0

---

[30] A helpful discussion of these differences can be found in Peijnenburg and Verhaegh's article "Analytic Women": https://aeon.co/essays/the-lost-women-of-early-analytic-philosophy.

10 SUSAN STEBBING

Stebbing is indexed in only two works: Urmson's 1956 *Philosophical Analysis* (four entries) and Passmore's 1957 *A Hundred Years of Philosophy* (sixteen entries). Urmson's mentions, however, are brief and cursory, though he does credit Stebbing for introducing logical positivism to Cambridge in the early 1930s. By contrast, Passmore's treatment is more generous: one full page of his compressed yet semi-comprehensive 500-page survey of philosophy— from Mill to Ordinary Language Philosophy—is devoted to discussing several of Stebbing's articles, including "The Method of Analysis in Metaphysics" (1932–33). (Passmore, however, misdates the article and incorrectly refers to it as "The Method of Analysis in Philosophy.")

Aside from this, Stebbing's work is only cited in the bibliographies or reference lists of five of the ten texts above. In the earliest of these— Pap's *Elements of Analytic Philosophy* (1949)—her work appears in the "Selected Literature" sections of five chapters.[31] Beyond the inclusion of her essay, "The Method of Analysis in Metaphysics" in the bibliography of Warnock's *English Philosophy since 1900*, and a brief mention of "Moore's Influence" (1942)—her contribution to the Schilpp volume on Moore—in Stroll's *Twentieth-Century Analytic Philosophy*, Stebbing goes otherwise unmentioned and undiscussed in the remaining works. Unsurprisingly, Moore, Russell, and Wittgenstein all have their pride of place.

Stebbing's erasure from the history of analytic philosophy is due to several factors, both philosophical and sociological.[32] Among philosophical ones, the demise of analysis as a focus of analytic philosophers' attention, after the 1930s, likely determined a wane of interest in Stebbing's most important contributions, many of which were on the nature and role of analysis.[33] Moreover, Stebbing's habit of often crediting others, especially Moore, for ideas that were in fact her own, or ostensibly different from those of her colleagues, obscured the originality of her thought and led many to think of her mostly, if not solely, as a "disciple of Moore."[34] There's also the fact that some of Stebbing's most important post-analysis work appears in her books, which take the form of textbooks or public philosophy. But these genres, particularly the latter, have often been undervalued in professional philosophy, viewed as either pedagogical or popular rather than as sites of serious

---

[31] This work includes one of her articles—"Logical Positivism and Analysis"—and two of her books—*A Modern Introduction to Logic* and *Philosophy and the Physicists*.

[32] For broader and more comprehensive accounts of the erasure of women philosophers from the analytic tradition, see Connell and Janssen-Lauret (2022) and Verhaegh and Peijnenburg (2022).

[33] See also Milkov (2003) and Coliva (2021) who suggest something similar.

[34] Ayer (1977: 157–158).

INTRODUCTION 11

philosophical engagement. This attitude, however, is beginning to shift—and for the better. Given this, and the fact that much of this work was produced in the final decade of Stebbing's life, it is plausible that commentators either overlooked it or chose to ignore it.

Sociological factors include the obvious ones, that women did not have access to elite institutions in the UK (and in many other countries too). Recall that Stebbing was unable to receive an actual degree from Cambridge, let alone teach there, and had to complete her studies and take a position elsewhere, in London, in a context that did not allow her to exert the same influence on colleagues and students. (Cambridge was the hotbed of philosophy during this time.) Stebbing's relatively early death at the age of fifty-seven may also have contributed to the limited uptake of her work in subsequent decades—a pattern not uncommon among philosophers, and intellectuals more broadly, whose careers are cut tragically short.[35]

Times are changing, though. In recent years, there has been a notable resurgence of interest in Stebbing's work. Much of this renewed interest is due to the pioneering efforts of Michael Beaney (2003, 2016), Nikolay Milkov (2003), Siobhan Chapman (2013), and Frederique Janssen-Lauret (2017).[36] But it's also a sign of the times: a growing interest in figures at the margins, figures of philosophy who have been blurred out, neglected, or otherwise forgotten, as well as the emergence of the "historical turn" in analytic philosophy,[37] which has brought about a wave of interest in studying the works of analytic philosophy in context.

It is in this spirit that we proudly present this volume—the first dedicated exclusively to the philosophy of Susan Stebbing.[38] Through eleven previously unpublished essays, this book examines the full range of Stebbing's philosophical contributions, reaffirming both her significance within the tradition of analytic philosophy and the enduring relevance of her ideas to issues still under dispute today. Stebbing, we believe, can be considered a "founding

---

[35] Gareth Evans and J. L. Austin are victims of similar circumstances, as their untimely deaths arguably put a sharp halt on their influence. Even so, their posthumous reputations remain considerably more prominent than Stebbing's.

[36] Eric Schliesser has also contributed to the recovery of Stebbing's legacy through a series of blog posts dating back to 2012, published on *Digressions and Impressions* and *New APPS*.

[37] See Reck (2013: 1–36).

[38] Compare this to *Philosophical Studies*, a memorial volume published in 1948 that collects essays written by several of Stebbing's friends and colleagues. However, as the reprint edition acknowledges—and as is evident upon reading—"Most of these essays do not bear directly on Professor Stebbings' work, but they deal with problems which she discussed time and again at the Society's meetings." Hence, while *Philosophical Studies* honors Stebbing's memory and influence, the present volume is the first to be dedicated explicitly and exclusively to her philosophical thought.

12 SUSAN STEBBING

mother" of analytic philosophy, whose work should be regularly taught and researched alongside the work of analytic philosophy's "founding fathers"— Bertrand Russell, G. E. Moore, and (the early) Ludwig Wittgenstein—and its "grandfather"—Gottlob Frege. Moreover, as we shall see, her engagement with what, nowadays, would be considered "public philosophy," and her critique of propaganda, as well as her original take on analysis, which prefigures in several ways today's preoccupations with metaphysics and not just language, and a critique of the analytic/synthetic distinction make her specially attuned to the "metaphysical" as well as the "social turn" taken by analytic philosophy more recently.

3 The Structure and Content of the Volume

3.1 The Significance of Susan Stebbing's Work on Analysis

The volume opens with a section titled "The Significance of Susan Stebbing's Work on Analysis," containing a chapter by the same title by Annalisa Coliva. Coliva acknowledges the crucial contributions made by Stebbing with respect to the nature and role of analysis in philosophy; the relationship between science, philosophy, and common sense; and her role in promoting what, today, would be called "public philosophy," yet she focuses on the first of these seminal contributions.

According to Coliva, Stebbing's metaphysical (or what Stebbing called "directional") analysis was an important and original contribution to the debate about analysis, which occupied philosophers such as Russell, Moore, Wittgenstein, Wisdom, and others, up to the end of the 1930s. Stebbing, Coliva argues, was clearer than any of her contemporaries about the various kinds of analysis—postulational, definitional, clarificatory, and directional. While the former three essentially concern language, concepts, and propositions, the last one is distinctively metaphysical and cannot be conducted solely a priori, according to Stebbing.

Connectedly, Stebbing was critical of those philosophers who thought that analysis could only aim at the clarification of the meaning of our ordinary words, or that it could be conducted merely by a priori means, or that analysis could subvert our commonsensical belief in the existence of physical objects. Metaphysical analysis, as she originally argued, distancing herself from all her colleagues, including Moore, aims at revealing the ultimate truth-makers of our true judgments. In Stebbing's words: "metaphysics aims at making precise the reference of all true beliefs" (1932–33: 70). If carried out, such analysis would thus contribute to our knowledge of the world and to the clarification of our thoughts. It must be stressed that, according to Stebbing, neither the objects that our commonsensical beliefs are about nor their ultimate truth-makers would be, in any sense, our construction. As she aptly quipped in "Logical Positivism and Analysis" (1933: 34): "*points* and *electrons* may be constructs, *tables* certainly are not." Even if at a deeper level of analysis it turns out that tables are composed of electrons, that does not mean that they are inferred from them, or that they are reducible to them, or that they have the properties of their constituents (e.g., lack of solidity); even less that the word "table" should be understood as a shorthand for a definite description ranging over such particles of physics, let alone sense data, *à la* Russell.

In this respect, according to Coliva, Stebbing may thus be seen as a precursor of the denial of the analytic/synthetic distinction. That is, according to Stebbing, we cannot hope to clarify our thoughts merely based on a priori, conceptual, even less, merely linguistic reflection. Rather, conceptual clarifications will be intertwined with empirical and even scientific discoveries (as in the case of the concept of simultaneity after Einstein's relativity theory) and will depend on what basic facts in the world make our commonsensical beliefs about physical objects true.

Still, Stebbing was also acutely aware of the limitations of metaphysical analysis. In particular, she denounced as problematic the ungrounded assumption that such basic facts exist and that we may be able to identify them. Indeed, after her seminal "The Method of Analysis in Metaphysics" (1932–33) she became increasingly aware of this problem, up to her stark rejection of metaphysical analysis in "Moore's Influence" where she stated: "I think there are good reasons for saying that the notion of basic facts is a hangover from the days when 'the problem of the external world' was envisaged as primarily a problem of justifying common sense beliefs" (1942: 57). This passage was preceded a few years earlier by the remark in "Some Puzzles About Analysis":

> I tried to show that, once the assumptions [of metaphysical analysis] were explicitly stated, they did not seem very plausible. It appears that I entirely failed to make this contention clear, for several writers have subsequently taken me to have been defending the use of the method of analysis in metaphysics. (1938–39: 72)

In the second chapter of this first section, Eric Schliesser, in his contribution, "Stebbing on Clarity," focuses on an often-neglected kind of analysis

14 SUSAN STEBBING

Stebbing had discerned, namely, what she called the *analytic clarification of a concept* (see Stebbing 1933). A paradigmatic example of it is Einstein's treatment of simultaneity. This kind of clarification is introduced to "handle instances where a previously relatively successful scientific theory requires non-trivial revision after what we would now call a 'paradigm change'" (Schliesser, this volume). In these cases, we may say something is true even if we do not quite well know what we mean; for it is what a concept like that of simultaneity amounts to becomes clear only after this kind of scientific discovery. Hence, according to Schliesser, "an analytic clarification can (or is) the *effect* of scientific development. The clarity achieved is the product of the growth of science" (Schliesser, this volume). Thus, he quips, "'Analytic clarification of a concept' may be in the running for the worst philosophical coinage for failure to convey what it is trying to describe!" (Schliesser, this volume).

This kind of clarification, however, "does not merely impact the scientific image, it also shifts the manifest image" (Schliesser, this volume). This happens gradually, but it entails that common sense too can "shift like quicksand" (Schliesser, this volume). This is yet another difference between Stebbing and Moore, for the latter, contrary to Wittgenstein in *On Certainty*, was very careful to avoid reference to truisms that could somewhat be seen as the product of scientific investigation percolated within common sense. Finally, since science is open-ended and a communal enterprise, the analytic clarification of a concept may be distributed among scientists and may be subject to continuous changes. Thus, according to Schliesser, "lurking in Stebbing's philosophy, [there is] a call for a kind of individual humility" (Schliesser, this volume), including individual scientists.

Schliesser then turns to what he dubs "democratic clarity," which he finds defended in Stebbing's *Thinking to Some Purpose* (1939). While this is the topic of two other papers in the third section of this volume, and its content will be expanded upon shortly, it merits note that he thinks that, in light of her previous discussion of the analytic clarification of a concept, Stebbing is strangely oblivious to the fact that political parties may play the role of experts in the division of cognitive labor and that deference to them may be a valuable heuristic that allows "individuals to remain in partial darkness while being part of collectives that can act with sufficient enough effectiveness" (Schliesser, this volume). In other words, while Stebbing did see that clarity could sometimes not be obtained by individual thinkers, she nevertheless

INTRODUCTION   15

preached it as an ideal in her later work, despite the fact that on many topics we can do no more and no better than defer to authorities.

3.2 Public Philosophy, Science, and Common Sense

Stebbing was very interested in physics and in its momentous developments at the beginning of the twentieth century. As it seems she was discouraged from formally pursuing it—perhaps due to her disability, which may have made extended lab work difficult[39]—she taught herself a great deal of it. In the 1920s, moreover, influenced by Whitehead's philosophy of science, she started to consider the relationship between modern physics—relativity theory and quantum theory especially—and common sense. In *Philosophy and the Physicists* (1937) Stebbing criticizes religious and idealist interpretations of modern physics as put forward by Sir Arthur Eddington and Sir James Jeans.[40] Stebbing thus places philosophy at the service of dispelling the confusions she identified in various interpretations of modern physics—an effort that, today, would be recognized as part of what we call "public philosophy."

Consistent with her work on analysis, Stebbing was especially critical of conflating the levels of common sense and everyday language with the level of physical analysis and scientific language. As a result of such conflation, Eddington famously claimed that there are

> two tables! . . . One of them has been familiar to me from earliest years. . . . [I]t has extension, it is comparatively permanent; it is coloured; above all, it is substantial [i.e. solid]. . . . Table No. 2 is my scientific table . . . . There is nothing substantial about my second table. It is nearly all empty space. Eddington (1928: xi–xii)

According to Stebbing, in contrast, there is only one table—the macro properties of which are described by Eddington with reference to his table No. 1, including solidity. While its constituents, as revealed by physics, are mostly subatomic particles arranged in largely empty space, Stebbing argues

---

[39] Though see note 9 for an alternative explanation.

[40] A passage from Eddington is representative: "All through the physical world runs that unknown content, which must surely be the stuff of our consciousness" (1928: 200).

16 SUSAN STEBBING

that it would be a mistake to infer the properties of the whole from those of its constituents. Thus, it is entirely coherent to claim that the table is solid, even though its constituents are not.

It also merits note that Stebbing didn't think that contemporary physics could adjudicate between idealism and materialism. Its findings, according to her, are compatible with both interpretations, and further empirical inquiries and levels of analysis would be needed to adjudicate the issue. Notice, however, that precisely in virtue of the fact that the properties of a whole cannot be inferred from those of its constituents, even if the latter were mental or spiritual in nature, it wouldn't follow that physical objects, as mind-independent entities, didn't exist, or that they did not have the properties that common sense assigns to them.

Such themes are further examined by Frederique Janssen-Lauret in her chapter "Susan Stebbing's Anti-Idealist Philosophy of Physics: Her Rebuttal of Eddington's Argument from Intrinsic Nature." Janssen-Lauret challenges the received "Moorean" reading of Stebbing—that she was a "follower of Moore" or a committed Moorean of sorts[41]—arguing that such readings are misplaced. She contends that the differences between Moore and Stebbing become especially clear when considering Stebbing's innovative contributions to analysis and its relationship to the philosophy of science, which, according to Janssen-Lauret, go beyond Moore's views. To bring these differences into sharper contrast, Janssen-Lauret focuses specifically on Stebbing's objections to Eddington's argument from intrinsic nature in *Philosophy and the Physicists*: that all matter is conscious (a view that we would now recognize as panpsychism) and, moreover, that our best physical theories support this conclusion. Janssen-Lauret shows that Stebbing doesn't rebut Eddington's argument by invoking any Moorean maneuvers— that is, by showing that we have reason to reject such a thesis because it offends common sense or because, upon analysis, such a thesis results in paradox. Rather, Stebbing concedes that our best physical theories are com- patible with idealism, but that nevertheless Eddington's premises don't pro- vide a positive reason to believe this conclusion. Stebbing's rebuttal turns on the rejection of two ideas that are implicitly assumed in Eddington's argu- ment: that the nature of a thing's parts is inherited by the nature of the whole, and that metaphysical analysis and "same-level" (conceptual) analysis are

---

[41] See, for example, Ayer (1977: 157–158), Milkov (2003), Beaney (2016), and Beaney and Chapman (2017).

the same. Yet, as we've seen Stebbing argue, both these assumptions are erroneous.

As commentators like Janssen-Lauret have drawn much attention to, the relationship between Stebbing and Moore—particularly with respect to common sense philosophy—is complex and, in some respects, elusive. While Stebbing never tires of crediting Moore for many ideas, in fact they had quite different views, certainly about analysis, as we just briefly considered (see Coliva 2021 and Janssen-Lauret 2022: 36–37), but also about common sense philosophy. Stebbing's commonsensical starting points were much more tied to perception than Moore's. In addition, Stebbing was interested in the relationship between physics and common sense, whereas Moore never addressed the relationship between science and common sense and rather used the latter, and the realism he saw inherent in it, to oppose idealism and skepticism.

In his chapter, "Making Sense of Stebbing and Moore on Common Sense," Louis Doulas offers a substantial reappraisal of this issue. According to him, both received readings of Stebbing and alternative readings rest on an oversimplified account of Moorean common sense. As a result, the reasons for favoring a "Moorean" reading of Stebbing—or for resisting such a reading—are both misplaced. In particular, Doulas argues that Moore's views on common sense are less monolithic than is typically assumed, shifting between what he calls "ecumenical" and "sectarian" conceptions. The ecumenical conception leaves room for metaphysically diverse analyses of common sense truths—even idealist ones—while the sectarian view treats such truths as tied to mind-independent realism. Doulas shows that, in fact, Stebbing directly engaged with and was influenced by this more ecumenical strand of Moore's thinking.

Yet Doulas also contends that Stebbing's common sense view ultimately diverges from Moore's in a crucial and decisive way: through what he calls Stebbing's *unity thesis*—the view that common-sense knowledge and scientific knowledge form a mutually informing, unified whole. This thesis, he argues, lies at the heart of "Stebbing's project of *integrating* this common-sense worldview with a scientific one" (Doulas, this volume). On Doulas's account, Stebbing conceives of common-sense knowledge as a form of probable knowledge—fallible, corrigible, yet continuous with the methods of science. As he emphasizes, Stebbing's view resists both scientific reductionism and uncompromising appeals to common sense. Thus, her view "involves neither a demand that common sense submit to the authority

18   SUSAN STEBBING

of science, nor a conservative rallying to shield it from the incursions of physics" (Doulas, this volume). The upshot is a distinctive, dynamic position in which common sense concepts may be clarified or revised by scientific progress, but not displaced wholesale. In this way, Doulas situates Stebbing as a philosopher whose "common sense view" emerges from Moore's influence but ultimately moves beyond him in scope, philosophical ambition, and in its sustained engagement with the scientific worldview.

As noted, *Philosophy and the Physicists* is a work of public philosophy. It therefore makes for an interesting case study in that genre, raising a number of questions about how philosophy ought to be done in the public eye—especially when it engages with figures and ideas outside of philosophy, as Stebbing does throughout the book. It also prompts reflection on the value that philosophy can bring to a broader, non-specialist readership. While *Philosophy and the Physicists* was generally favorably reviewed,[42] many reviewers felt its greatest shortcoming was that it offered no positive contribution. Indeed, readers of *Philosophy and the Physicists* will know that Stebbing's critique of Eddington and Jeans is often scathing; "a devastating refutation of the philosophical confusions of the scientists" writes one reviewer.[43] Stebbing's unforgiving tone throughout the book can easily be read as defensiveness.

Seizing upon this aspect of *Philosophy and the Physicists*, in "Susan Stebbing's Critique of Popular Science: Guiding or Gatekeeping?" Karl Egerton writes that "one might feel unease [with *Philosophy and the Physicists*] which seems either a defensive move on philosophers' behalf, arguing that scientists ought to leave certain work to them, or an attempt to school scientists on the significance of their own results" (Egerton, this volume). This, for Egerton, raises the following pressing question: is Stebbing's contribution in *Philosophy and the Physicists* "guiding" or "gatekeeping"? Egerton ultimately argues that Stebbing's intervention is guiding, and that she keeps in check the overexcitement produced by the "new" physics brought to the early twentieth century. Indeed, the metaphors and equivocations that Eddington and Jeans hide behind obscure and obfuscate the premises from which they draw their conclusions, conclusions that are

---

[42] Within philosophical circles at least. Outside of such circles, the book was more critically received. See Chapman (2013: 116–119).
[43] See Burns (1938).

in the end, according to Stebbing, not actually warranted. For Egerton, then, *Philosophy and the Physicists* is a necessary intervention into philosophical speculation gone astray and unchecked.

Closing this section of the volume, Peter West further examines the regulatory role of the *Philosophy and the Physicists* that Egerton alludes to above. In "Stebbing's Pelicans: Public Philosophy in *Philosophy and the Physicists* and *Thinking to Some Purpose*" West compares *Philosophy and the Physicists* to another of Stebbing's public philosophy works: *Thinking to Some Purpose* (1939). These books can seem quite different from one another at first glance. *Philosophy and the Physicists*, after all, is concerned with undoing the philosophical muddles arising out of the revisionary metaphysical views that two prominent scientists hastily "read off" of the new physics. *Thinking to Some Purpose*, by contrast, is a kind of handbook that endeavors to defend democratic ideals by instructing people how to think more clearly by paying attention to how language is used by politicians and journalists (and the media more broadly). Yet, West argues that these books are largely of a piece and are, in fact, part of a unified philosophical project: "that of ensuring that the citizens of a democracy are in a position to think clearly" (West, this volume). West then goes on to develop Stebbing's philosophy of public philosophy, contrasting it with another great popularizer of philosophy, Bertrand Russell, and his own approach. Russell, according to West, has a loftier vision of public philosophy than Stebbing, promoting the Aristotelian idea that leading a good life entails cultivating and accruing wisdom: "that if everyone were equipped with philosophical training . . . there would be considerably fewer disputes and . . . we would all lead more peaceful and fulfilling lives" (West, this volume).

Loftier, however, doesn't necessarily mean better. As West remarks, while Russell's vision is much more idealistic, Stebbing's is much more practical and actionable. Unlike Russell, Stebbing offers her readers *actual* tools for philosophical thinking—how to detect fallacies in the speeches of politicians and spot inconsistencies in news stories, among other things. That is, Stebbing adopts what West calls a "skills and training" approach to public philosophy, rather than a "transfer of knowledge" approach in which a non-specialist is presented with simplified or condensed introductions to certain philosophical theses and arguments by some expert specialist. According to West, Stebbing "focuses on the *way* we think rather than *what* certain philosophers think or have thought" (West, this volume). "After all," remarks West, "for Stebbing, all thinking is *thinking to some purpose*" (West, this volume). And

20 SUSAN STEBBING

this is just as true of *Thinking to Some Purpose* as it is for *Philosophy and the Physicists*.

3.3 The Logic and Politics of Everyday Language

The third section of the book is titled "The Logic and Politics of Everyday Language." With the rise of Fascism and Nazism in the 1930s, Stebbing took an active role in supporting Jewish colleagues in finding academic jobs. She also admitted many Jewish refugee children at the school in London she had founded with her sister and friends. Not only was she an activist against Nazi-fascism, but she also contributed to public philosophy by considering her duty to help counter the effects of political propaganda by writing a book of critical thinking aimed at the general public. The book appeared in print in 1939, with the title *Thinking to Some Purpose*. With examples from political debates of her time, Stebbing denounced several common fallacies which are regularly present in political propaganda, such as special pleading and what she called "potted thinking"—that is, simplistic thinking that betrays what others are saying and makes it susceptible to facile rebuttal. The aim of the work was thus to help people think clearly and, by so doing, become free— that is, capable of forming independent, considered judgments—rather than be surreptitiously influenced and deceived by political propaganda.

Stebbing's unfaltering faith in the civic role of philosophy—including logic—is here considered from a variety of perspectives. Nikolay Milkov's "Susan Stebbing and Some Poorly Explored Venues of Analytic Philosophy" claims that "like nobody else before or after her," Stebbing considered "the ultimate objective of analytic philosophy . . . to obtain a clear and precise grasp of words' and phrases' meaning in order to improve human *thinking*" (Milkov, this volume). That, in turn, was at the service of "apprehend[ing] how the *facts* were interconnected and how they developed" (Milkov, this volume).

According to Milkov, Stebbing was a "logical interventionist" *ante litteram*, for she thought that logic was not just an exploration of abstract systems but could be brought to bear on problems and issues of modern life. Starting with her *Logic in Practice* (1934a), she considered examples from everyday life to illustrate logical principles. In *Thinking to Some Purpose*— Stebbing's most famous work aimed at bringing logic to bear onto real-life issues—she maintained that "to think logically is to think relevantly to the

INTRODUCTION 21

purpose that initiated the thinking" (1939: 10), based on exact connections between the relevant facts. Whereas in the *Philosophy and the Physicists*, Stebbing had applied her conception of analytic philosophy to clarifying the muddles caused by trying to convey "exact thought" with "inexact language" (1937: 14), in *Thinking to Some Purpose* she attacked "the tricks of the fascist totalitarian ideology and its propaganda" (Milkov, this volume). In her view, "propaganda was just a weak form of argument" (Milkov, this volume).

Furthermore, Stebbing held that politics is a battle of *ideals* which are neither categorical imperatives nor principles, but are "regulative ideas" and are "relative a priori" (Milkov, this volume), so that they may and do change in time. In *Ideals and Illusions* (1941), Stebbing denounced religion as an illusion, whereas she considered democracy a true ideal. According to her, democracy consists in "freedom, respect for other men issuing in tolerance and humanity, respect for truth and delight in knowledge" (1941: 151). Democracy considers all human beings equal and aims at everyone's happiness. By contrast, Nazis and Fascists pursued ideals that are contrary to democracy, which should be fought against and replaced with true ones.

In "Susan Stebbing and the Politics of Symbolic Logic," David Dunning too considers Stebbing a logical interventionist, but more a "dialogical" one than an umpire. Her political aims did not manifest themselves in aligning logic to a specific political agenda. Rather, she thought of it as a professional discipline, with respect to which there are different levels of proficiency, the basics of which should be taught to everyone. That is to say, logic, for Stebbing, should be part of general education, even if its highest peaks could be pursued only by (prospective) professional logicians. Before *Thinking to Some Purpose,* Stebbing had thought of logic as a "science of pure forms, not of individual reasoning" (Dunning, this volume). Due to the political changes in the late 1930s, Stebbing took a more practical turn and stated that "It is, we need to remember, persons who think, not purely rational spirits" (1939: 21). She was fully aware that politicians are more interested in persuasion than in proof and that their audiences are in general not well equipped to follow arguments. Yet, she could not condone a "complacent attitude towards this deficiency" (Dunning, this volume). Democracy, for Stebbing, is worthwhile only if people cast their vote after "due deliberation" (1939: 11), which can be achieved only by knowing the facts, assessing the evidence for them, and by being able to discount "the effects of prejudice and to evade the distortion produced by unwarrantable fears and by unrealizable hopes" (1939: 11). This is what thinking "relevantly" or "to some purpose"

22 SUSAN STEBBING

consists in. Teaching logic, therefore, was a powerful political tool, according to Stebbing, as it could help counter the effects of political propaganda and be at the service of making people free.

3.4 Natural Language, Definitions, and Verbal Disputes

Finally, in the book's fourth section, "Natural Language, Definitions, and Verbal Disputes," Stebbing's views on natural language are examined. In contrast to some dominant tendencies within mainstream early analytic philosophy—particularly among key figures of the Cambridge school such as Russell and the early Wittgenstein, who were largely following in Frege's footsteps—Stebbing paid close attention to natural language in its own right. She was fully aware of the discrepancies between natural language and logic with respect to connectives (e.g., "and," "or," "if then," etc.), which she treated at length in several of her logic textbooks. Yet, she did not think that natural language had to be reformed or regimented; rather, it should be studied for its own sake. She thus anticipated key moves characteristic of later Oxford ordinary language philosophy, as well as of the pragmatic turn in the philosophy of language. Furthermore, in *Thinking to Some Purpose*, by analyzing political discourse with the aim of unveiling its implicit ideological commitments made to pass as common sense, she anticipated key moves of Critical discourse analysis in linguistics.

In her "Susan Stebbing: Philosophy, Pragmatics and Critical Discourse Analysis," Siobhan Chapman focuses on Stebbing's original outlook on natural language. She stresses how Stebbing's treatment of material implication as unsuitable to convey the meaning of "if then" in natural language, where "the meaning of the premise must be relevantly connected with the meaning of the conclusion" (Stebbing 1943: 145), prefigured a key move in subsequent relevance theory, developed over fifty years later by Sperber and Wilson (1995). For Stebbing recognized that relevance is outside the scope of logic but held that it is worth studying in its own right. Furthermore, in *Thinking to Some Purpose*, Stebbing undertook a detailed analysis of ordinary language by looking at "newspaper reports, political speeches and advertisements" to reveal "the ideology behind the production of such texts and the persuasive devices employed in them" (Chapman, this volume). This was highly unusual at her time and anticipated by several decades a key tenet of Critical

INTRODUCTION 23

discourse analysis, which studies the relationship between language, power, and ideology by looking at concrete linguistic sources. Beside commenting on specific words' choices, she denounced "potted thinking" and the (mis) use of analogies. As Quassim Cassam recognizes, Stebbing was thus acutely aware of what he calls "epistemic vices" and was "right to insist that some of our failures in thinking can be overcome and that there is an urgent need to overcome them to the extent that this is possible" (Cassam 2019: 187).

Bryan Pickel in "Stebbing on Linguistic Convention: Understanding, Definition, and Verbal Disputes" reconstructs Stebbing's views on linguistic convention across several of her texts, illuminating important features of her philosophy of language—a somewhat elusive and neglected topic in Stebbing scholarship—and on how such features bear on various aspects of philosophical and scientific inquiry. Pickel takes readers on a tour through Stebbing's account of linguistic signs and symbols, sentence meaning, and definition, among other similar topics. Undergirding each of these topics, however, is Stebbing's views about the conventionality of language, the idea that "[w]ords bear no inherent relations to their referents" Pickel writes, paraphrasing Stebbing (Pickel, this volume). Indeed, that language is conventional seems like a truism hardly worth stating. Yet, this innocuous sounding thesis has been used by philosophers to derive radical philosophical conclusions—that, for example, necessity and certainty can be explained by convention (A. J. Ayer) or that the principles of logic are themselves conventional (C. I. Lewis).

Stebbing, however, finds such conclusions hasty, ultimately turning on misconceptions about the nature of linguistic convention. For example, it might be thought that the conventionality of language has a kind of "trickle down" effect, rendering arbitrary related notions in the vicinity like *definition*. But while language may be conventional, definition isn't. Writes Pickel on Stebbing: "even though language is conventional, the process of definition requires substantive investigation [into] the referents of the expressions" (Pickel, this volume). While allowing that there may be cases in which an arbitrary definition may be given or simply stipulated, there is still no guarantee that the definition will be true "and thus no guarantee that the defining and defined expressions are equivalent" (Pickel, this volume). In this way, Pickel sees Stebbing as anticipating Quine's discussions of "legislative definition." A physicist, for example, might legislatively *define* an expression for a force, yet be led to reject it as false after discovering that nothing corresponds

24 SUSAN STEBBING

to it. As Pickel explains, given that for both Quine and Stebbing legislative definitions are corrigible, it would be a mistake to characterize them as strictly conventional.

Picking up on related linguistic themes in Stebbing's work, Teresa Kouri Kissel's chapter "Stebbing, Translations, and Verbal Disputes" argues that Stebbing may have to some extent anticipated present-day discussion concerning the philosophical significance of merely verbal disputes—that is, debates that are taken to be neither substantive nor deep and that seem largely terminological. The source, Kouri Kissel reveals, is found in a somewhat unexpected place: Stebbing's *Ideals and Illusions* (1941). While Stebbing's concerns in that book are largely of a piece with the themes of *Thinking to Some Purpose* (that clear and critical thinking go hand in hand with social emancipation), Kouri Kissel shows that, after some necessary modification and augmentation—which, according to Kouri Kissel, Stebbing's previous work on analysis has the resources to provide—what we get is a compelling translation test that seems to predict when a specific debate is a merely verbal one. This is what Kouri Kissel calls Stebbing's "directional translation test." Though the context in which Stebbing's test is developed is no doubt different from contemporary discussions of merely verbal disputes, Stebbing's directional translation test nevertheless appears to solve some problems that have been raised for David Chalmers's own more formal test for merely verbal disputes. Indeed, as Kouri Kissel urges, Chalmers could address these worries by incorporating Stebbing's insights. As such, Stebbing emerges as "an integral member of the tradition that gives rise to the idea of merely verbal disputes, and should be treated as such" (Kouri Kissel, this volume).

* * *

We think the preceding should have made abundantly clear that, far from being a marginal figure, Stebbing was clearly a founding mother of analytic philosophy, whose ideas are of relevance also to present-day debates and are particularly attuned to the "social turn" analytic philosophy has taken in the last few years. If some reasons could be adduced to explain why she did disappear from the canon after her death, such as the demise of the centrality of analysis among the core issues of analytic philosophy, this volume should make apparent that there are none, nowadays, to not reinstate Stebbing where she belongs.

INTRODUCTION 25

References

For a comprehensive biography and bibliography of Stebbing's works see Chapman 2013.

Ayer, A. J. 1977. *Part of My Life*. Oxford: Oxford University Press.

Beaney, Michael, and Siobhan Chapman. 2017. "Susan Stebbing." In Edward N. Zalta, ed., *The Stanford Encyclopedia of Philosophy* (Summer 2017 Edition). https://plato.stanford.edu/archives/sum2017/entries/stebbing/.

Beaney, Michael. 2016. "Susan Stebbing and the Early Reception of Logical Empiricism in Britain." In Christian Damböck, ed., 233–256, *Influences on the Aufbau*. Cham: Springer.

Beaney, Michael. 2017. *Analytic Philosophy: A Very Short Introduction*. Oxford: Oxford University Press.

Beaney, Michael. 2013. "The Historiography of Analytic Philosophy." In Michael Beaney, ed., 30–60, *The Oxford Handbook of the History of Analytic Philosophy*. Oxford: Oxford University Press.

Beaney, Michael. 2003. "Susan Stebbing on Cambridge and Vienna Analysis." In Friedrich Stadler, ed., 339–350, *The Vienna Circle and Logical Empiricism: Re-evaluation and Future Perspectives*. Cham: Springer.

Burns, C. D. 1938. "Review of *Philosophy and the Physicists* by L. Susan Stebbing." *Ethics* 48: 559–560.

Cassam, Quassim. 2019. *Vices of the Mind: From the Intellectual to the Political*. Oxford: Oxford University Press.

Chapman, Siobhan. 2013. *Susan Stebbing and the Language of Common Sense*. London: Palgrave Macmillan.

Coliva, Annalisa. 2021. "Stebbing, Moore (and Wittgenstein) on Common Sense and Metaphysical Analysis." *British Journal for the History of Philosophy* 29: 914–934.

Connell, Sophia, and Frederique Janssen-Lauret. 2022. "Lost Voices: On Counteracting Exclusion of Women from Histories of Contemporary Philosophy." *British Journal for the History of Philosophy* 30: 199–210.

Day, Ivory. 2023. "Stebbing and Russell on Bergson: Early Analytics on Continental Thought." In C. C. Harry and G. N. Vlahakis, eds., 129–50. *Exploring the Contributions of Women in the History of Philosophy, Science, and Literature, Throughout Time*. Cham: Springer.

Douglas, Alexander X., and Jonathan Nassim. 2021. "Susan Stebbing's Logical Interventionism." *History and Philosophy of Logic* 42: 101–117.

Dummett, Michael. 1993. *Origins of Analytic Philosophy*. Cambridge, MA: Harvard University Press.

Eddington, A. S. 1928. *The Nature of the Physical World*. Cambridge: Cambridge University Press.

Franco, P. L. 2024. "Susan Stebbing on Logical Positivism and Communication." *Ergo* 10: 1378–1402.

Glock, Hans-Johann. 2008. *What Is Analytic Philosophy?* Cambridge: Cambridge University Press.

Janssen-Lauret, Frederique. 2022. *Susan Stebbing*. Cambridge: Cambridge University Press.

Janssen-Lauret, Frederique. 2017. "Susan Stebbing, Incomplete Symbols, and Foundherentist Meta-Ontology." *Journal for the History of Analytical Philosophy* 5: 6–17.

Kremer, Michael. 2017. "Ryle's 'Intellectualist Legend' in Historical Context." *Journal for the History of Analytical Philosophy* 5: 16–39.

Körber, Silke. 2025. "Scientific Humanism in Practice—L. Susan Stebbing and Otto Neurath." In G. Schiemer, ed., 67–84. *The Legacy of the Vienna Circle*. Cham: Springer.

Körber, Silke. 2019. "Thinking About the 'Common Reader': Otto Neurath, L. Susan Stebbing and the (Modern) Picture-Text Style." In J. Cat and A. T. Tuboly, eds., 451–70. *Neurath Reconsidered: New Sources and Perspectives*. Cham: Springer.

26 SUSAN STEBBING

Körber, Silke, and Adam Tamas Tuboly. 2025. "Susan Stebbing on the Scientific Attitude and Moral Philosophy Context and Comments." In G. Schiemer, ed., 187–203. *The Legacy of the Vienna Circle*. Cham: Springer.

Milkov, Nikolay. 2003. "Susan Stebbing's Criticism of Wittgenstein's *Tractatus*." In F. Stadler, ed., 351–363. *The Vienna Circle and Logical Empiricism*. Cham: Springer.

Moravec, Matyáš, and Peter West. 2023. "Stebbing and Eddington in the Shadow of Bergson." *History of Philosophy Quarterly* 40: 59–84.

Pap, Arthur. 1949. *Elements of Analytic Philosophy*. New York: The Macmillan Company.

Passmore, John. 1957. *A Hundred Years of Philosophy*. London: Duckworth.

Pickel, Bryan. 2022. "Susan Stebbing's Intellectualism." *Journal for the History of Analytical Philosophy* 10: 1–24.

Reck, Erich H. 2013. "Introduction: Analytic Philosophy and Philosophical History." In E. H. Reck, ed., 1–36. *The Historical Turn in Analytic Philosophy*, London: Palgrave-Macmillan.

Richardson, Alan. 2017. "From Scientific to Analytic: Remarks on How Logical Positivism Became a Chapter of Analytic Philosophy." In A. Preston, ed., 146–159. *Analytic Philosophy: An Interpretive History*. Oxon: Routledge.

Schwartz, Stephen P. 2012. *A Brief History of Analytic Philosophy: From Russell to Rawls*. Malden, MA: Wiley-Blackwell.

Soames, Scott. 2003a. *Philosophical Analysis in the Twentieth Century*, vol. 1, *The Dawn of Analysis*. Princeton NJ: Princeton University Press.

Soames, Scott. 2003b. *Philosophical Analysis in the Twentieth Century*, vol. 2, *The Age of Meaning*. Princeton, NJ: Princeton University Press.

Sperber, Dan, and Deirdre Wilson. 1995. *Relevance: Communication and Cognition* 2nd ed. Oxford: Blackwell.

Stebbing, L. S. 1913. "The Notion of Truth in Bergson's Theory of Knowledge." *Proceedings of the Aristotelian Society* 13: 224–256.

Stebbing, L. S. 1914. *Pragmatism and French Voluntarism*. Cambridge: Cambridge University Press.

Stebbing, L. S. 1915. "A Reply to Some Charges Against Logic." *Science Progress* 10: 406–412.

Stebbing, L. S. 1916–17. "Relation and Coherence." *Proceedings of the Aristotelian Society* 17: 459–480.

Stebbing, L. S. 1917–18. "The Philosophical Importance of the Verb 'To Be.'" *Proceedings of the Aristotelian Society* 18: 582–589.

Stebbing, L. S. 1928. "Materialism in the Light of Modern Scientific Thought." *Proceedings of the Aristotelian Society* 8: 99–142.

Stebbing, L. S. 1930. *A Modern Introduction to Logic*. London: Methuen.

Stebbing, L. S. 1932–33. "The Method of Analysis in Metaphysics." *Proceedings of the Aristotelian Society* 33: 65–94.

Stebbing, L. S. 1933. "Logical Positivism and Analysis." *Proceedings of the British Academy* 19: 53–87.

Stebbing, L. S. 1934a. *Logic in Practice*. London: Methuen.

Stebbing, L. S. 1934b. "Directional Analysis and Basic Facts." *Analysis* 2: 33–36.

Stebbing, L. S. 1937. *Philosophy and the Physicists*. London: Methuen.

Stebbing, L. S. 1938–39: "Some Puzzles About Analysis." *Proceedings of the Aristotelian Society* 39: 69–84.

Stebbing, L. S. 1939. *Thinking to Some Purpose*. Harmondsworth: Penguin.

Stebbing, L. S. 1941. *Ideals and Illusions*. London: Watts and Co.

Stebbing, L. S. 1942. "Moore's Influence." In P. Schillp, ed., 17–532. *The Philosophy of G. E. Moore*. Evanston, IL: Northwestern University Press,

Stebbing, L. S. 1943. *A Modern Elementary Logic*. London: Methuen.

Stebbing, L. S. 1944. *Men and Moral Principles*. Oxford: Oxford University Press.

Stroll, Avrum. 2000. *Twentieth-Century Analytic Philosophy*. New York: Columbia University Press.

INTRODUCTION 27

Tuboly, Adam Tamas. 2020. "Knowledge Missemination: L. Susan Stebbing, C.E.M. Joad, and Philipp Frank on the Philosophy of the Physicists." *Perspectives on Science* 28: 1–34.

Urmson, J. O. 1956. *Philosophical Analysis: Its Development Between the Two World Wars.* Oxford: Oxford Clarendon Press.

Verhaegh, Sander, and Jeanne Peijnenburg. 2022. "Introduction: Women in the History of Analytic Philosophy." In S. Verhaegh and J. Peijnenburg, eds., *Women in the History of Analytic Philosophy.* Cham: Springer, pp. 1–21.

Vrahimis, Andreas. 2022. *Bergsonism and the History of Analytic Philosophy.* Cham: Springer.

Warnock, G. J. 1948. *English Philosophy since 1900.* Oxford: Oxford University Press.

Wisdom, John. 1934. "Is Analysis a Useful Method in Philosophy?" *Proceedings of the Aristotelian Society* 13: 65–89.

Wisdom, John. 1948. "L. Susan Stebbing, 1885–1943." *Philosophical Studies: Essays in Memory of L. Susan Stebbing.* London: Harrison and Sons Limited, pp. 1–4. Originally published in *Mind* 53: 283–285 1943.

SECTION I

THE SIGNIFICANCE OF SUSAN STEBBING'S WORK ON ANALYSIS

The Significance of Susan Stebbing's Work on Analysis

Annalisa Coliva

1 Introduction

In this chapter, I address the issue of the significance of Susan Stebbing's philosophy.* This is a particularly crucial question because, up to a few years past, Stebbing has been one of the Early Analytic women philosophers who have been erased from the canon. This is all the more remarkable because Stebbing was the first woman philosophy professor in the United Kingdom and had leading roles within the philosophical community of her time. She also made crucial contributions to the understanding of analysis; furthered the relationship between science, philosophy, and common sense; and played a major role in promoting what today would be called "public philosophy."

Here, I focus mainly on the first of these crucial contributions, while several other chapters in this volume explore the latter two, with special attention to her contribution to public philosophy. This should not surprise us, since it is a raising mission of present-day philosophy to address issues of public concern while making itself accessible to a non-specialist audience. In this respect, Stebbing has been a precursor to today's movement within analytic philosophy. For she conceived logic and analysis as ways to clarify our ideas. This, for her, would be at the service of unmasking political propaganda, thereby freeing us, at least in thought, from its nefarious influence.

Regarding Stebbing's major work on analysis, its erasure may be explained by reference to the declining role of this issue within debates in analytic philosophy starting in the 1940s. Yet, revisiting it will bring out the novelty and

---

* Sections 2–3 are borrowed from Coliva (2021). Sections 1 and 5 are new; section 4, while drawing on Coliva (2021), has been substantially reworked.

Annalisa Coliva, *The Significance of Susan Stebbing's Work on Analysis* In: *Susan Stebbing*. Edited by: Annalisa Coliva and Louis Doulas, Oxford University Press. © Oxford University Press 2025. DOI: 10.1093/9780197682371.003.0002

32   SUSAN STEBBING

clarity of her position, which, I believe, resonates with present-day philosophical interests and methodology.

2 Stebbing on Metaphysical Analysis

Stebbing's views on analysis were presented in several articles published in the 1930s. The most important of these papers is "The Method of Analysis in Metaphysics" (henceforth MAM), read at a meeting of the Aristotelian Society on London, on December 12, 1932.

The starting point is a criticism of British idealism. Stebbing takes issue with John McTaggart's claim in *Some Dogmas of Religion* (1906, p. 1) that metaphysics is "the systematic study of the *ultimate* nature of reality" (my emphasis). According to Stebbing, this way of conceiving of metaphysics is problematic because it depends on thinking that the nature of reality is neither as it appears nor as is empirically discoverable by science, or through analysis. Rather, it is discovered through a priori, deductive reasoning, which starts from what is ultimate—Spirit, Reason—to derive appearance. Metaphysics then consists in the construction of a deductive system, predicated on the distinction between appearance and reality (possibly with capital "A" and "R"), which is either embraced or rejected *en bloc* (p. 68). According to Stebbing, the value of such systems, if they are coherent, is like the value of works of art (p. 68 and p. 94). They have beauty and therefore have spiritual significance (p. 94). "They heighten the joy of living, but they do not give knowledge; they are the source of inspiration, but they do not yield understanding" (p. 94). To such a conception Stebbing objects: "In my opinion, however, metaphysics does not consist in creation, but in investigation" (p. 68).

Notice that Stebbing is not of the opinion that metaphysics is an investigation leading to the discovery of any new fact. In this, metaphysics differs from natural and social sciences (p. 65). Rather, "the aim of metaphysics is to reveal the *structure of that to which reference is made in true statements*" (p. 65, my emphasis). The investigation, therefore, is not meant to discover any new facts, but to clarify the nature of facts to which we ordinarily refer in our everyday statements, such as when we say "I am sitting at a table," or "Here is a pen," etc.

According to Stebbing, traditional metaphysics errs because it partakes in "a very common view of the nature of philosophy. This is the view that the business of the philosopher is to find reasons for our commonsense beliefs that certain things are the case; that if he cannot find these reasons, these beliefs must be abandoned" (p. 68). To put it with Francis Herbert Bradley in *Appearance and Reality* (1893/1897, p. 1), "metaphysics is the finding of bad reasons for what we believe upon instinct." In other words, if one engages in the epistemological project of justifying our commonsensical beliefs, one will be led to search for beliefs or principles that are allegedly more certain than what they are supposed to justify, and then to either proclaim that our commonsensical beliefs are unjustified after all or that they are derivable from those more certain bases. Descartes's cogito is a clear example of that conception of metaphysics, according to Stebbing; and we could add Hume's empiricism as another example of that, albeit with skeptical outcomes.

According to Stebbing, in contrast, metaphysics should not be conducted under the aegis of this kind of epistemological project. Rather, it should take it for granted that our commonsensical beliefs are for the most part correct and then proceed to analyze what facts exactly make them true. We could dub her approach "the metaphysics first" approach and the one she opposes "the epistemology first" approach to metaphysics. The former, takes commonsensical beliefs to be mostly correct and aims at investigating what makes them true; whereas the latter starts from allegedly more secure philosophical presuppositions and it either derives—that is, epistemologically grounds—commonsensical beliefs or else revokes them into doubt. As Stebbing puts it:

> I am concerned to maintain that the contention that the proper method of metaphysics is the method of analysis involves, and is involved by, the denial of the view that the problem of metaphysics is to find reasons for our beliefs. I hold that such a belief, as, for example, that there is a table in this room, or that I am now sitting at this table, or that putting my hand in the flame was unpleasant, must afford a starting point....
>
> On this view, the business of metaphysics is to show (i) what exactly we are believing when we believe that there is a table in this room, that it was here three hours ago, and so on; (ii) *how* our various beliefs are inter-related; (iii) how our inconsistent beliefs may be adjusted, and which should be rejected. Thus metaphysics aims at making precise the reference of all true beliefs. For this purpose analysis is indispensable. (p. 70)

Importantly, Stebbing points out that "we cannot demonstrate that *this* given belief is true; we cannot find premises more certain than the belief itself *from*

34   SUSAN STEBBING

which it may be *deduced*. Either there is no guarantee of truth or there are some instantial premises which I can know to be true" (p. 70). Notice that here Stebbing is not merely saying that commonsensical beliefs are accepted without proof, or that we are more certain of them than of any contrary philosophical thesis, or of the premises of arguments which should allegedly prove them. Rather, she is making a modal claim about the fact that no proof of them could be given, for it would necessarily rest on premises the truth of which is disputable, while the truth of these commonsensical beliefs isn't. Furthermore, she is saying that, alternatively, such a proof would depend on already taking for granted the very thing one is supposed to thereby prove, e.g., knowledge of having hands, for instance.

3 The Epistemological Significance of "The Method of Analysis in Metaphysics"

Stebbing's former point—i.e., that no proof of commonsensical beliefs could be given, for it would necessarily rest on premises the truth of which is disputable, while the truth of these beliefs isn't—definitely resonates with Moore, who, in "Proof of an External World" (henceforth PEW) states: "I can know things, which I cannot prove; and among things which I certainly did know, even if (as I think) I could not prove them, were the premises of my [proof]" (PEW, p. 150)—that is, "Here is my hand" and "Here is another." Yet, as is apparent, Moore is not explicit as to why a proof of the premises of his proof cannot be given.

Stebbing's latter claim—i.e., that a proof would depend on already taking for granted the very thing one is supposed to thereby prove—also resonates with what Wittgenstein writes in *On Certainty* (henceforth *OC*): "If a blind man were to ask me 'Have you got two hands?' I should not make sure by looking. If I were to have any doubt of it, then I don't know why I should trust my eyes. For why shouldn't I test my eyes by looking to find out whether I see my two hands? What is to be tested by what? (Who decides what stands fast?)" (*OC*, p. 125). Yet, Wittgenstein is just insisting on the fact that a proof of commonsensical beliefs would likely take them for granted. Still, he is not taking issue with the idea of providing a proof of them which started from allegedly more secure philosophical theses (e.g., like Descartes's cogito).

Be that as it may, it must be stressed that PEW was written seven years after MAM, and *OC* was composed between 1949 and 1951, so over seventeen years after MAM. True, in "Hume's Philosophy" (1909, pp. 159–160, henceforth HP) Moore had already made the point that any proof aimed at proving that we know that there are external facts will proceed by considering a specific instance of knowledge, such as I know I have hands. It would thus beg the question since it would assume that we do have knowledge of at least that fact about the external world. Yet, HP is not referenced in MAM and it is not clear that Stebbing had read it at the time. The reference we find to HP in her writings is much later, in "Moore's Influence" (1942, henceforth MI).[1]

In "A Defence of Common Sense" (henceforth DCS), which Stebbing refers to repeatedly in MAM, the problem of a proof of the truth of our commonsensical beliefs is not even in view, for the paper is concerned with the defense of common sense, and not with the proof of it. In DCS, Moore first specifies which truisms characterize common sense and then goes on to claim that philosophers who either deny propositions entailed by them, like idealists, or who claim that they don't know them, like skeptics, are saying something either false or self-contradictory (DCS, pp. 38–43). The insistence on the truth of commonsensical beliefs, even though no proof of them can be given, is not to be found in DCS, but only in PEW.

In DCS (p. 40), Moore very briefly outlines a reason against idealism that resembles but isn't identical to Stebbing's argument for considering it impossible to deduce commonsensical beliefs from other ones. For Moore asserts that any philosophical position that *denies* or entails the denial of commonsensical beliefs (and/or of what they entail, such as the existence of an external world) would reach a conclusion that is less certain than those very truisms and should therefore be rejected. Yet, notice that Moore is concerned neither with the derivation or justification of those philosophical theses nor with the derivation or the justification of truisms themselves. Rather, he is merely pointing out that since commonsensical beliefs and what they entail are maximally certain, anything incompatible with them is less certain and should therefore be rejected. This is in fact commonly referred to as "Moore's gambit."

Furthermore, the "metaphysics first approach" that characterizes Stebbing's position is echoed in Moore's PEW. For despite the fact that generations of interpreters have tended to read it as an epistemological paper,

---

[1] Stebbing and Moore had been interacting since 1917 and there are indications that Stebbing was familiar with Moore's writings before "A Defence of Common Sense." Yet, in MAM there is no reference to HP or to any other paper by Moore.

36 SUSAN STEBBING

meant to address skepticism, Moore (1942, p. 668) emphatically denied that and maintained that the paper was to be read as an anti-idealist one. However, if the topic of PEW is metaphysics, it no longer involves analysis. Indeed, a *proof* of the existence of the external world is attempted in PEW— against Stebbing's claim that commonsensical beliefs couldn't be proved. True, the proof starts with commonsensical premises that aren't proved. And true, Moore says that a proof of them cannot be given (PEW, p. 149; cf. also Moore 1909, pp. 159–160). Yet, he goes on to say that such a proof would depend on proving that one isn't now dreaming (PEW, p. 149). He claims that he has plenty of conclusive evidence that he isn't dreaming but that such evidence would not amount to a proof. Yet, the absence of such a proof is no reason for him to doubt that he knew those premises to be true. As I have claimed elsewhere,[2] this is indeed Moore's central contention in PEW—that is, that a proof remains a good and cogent one even if its premises aren't proved, as long as they are known, as they are in this case.

Turning to Wittgenstein, as is well known, he was greatly influenced by Moore's writings in *OC*, particularly DCS, while he was more critical of PEW precisely because it attempted to *prove* the existence of an external world. It is less clear if he was aware of Stebbing's or whether he interacted (philosophically) with her. What he took to be the central insight in DCS was the anti-Cartesian idea that there are propositions, which look like ordinary empirical ones, yet are not subject to doubt or verification. In ordinary circumstances, we do not verify that we have hands by looking at them, and it is no more certain that we do have them after looking. Nor do we have or would we accept any reason to doubt that we have them (in said circumstances). Furthermore, we do not derive that belief from an allegedly more secure one about our sensory experience. That belief, like a myriad other ones he lists in *OC*, is, for Wittgenstein, like Moore and Stebbing, as secure as "2+2=4."[3] He was likewise highly critical of the attempt at proving them: either because an alleged proof would start with premises that would be no more secure than them; or else because the proof would be epistemically circular.[4] For these reasons, he ended up holding that, despite appearances, these were not ordinary

---

[2] See Coliva 2010 (chapter 1), Coliva 2018a,b, and Coliva, 2024.

[3] For the point of this mathematical analogy, see Coliva 2020a.

[4] The former structure would be instantiated by a proof aimed at proving "I have hands" starting with my current sensory experience. The latter structure would be exemplified by a proof, like Moore's, that, starting with commonsensical beliefs, aimed at deriving a justification for "There is an external world," which needs in fact to be presupposed in order to have a justification for its premises. On this, see Coliva (2010, chapter 2).

empirical propositions but were more like rules—they are like "hinges" that need to stay put if we want the door, that is our ordinary epistemic trafficking in genuinely empirical investigation, to be possible at all.[5] This was in the end the new and original contribution made by Wittgenstein—that is, the claim about the different epistemic and semantic status of these propositions—not to be found in MAM. Still the motivations behind such a radical move are indeed very similar to the ones presented by Stebbing.

Another key anti-skeptical claim in MAM appears toward the end of the paper. After clarifying the purpose of the method of analysis in metaphysics, which, as we have seen, should not aim at grounding our commonsensical beliefs in allegedly more secure ones, Stebbing returns on the possibility of being mistaken about beliefs such as "I am sitting a table," "This is a pen," "I am seeing a piece of paper," etc., in ordinary circumstances. She acknowledges that we may be mistaken in asserting that we know such things, but she adds:

> But it does not follow from this that we can never know that we are not mistaken. Descartes' argument . . . seems [to me] one of his weakest. . . . His mistake was to attempt to doubt simultaneously *all* those propositions concerning the external world, which he had formerly *known* to be true. One feels Descartes knew too much about the characteristics of malignant demons to satisfy the requirements of his own method. Methodic doubt must proceed step by step. Such step-by-step doubting is not inconsistent with the assumption that I do *now know* that I am seeing a piece of paper. (p. 93)

The idea, then, is that we cannot doubt all our commonsensical beliefs at once. Stebbing seems to be claiming, in a Moorean spirit, that there is a form of incoherence in taking oneself to have known them and then in calling all of them into question at once.[6] More importantly, she seems to be saying that doubt can only sensibly target specific beliefs and must presumably be supported by reasons. Thus, it is compatible with the assumption (or the fact) that we do now know such things as "I am seeing a piece of paper," when we are holding one in our hands.

---

[5] For a discussion, see Coliva 2010 (chapters 2–4).

[6] Stebbing was also familiar with the pragmatist rejection of Cartesian global skepticism and might have drawn inspiration from that for her criticism of it. Thanks to Alexander Klein for drawing my attention to this point.

38   SUSAN STEBBING

The latter is an idea that we do not find in Moore's writings but which will be elaborated at length by Wittgenstein in *OC*. Sure, Moore does claim in PEW, but also in writings that predate MAM, like HP, that it would be absurd to doubt that he knows the premises of his proof or that he is not now dreaming. Yet, he is not taking issue with Descartes's *global* skepticism as such. That is, he is not claiming that calling all our beliefs into question *at once* is impossible or otherwise problematic. Wittgenstein, in contrast, insists on the fact that a doubt that doubted everything would be self-defeating in that it would equally annihilate both the reasons for doubt (*OC* 115, 450, 519, 625) and the possibility of meaning (*OC* 506). Hence, it would be irrational—in the sense of not being supported by reasons—and meaningless (*OC*, pp. 302, 383, 392, 606, 676).[7]

Thus, to sum up: Stebbing anticipates in MAM key points in both Moore's more mature writings and in Wittgenstein's and makes a more definitive claim about the epistemic status of commonsensical beliefs than Moore, at least in DCS. Indeed, her views are very close to Wittgenstein's, with respect to both the unprovability of commonsensical beliefs and the impossibility of global skepticism. Yet, Wittgenstein would develop his position only almost two decades after MAM.

So why did Stebbing's seminal contribution to epistemology, as it happens, go unnoticed? Three reasons immediately stand out. First, Stebbing is not elaborating the epistemological significance of those points further, for, by being interested in metaphysics and in the particular kind of metaphysics that is concerned with finding the structure of facts referred to by the propositions that are the content of those beliefs, she was critical of foundationalist epistemological projects and uninterested in epistemology at large. Second, she was writing in a philosophical *milieu* that was mostly concerned with the issue of analysis: that issue was at the core of Russell's, Moore's, Wittgenstein's, and the Vienna Circle's investigations. Remarks that were significant for epistemology were simply not the focus of the ongoing debate with which she was engaging and which she contributed to spur. Last, Stebbing's influence faded with the waning away of interest in the debate on analysis. Thus, also the contributions she made to epistemology in her writings on analysis went unnoticed by subsequent generations of philosophers.

---

[7] For a discussion of Wittgenstein's anti-Cartesian strategies in *OC*, see Coliva 2010 (chapter 3).

SUSAN STEBBING'S WORK ON ANALYSIS   39

4 The Significance of Metaphysical Analysis, Its Aims and Limitations

In MAM, Stebbing distinguishes two main kinds of analysis: one is symbolic (p. 76) or same-level analysis; the other one is metaphysical or new-level analysis (p. 76). The former is what occurs in postulational systems—whence its other title of "postulational analysis."[8] This kind of analysis aims at giving a clear and unambiguous formulation of key notions and concepts and at deductively deriving whatever follows from the initial set of definitions (p. 83). An axiomatic system would be a good example of what Stebbing calls "postulational analysis."[9] According to Stebbing, logical positivists pursued this kind of analysis. Postulational analysis is typically a priori.

The latter, metaphysical analysis, in contrast, aims at determining which facts make our commonsensical beliefs true. According to Stebbing, metaphysical analysis has been practiced and championed by Bertrand Russell, John Wisdom, Moore, and probably Wittgenstein in the *Tractatus* (p. 74)—and could be considered the characteristic trait of "Cambridge analysis," as opposed to "Vienna analysis." Since, as we shall see, it aims at determining the basic, not further analyzable facts, which are truth-makers of commonsensical propositions about physical objects, it cannot be conducted purely a priori. Nor is it merely analytic, since it differs from linguistic and conceptual analyses.

These attributions should be taken with more than a grain of salt, however. For instance, Stebbing lists Wittgenstein in the main text but then adds a cautionary footnote. The main reason for that is that Wittgenstein's atomism in the *Tractatus* is driven by the transcendental aim of determining the conditions of possibility of meaning. Stebbing stands opposed to such transcendental aims and to assigning language a preeminent role in metaphysics. For her, words mean what they mean, and metaphysics should determine what facts, if any, ultimately make our true beliefs true. Wittgenstein was considered by Stebbing to be at crossroads between Vienna and Cambridge analysis, and she was very critical of the former.[10] Yet, it is also doubtful that

---

[8] This was Stebbing's (1933) preferred terminology. This level of analysis is sometimes called "grammatical."

[9] As long as it is merely formal. *Principia Mathematica* is not, according to Stebbing; see pp. 90–91. See also Beaney (2003, pp. 339–340) for a useful elucidation of postulational analysis (which, following Bentham and Wisdom, he dubs "paraphrastic").

[10] See also "Logical Positivism and Analysis" (*LPA* hereafter) where she is very critical of Wittgenstein's approach to analysis. On the differences between Vienna and Cambridge analysis, see Beaney (2003).

40 SUSAN STEBBING

Moore engaged in metaphysical analysis, as Stebbing herself recognized in "Some Puzzles About Analysis" as well as in MI (p. 528). While Moore was not interested in linguistic analysis (even though his terminology, especially his reference to meaning, often obscured this point), it is quite difficult to attribute to him the view that, like Stebbing, he was interested in analyzing facts. For he never claimed that analysis should be first and foremost the analysis of true propositions (on the assumption that true propositions are facts), and he did not clarify what the constituents of propositions were in his view.[11] Rather, it was Wisdom who made such an attribution to Moore, when he wrote, in "Logical Constructions," "Philosophy is concerned with the analysis of facts—a doctrine which Wittgenstein has lately preached and Moore long practiced" (1931–1933, I, p. 195). Furthermore, as we will briefly see, Stebbing was critical of Russell's idea that physical objects are constructions out of sense data. Thus, the main precedent of Stebbing's metaphysical analysis was probably Wisdom's "Logical Constructions." Wisdom, however, credits Stebbing with the idea contained in MAM, and MAM was published when the publication of Wisdom's paper was still in progress.

Be that as it may, metaphysical analysis has a characteristic direction—whence its further label of "directional analysis." It goes from the more complex to the less complex and bottoms out in facts that are basic because they cannot be further analyzed into simpler ones.[12]

Take "I see a pen." No matter whether there is a pen or whether I am right about the fact that what I am seeing is in fact a pen, "I must continue to contend that I see something black and (roughly) cylindrical. This contention must be granted. *This, that is black and cylindrical*, which I now see, has often been called a 'sense-datum'" (p. 71). Stebbing goes on to claim that she is only adopting the word, without endorsing any theory about the nature of sense data and their relations to physical objects.

It is then clarified that sense data cannot be identical to physical objects because they are what "is directly presented to me in a given, determinate, perceptual situation" (p. 71) and, at most, only parts of objects are so given

---

[11] For further details on this, see Coliva (2021) and Janssen-Lauret (2022, pp. 45–53). For a contrary interpretation, see Milkov (2003).

[12] A common illustration of directional analysis is the analysis of committees into the individuals that compose them (cf. Stebbing (1934, pp. 34–35)), where we go from a complex group entity to a set of less complex entities like individuals. Yet, this is no more than an illustration, since facts about individuals are not ultimate. Directional analysis is not just "new level" analysis. Rather, as Stebbing points out in MAM, it is that kind of new level analysis that bottoms out in basic facts—that is, in facts that cannot be further analyzed.

SUSAN STEBBING'S WORK ON ANALYSIS 41

to us, while many of their other parts aren't. Furthermore, seeming to be aware of a sense datum and being aware of it are one and the same thing. Thus, there is no room for an appearance/reality distinction with respect to sense data (p. 71). Yet, we don't infer the presence of the physical object from the sense datum, according to Stebbing. Such an inference would be open to mistake and this would quickly lead to considering the existence of physical objects, or our belief in it, problematic (as for instance Hume (1739, I, iv, 2) and Russell (1912) did). Rather, the physical object (Stebbing calls it "perceptual object," p. 72) is *discerned* within a given perceptual situation" (p. 72, my emphasis). It is not further explained what "discerning" a physical object in a perceptual situation consists in. One way of making sense of this idea would be to think that the sense datum is that part of the surface of a physical object which is given to us in a specific perceptual situation. It wouldn't be the whole object, yet it would be a part of it, and not a mental entity. This would entail a certain view of sense data—one Moore is often associated with, even though he never committed to it and was indeed critical of, as is clear from DCS, IV.[13] If so, however, Stebbing herself could not be noncommittal about the nature of sense data, after all.[14]

Notice, furthermore, that the sense datum is not even what "this pen" signifies (p. 71). "Pen" for Stebbing means the physical object, not the sense datum. Yet the judgment, "This is a pen" or "I am seeing a pen," is *based on* and *refers to* the sense datum—it is based on that of which I am aware in the perceptual situation (MAM, p. 73)—whether I pay attention to it or not.

Echoing Russell, Stebbing maintains that philosophers have been drawn to this way of analyzing the fact that this is a pen because "a demonstrative symbol can be used only when the using of it is co-present with its referend" (p. 72). The whole physical object is never completely given in the perceptual scene; therefore, it cannot be the referent of "this" in the judgment "This is a pen." The reference we make to sense data is thus direct, whereas the reference we make to physical objects is always and necessarily indirect (p. 73). Still, contrary to Russell, Stebbing is clear, in "Logical Positivism and

---

[13] In DCS, IV Moore objects to such a conception of sense data.

[14] In later work, Stebbing writes: "Perceiving, I should contend, is neither direct nor inferential. To suppose that these alternatives are exhaustive is a prime mistake of Logical Positivism. Perceiving is certainly *indirect*; but it is a non-inferential, indirect *knowing*" (Stebbing 1933, p. 78). By perceiving a pen indirectly, since the direct object of perception is a sense datum, we nevertheless know, and know non-inferentially, that there is a pen in front of us. It seems to me that for this idea to have some prospects of success, the sense datum should be considered identical to the part of the object perceived. Yet, this is no more than a tentative conjecture.

42 SUSAN STEBBING

Analysis" (*LPA* hereafter, p. 34), that physical objects, like pens and tables, are not constructs of sense data. As she writes "*Points* and *electrons* may be constructs, *tables* certainly are not."[15] Yet, until the nature of sense data is clarified, the relation between physical objects and sense data is going to be unclear and potentially problematic (pp. 73–74).

What is clear to Stebbing (like to Moore, see DCS, IV), on the contrary, is that we cannot hope to answer the general question "What is a physical object?" before answering the question "What is a pen?" (or some other relevant instance of the category of physical object), and that an answer to that question depends on knowing facts about this pen I am now seeing. To suppose otherwise would entail being content.

> with a definition, which leads us nowhere. . . . It is useless first to define "material thing" . . . and then to ask whether [that term is] exemplified in the world. Yet this is what the deductive metaphysician does, unless he takes the easier course of defining the terms, and then ruling out whatever does not conform to the definition as 'mere appearance.' (p. 74)

Now, while Moore in DCS, IV, is adamant that he is interested in analyzing *propositions* like "This is a pen," Stebbing is interested in analyzing the *fact* that this is a pen (p. 77, see also p. 82). The reason she gives is that propositions are what sentences in different languages can all express and their elements "are constituents of the world; if the proposition is *true*, these constituents of the proposition are the elements of the *facts* to which the proposition refers" (p. 78, my emphasis). Moreover, metaphysical analysis is concerned primarily with true propositions, because it aims at knowledge. Hence, it is, at least primarily, an analysis of facts (on the assumptions that true propositions are facts). Notice, however, that this argument presupposes a particular take on the nature of propositions, which is incompatible with a Fregean account of propositions as composed of the *senses* of the words that occur in the sentences that express them. It is also incompatible with the *Tractarian* view that propositions are pictures composed of (logically proper) *names* which *stand for* objects, sharing the same logical form with the states of affairs they depict. Yet, it is compatible with a Russellian conception of propositions, at least at a structural level. That is, Stebbing seems to agree with Russell that at a structural level propositions are composed of

---

[15] Constructs, moreover, aren't fictions, for Stebbing.

worldly items. This is compatible with taking different views about the nature and identity of these worldly items. This account of propositions clearly raises problems of its own, concerning vacuous or fictional proper names, for instance. Yet, Russell's theory of description was meant precisely to overcome them.[16] Be that as it may, we can put the point by saying that Stebbing's metaphysical analysis would aim at clarifying the structure of *truth-makers*, rather than of truth-bearers.[17]

Now, the point of analysis, for Stebbing, like for Moore and Wittgenstein, is not to discover the immediate reference of a proposition since we know it already simply in virtue of understanding the proposition (pp. 78–79). Rather, it is to discover "what *exactly* it asserts"—that is, what it *refers to* "however indirectly" (pp. 78–79). To know this "is to know what must be the case if we are asserting truly" (p. 79). Stebbing exemplifies this idea with the proposition that *every economist is fallible*. What I am asserting exactly by that entails that Maynard Keynes is fallible, Karl Marx is fallible, *and so on*. So reference is made to Keynes, as well as to any other economist, even if none of them is the immediate reference of the proposition.[18] Analysis is then directional because it identifies those more basic facts—like the fact that Keynes is fallible, that Karl Marx is fallible, that Amartya Sen is fallible, etc.—which must obtain for the proposition that all economists are fallible to be true. These facts may be based on even more basic ones, where "a fact F is based upon F' when F cannot be unless F' is" (p. 80). Metaphysical analysis ultimately bottoms out in *basic facts*—that is, in facts that are not based on any other fact. Stebbing's basic facts are clearly reminiscent of "atomic facts" in the *Tractatus* (*TLP* 2) that are depicted by "atomic propositions" (as Russell (1922) calls them), also because, like in the *Tractatus*, for Stebbing if "we could express" them, "there would be complete isomorphy between these *facts* and their expression" (p. 82; cf. *TLP* 2.18, 2.2, 4.121).

Metaphysical analysis thus "presupposes certain assumptions with regard to the constitution of the world ... [which] are not logically necessary" (p. 80, cf. p. 87). It presupposes the existence of such atomic or basic facts that serve as building blocks of all other facts.

---

[16] Black (1933) is a sustained critique of Stebbing's idea that analysis should reveal the structure of facts. According to Black, analysis can only reveal the underlying logical structure of propositions. For a discussion of Black's criticism of Stebbing, see Beaney (2003, §3).

[17] I am indebted to Sandra Lapointe for this incisive formulation.

[18] Stebbing also distinguishes between referring to Keynes, in this case, and being acquainted with him, and holds that reference does not presuppose acquaintance.

44 SUSAN STEBBING

According to Stebbing, we cannot analyze what we don't or even can't understand (p. 80). She credits Moore with this crucial insight,[19] even if there is no trace of it in DCS. As she will state in later writings (MI, pp. 519–520), Moore's insistence on attaining a clear understanding of what is meant by certain philosophically germane expressions (e.g., "external world"), acquires its significance in this context. That is, it is the first necessary step toward giving a satisfactory analysis.[20]

An important corollary of this is that metaphysical analysis is incompatible with explicationism *à la* Carnap. Writes Stebbing: "we cannot hope to solve metaphysical problems by assigning out-of-the-way meanings to ordinary expressions" (MAM, p. 86). That is, we must make clear what is meant by our *ordinary* way of speaking, if we want to find out what facts the propositions expressed by our sentences refer to. If, in contrast, we substitute those ordinary words with new ones, or select only a subset of their ordinary meaning, then our analysis would not clarify what we referred to exactly in the first place, but it would clarify, at most, what the propositions expressed by these precisified expressions refer to.[21] In this sense, metaphysical analysis is tied to the analysis of ordinary language and is not the analysis of an ideal, or curbed, or regimented, or more precise, or more scientific language.

Yet, in *LPA* (p. 31), Stebbing also insists that our understanding may be a matter of degree. She writes, "I want to urge that it is a grave mistake to suppose that the alternatives are *understanding*, on the one hand, and *simply not understanding*, on the other. We understand more or less clearly." Stebbing is thus critical of Wittgenstein's idea, in the *Tractatus*, that either what we think can be stated clearly, or else it is nonsense. For, according to Stebbing, even if we have a partial understanding, we may still engage in directional analysis, because we "know that what we say is true" (ivi, p. 34). By inquiring "what must be the case if what we have said is true . . . we may come to see more clearly what it is we were knowing" (ivi, p. 34). Thus, even if it is correct to "assert that scientific concepts must be clarified, . . . it is a muddle to suppose

---

[19] As remarked by Janssen-Lauret (2022, p. 12): "Stebbing was generous with acknowledgements where she took her views to originate with others, a trait typical of early analytic female philosophers. . . . Although this trait is, in general admirable, Stebbing at times gives herself insufficient credit for originality."

[20] Stebbing makes this point also in *LPA* (p. 30). For a critical appraisal of this point, see Beaney (2003, pp. 340–341).

[21] This clearly anticipates the objection made by Strawson against Carnap's explicationism, and nowadays customarily raised against conceptual engineering projects, that they would entail a change in topic.

that this clarification is a pursuit of meaning." Rather, Stebbing seems to suggest, it is a pursuit of what in the world makes our judgment true. Hence, to stress, metaphysical analysis is not, in and of itself, meant to reveal to us what we mean by the words we use. On the contrary, it is meant to clarify what facts in the world make our judgements true. Hence, "the task of philosophy [is] to render our thoughts clear. . . . [Yet] we cannot clarify our thoughts by thinking about thinking, nor by thinking about logic. We have to think *about* what we *were* thinking about" (ivi, p. 36).

To put it provocatively, and somewhat misleadingly, as we shall see, Stebbing is hereby suggesting that clarifying our thoughts is intertwined with acquiring knowledge of facts in the world. More specifically, it is intertwined with determining what basic facts make our judgments true. In this sense, she comes close to the rejection of the analytic/synthetic distinction, whereby the clarification of our thoughts consists merely in carrying out conceptual analysis from the armchair.[22] Indeed, what she calls "analytic clarification of a concept" (*LPA*, pp. 29–30) is already intertwined with knowledge of the facts in the world. For, in the way of an example, Stebbing claims that Einsteinian physics brought about a change in our concept of simultaneity. Yet, metaphysical analysis is directed at the world by seeking to determine the basic facts that make our judgments true.

Further, Stebbing notes that if the *point* of metaphysical analysis is to acquire *knowledge* of the structure of facts (of a higher order), some of the propositions we analyze must be true and known to be true. Or, to put it differently, if metaphysical analysis is to yield knowledge of how nature is carved at its joints (facts of a lower, more fundamental order), and if it starts with propositions about, for instance, middle-size objects in our surroundings, which are based on, and are made true by these more fundamental facts, it must itself start with some true proposition, or fact that we know (see MAM, p. 92).

Now, Stebbing rightly points out that what is problematic in the method of analysis, once we are clear about its presuppositions, are the metaphysical assumptions it depends on, particularly that it bottoms out in absolutely specific basic facts (cf. also *LPA*, p. 32). For these presuppositions are not logically necessary (MAM, p. 87, cf. p. 80). Writes Stebbing:

---

[22] Milkov (2003, p. 358) claims that Stebbing (and Moore) were denying the analytic/synthetic distinction well before Quine's rejection of it. Yet, as we shall see, Stebbing is ultimately skeptical of the very possibility of metaphysical analysis. Thus, it is unclear to what an extent she would have rejected the analytic/synthetic distinction.

46   SUSAN STEBBING

> These assumptions entail certain consequences with regard to the con-
> stitution of the world. It cannot be maintained that the world is certainly
> so constituted. If it could, then the method of metaphysics might be de-
> ductive. But unless the world *is* so constituted metaphysical analysis is not
> possible. Hence, those who employ this method ought to attempt to de-
> termine to what extent, if any, it is reasonable to grant these assumptions.
> (MAM, p. 87)

Notice that Stebbing is here introducing a powerful idea *against* the very possibility of metaphysical analysis. This point may go unnoticed because the first part of the paper is devoted to what looks like not simply a characterization and a methodological clarification of metaphysical analysis, but a defense of it.[23] Yet, this is not in the end or the aim of the paper. Its goal is to clarify in detail the presuppositions on which metaphysical analysis rests and then evaluate whether they are plausible. As we have just seen, Stebbing ultimately returns a negative verdict on this latter issue. Yet, she does not dismiss it out of hand. Rather, she gives it its best shot, and, even if she is skeptical of its prospects, she never sounds dismissive. Probably, at the time of MAM, she still wished to remain somewhat open to the possibility that it could be shown that the world is as metaphysical analysis requires it to be, if that kind of analysis is to be possible at all.[24]

Let us return now to the reasons that she thinks that metaphysical analysis is ultimately not viable. Since it cannot be wholly deductive and a priori, unless there are good reasons to think that the world contains basic, non-further reducible and analyzable facts, metaphysical analysis is simply impossible. That is, if the world is not like that, then directional analysis is impossible, for it cannot reach an end point and is destined to proceed in a

---

[23] In "Some Puzzles About Analysis" (henceforth SPA, 1938–1939, p. 72) Stebbing states: "I tried to show [in MAM] that this metaphysical use of the method of analysis rested upon certain assumptions which, so far as I knew, had not been explicitly stated. . . . I tried further to show that, once the assumptions were explicitly stated, they did not seem very plausible. It appears that I entirely failed to make this contention clear, for several writers have subsequently taken me to have been defending the use of the method of analysis in metaphysics."

In "Moore's Influence" (1942, p. 527) Stebbing states: "I think there are good reasons for saying that the notion of basic facts is a hang-over from the days when 'the problem of the external world' was envisaged as primarily a problem of justifying common sense beliefs, although it is Moore himself who has clearly shown us that these beliefs do not stand in need of justification but only of analysis."

[24] I therefore fully concur with Chapman (2013, pp. 70–71; cf. also p. 93), and Beaney and Chapman (2017, §3), who point out that Stebbing is not endorsing metaphysical analysis but is adopting "it as a hypothetical possibility, in order to establish what would follow from it" and to clarify "the assumptions on which it rests and the principles by which it must proceed."

circle (or be open-ended and infinite). Yet, it is of the essence of directional analysis—as opposed to symbolic analysis (p. 87)—that it be non-circular and that it would reach an end point.

Now, one might suggest that the end point could be determined arbitrarily. That is, one might say something like *"for our current purposes*, let arrangements of atoms be the simple facts on which all other facts are based," where this is compatible with saying *"for these other purposes of ours*, let us consider what atoms are composed of." The operator "for our purposes," however, would give the game of metaphysical analysis away, according to Stebbing. For, if the adjective "metaphysical" is to do any serious work at all, it cannot be up to us, even less to our purposes, how we carve up nature at its joints, as it were (MAM, p. 89).

Symbolic analysis allows us to treat complexes as simples (for instance, when we take a more complex formula and indicate it with a letter and operate on it), but metaphysical analysis worth its name is supposed to give us knowledge about mind- and representation-independent facts. Thus, it is of its essence that the world be as it needs to be for it to be possible. Yet, we have no guarantee whatsoever that the world be that way.

Stebbing then concludes:

> My difficulty is not that these assumptions are involved in metaphysical analysis; it is whether they can be justified. When we have made explicit what is entailed by directional analysis, we find we must make assumptions which so far from being certainly justified, are not even very plausible. Yet, unless they can be justified, the method of metaphysical analysis cannot yield results capable of solving our problems. (pp. 91–92).

In later writings, such as SPA and MI, Stebbing returns on the issue of whether there are basic facts, that could be the end point of metaphysical analysis and denies that. In MI, she clearly states that sense data, which, according to metaphysical analysis, should be the constituents of basic facts, are

> elements discriminated within a context, and the discrimination is relative to the specific set of questions arising out of that context. Within that context the sense-data can be taken as basic, but, even so, they are not the termination of a directional analysis of common sense propositions. . . . [W]hat is basic is to be determined by the purpose of the investigation. (1942, pp. 527–528)

48   SUSAN STEBBING

What Stebbing is in fact claiming, already in MAM and throughout her career, is that the idea of "basic facts," or of simple and unanalyzable elements of reality, is a philosophical myth. In a very Wittgensteinian spirit—this time in the vein of *Philosophical Investigations* (henceforth *PI*. See *PI* §§38–79, especially 47–48)—she notices that considering something as simple or complex is an arbitrary choice, constrained only by the purposes of the investigation at hand.[25] The significance of this claim is not to expose the fact that the distinction is impossible but that it is not metaphysically serviceable—that is, that there is no prospect in the kind of metaphysical analysis which is meant to carve nature at its joints. Clearly if that is the project metaphysics as a whole identifies as central, then so much the worse for metaphysics. Thus, contrary to logical positivists, Stebbing is not saying that metaphysics is nonsense, or that so-called metaphysical truths are at most grammatical—that is, conceptual—necessities. Rather, she is criticizing its fundamental methodological assumption—namely, that there are metaphysically basic facts.

In sum, in MAM, Stebbing clearly spells out the project of metaphysical analysis and raises crucial objections against it. Neither the methodological clarity nor the critique of the entire project is to be found in Moore's writings, particularly DCS, which Stebbing—contentiously, as we have seen—considers the best example of metaphysical analysis. Her critique is in fact similar, yet prior, to Wittgenstein's in *Philosophical Investigations*. Finally, since metaphysical analysis, for Stebbing, would be the best way of pursuing metaphysics, far superior to the kind of metaphysics that, since Descartes and Hume, up to British Idealism, has tried to provide a justification for our commonsensical beliefs, its demise is, in fact, the demise of metaphysics, as Stebbing sees it. Stebbing did not explicitly draw that conclusion in MAM, probably because she wished to remain open to the idea that it might be shown that the world is constituted by basic facts. In time, however, it became clear to her that that residual hope was indeed vain—"a hangover from

---

[25] Compare Wittgenstein's *PI*, 47: We use the word "composite" (and therefore the word "simple") in an enormous number of different and differently related ways. (Is the colour of a square on a chess board simple, or does it consist of pure white and pure yellow?) And is white simple or does it consist of the colours of the rainbow? Is this length of 2 cm simple, or does it consist of two parts each 1 cm long? But why not of one bit 3 cm long, and 1 bit 1 cm long measured in the opposite direction? To the philosophical question: "is the visual image of this tree composite and what are its component parts?" the correct answer is: "That depends on what you understand by 'composite.'" (And that is of course not an answer but the rejection of the question). For a discussion of Wittgenstein's rejection of his earlier atomism, see Coliva 2020b.

the days when 'the problem of the external world' was envisaged as primarily a problem of justifying common sense beliefs" (MI, p. 527), but also from the days when eminent analytic philosophers engaged themselves in the project of analysis—metaphysical or otherwise.

5 Conclusions

As the preceding should have made abundantly clear, Stebbing's metaphysical analysis was a major and original contribution to the debate about analysis that occupied so many philosophers up to the end of the 1930s. Stebbing was clearer than any of her contemporaries about the various kinds of analysis we may engage in, and she was critical of those philosophers who thought that analysis should (only or mainly) aim at the clarification of the meaning of our ordinary words, or that it could be conducted merely with a priori means, or that thought that analysis could subvert our commonsensical belief that there are physical objects. Rather, the task of philosophy for her consisted in carrying out metaphysical analyses that could reveal the ultimate truth-makers of our true judgments. By so doing, metaphysical analysis would contribute to our knowledge of the world as well as to the clarification of our thought. In that, Stebbing may be seen as a precursor of the rejection of the analytic/synthetic distinction. Still, Stebbing was also acutely aware of the limitations of metaphysical analysis, which inevitably rests on the ungrounded assumption that such basic facts exist and that we may identify them. Furthermore, Stebbing also surprisingly anticipated many points against skepticism and the possibility of proving commonsensical beliefs that are usually associated with Moore's epistemological writings and Wittgenstein's *On Certainty* (to some extent).

If, as I have claimed elsewhere,[26] a philosophical classic is such because of the questions and prospects it raises, Stebbing's "The Method of Analysis in Metaphysics" should be considered a classic of Early Analytic Philosophy, for its contributions to both epistemology and metaphysics, on par with much more celebrated works by a whole host of male colleagues of hers.

---

[26] Coliva 2010, p. 5.

References

Beaney, M. 2003. "Susan Stebbing on Cambridge and Vienna Analysis" In F. Stadler, ed., 339–350, *The Vienna Circle and Logical Empiricism: Re-evaluation and Future Perspectives.* Dordrech: Kluwer.

Beaney, M., and S. Chapman. 2017. "Susan Stebbing," *The Stanford Encyclopedia of Philosophy* (Summer Edition), Edward N. Zalta, ed. https://plato.stanford.edu/archives/sum2017/entries/stebbing/.

Black, M. 1933. "Philosophical Analysis." *Proceedings of the Aristotelian Society* 33 (1932–33): 237–258.

Bradley, F. H. 1893–1897. *Appearance and Reality.* Oxford: Clarendon Press, 1930.

Chapman, S. 2013. *Susan Stebbing and the Language of Common Sense.* London: Palgrave.

Coliva, A. 2010. *Moore and Wittgenstein. Scepticism, Certainty and Common Sense.* London: Palgrave.

Coliva, A. 2018a. "Moore and Mooreanism." In D. E. Machuca and B. Reed, eds., 467–480, *Skepticism. From Antiquity to the Present.* London: Bloomsbury.

Coliva, A. 2018b. "What Do Philosophers Do? Maddy, Moore and Wittgenstein." *International Journal for the Study of Skepticism* 8 (3): 198–207.

Coliva, A. 2020a. "Are There Mathematical Hinges?" *International Journal for the Study of Skepticism* 10(3–4): 346–366.

Coliva, A. 2020b. "Logical Atomism and Wittgenstein." In U. Zilioli, ed., 301–311, *Atomism in Philosophy.* London: Bloomsbury.

Coliva, A. 2024. "What Do Philosophers Do? Maddy, Moore (and Wittgenstein) II." In J. Kennedy and S. Arbeiter, eds., 299–310, *The Philosophy of Penelope Maddy.* Cham: Springer.

Coliva, A. 2021. "Stebbing, Moore (and Wittgenstein) on Common Sense and Metaphysical Analysis." *British Journal for the History of Philosophy* 29 (5): 914–934.

Hume, D. 1739. *Treatise on Human Nature.* Oxford: Clarendon Press, 1978.

Janssen-Lauret, F. 2022. *Susan Stebbing.* Cambridge: Cambridge University Press.

McTaggart, J. 1906. *Some Dogmas of Religion.* London: Edward Arnold Press.

Milkov, N. 2003. "Susan Stebbing's Criticism of Wittgenstein's *Tractatus.*" In F. Stadler, ed., 351–363, *The Vienna Circle and Logical Empiricism: Re-evaluation and Future Perspectives.* Dordrecht: Kluwer.

Moore, G. E. 1909. "Hume's Philosophy." In his *Philosophical Studies* 1922, 147–167. London-New York: Kegan Paul.

Moore, G. E. 1925. "A Defence of Common Sense." In *Philosophical Papers*, 32–59. London: George Allen and Unwin, 1959.

Moore, G. E. 1939. "Proof of an External World." In *Philosophical Papers.* London: George Allen and Unwin, 1959, 127–150.

Moore, G. E. 1942. "A Reply to My Critics." In P. A. Schilpp, ed., 535–677, *The Philosophy of G. E. Moore.* Evanston: Northwestern University Press.

Russell, B. 1912. *The Problems of Philosophy.* London: Williams and Norgate; New York: Henry Holt.

Russell, B. 1922. "Introduction." In L. Wittgenstein *Tractatus Logico-Philosophicus.* London: Kegan Paul, 7–19.

Stebbing, S. 1932. "The Method of Analysis in Metaphysics." *Proceedings of the Aristotelian Society* 33: 65–94.

Stebbing, S. 1933. "Logical Positivism and Analysis." *Proceedings of the British Academy* 19: 53–87.

Stebbing, S. 1934. "Directional Analysis and Basic Facts." *Analysis* 2: 33–36.

Stebbing, S. 1938–1939. "Some Puzzles About Analysis." *Proceedings of the Aristotelian Society* 39: 69–84.

Stebbing, S. 1942. "Moore's Influence." In P. Schillp, ed., 517–532, *The Philosophy of G. E. Moore.* Evanston: Northwestern University Press.

SUSAN STEBBING'S WORK ON ANALYSIS   51

Wisdom, J. 1931–1933. *Logical Constructions*, Parts I–V. *Mind*, 40–42: Parts I–II, 40, pp. 188–216; Part III, 41, pp. 441–64; Part IV, 42, pp. 43–66; Part V, 42, pp. 186–202. Repr. together as *Logical Constructions*, J. J. Thomson, ed. New York: Random House, 1969.

Wittgenstein, L. 1921. *Tractatus Logico-Philosophicus*. Oxford: Blackwell.

Wittgenstein, L. 1953. *Philosophical Investigations*. Oxford: Blackwell.

Wittgenstein, L. 1969. *On Certainty*. Oxford: Blackwell.

Stebbing on Clarity

Eric Schliesser

The main aim of this chapter is to analyze Susan Stebbing's views on the nature of clarity in the 1930s.[1] I limit myself to this period because it allows for a contrast between her sophisticated and significant views on what I call "the standard conception of clarity" with her view on "democratic clarity" developed in her (1939) *Thinking to Some Purpose*. I contextualize her views with some alternative characterizations of clarity on offer among other early analytic philosophers (including brief discussions of Carnap, Quine, Price, and Nagel). While my focus is on Stebbing, I show, thereby, that in the great age of clarification in early analytic philosophy there was no consensus on the nature of clarity. This helps illuminate some of the by now well-known difficulties in treating analytic philosophy as a unified project. The other pay-off of my approach should be the start of a taxonomy of the kinds of clarity.

Before I give a summary of the main sections, here is a cautionary note by way of some terminological clarification. In what follows I am largely unconcerned with the origin and value placed on writing perspicuously or expressing oneself lucidly, that is what hereafter I shall call, "presentational clarity." Some analytic philosophers quite clearly prized such presentational clarity, especially in the context of polemics with (say) Bradley and his followers or, later, Heidegger and his followers.

In the first section, I focus on the early modern ways of ideas, and Pierce's discussion and criticism of it, in order to set up discussion of the structure of what I call "the standard conception of clarity" in early analytic philosophy. In the second section, I show that the standard conception of clarity is indeed standard and with the help of Stebbing's interpretation of Wittgenstein I point to an ambiguity in it. In the third section, and drawing

---

[1] I am grateful to the editors of this volume for the invitation, their encouragement, and comments.

Eric Schliesser, *Stebbing on Clarity* In: *Susan Stebbing*. Edited by: Annalisa Coliva and Louis Doulas, Oxford University Press. © Oxford University Press 2025. DOI: 10.1093/9780197682371.003.0003

on her fourfold characterization of analysis, I also show that the standard conception smooths over considerable heterogeneity. I develop this point by looking at the significance of Stebbing's largely—despite Ayer's alertness to it—overlooked treatment of what she calls "analytic clarification of concepts." I show that Stebbing anticipates themes commonly associated with Quine and Kuhn. In the fourth section I put the distinctiveness of Stebbing's accounts of clarity in context by looking at Ernest Nagel's and a Carnapian conception of clarity. In the fifth section, I focus on the role and nature of what I call "democratic clarity" in *Thinking to Some Purpose*. It turns out that this is quite distinct from the standard conception of clarity. I emphasize Stebbing's contribution to articulating the pre-conditions of deliberative democracy, but I also highlight some lacunae in her approach.

1 Prelude; From the Way of Ideas to How to Make Our Ideas Clear

From Descartes to Hume, the so-called way of ideas was devoted to the notion that clarity is a desirable property or quality of ideas. I do not mean to suggest that after this way was abandoned clarity disappeared wholly as a philosophical ideal; the subsequent German age embraced, at least briefly, *Aufklärung* for individuals and society alike. One cannot help notice that *Aufklärung* shares a common root with clarification [*klärung*]. But while clarity was not ignored during the nineteenth century altogether, until our ongoing "age of analysis" clarity was at best a lower, philosophical virtue.

Somewhat frustratingly, other than being a desirable quality of our ideas because clarity is a mark or a sign of truth, it's much harder to say what clarity is in the way of ideas.[2] In his (1878) "How to Make Our Ideas Clear," Peirce mocks a definition that he attributes to Leibniz—to wit, that clarity is "the clear apprehension of everything contained in the definition" of the notion one is clear about. I'd be surprised this idea is really found in Leibniz.[3] But fairly or not, Peirce does put his finger on one of the problems with the way of

---

[2] *Locus classicus* on the way of ideas is Yolton 1956. This also includes non-trivial discussion of what different thinkers might have meant by "clarity" and its cognates. I am unaware, alas, of a standard account of the evolving ideas notions of clarity in the way of the ideas.

[3] For a sophisticated account of Leibniz's views on clarity, see Smith 2003, especially note 38 (on p. 63), and McQuillan 2017. I thank John Callanan and Stefan Heßbrüggen for the suggestions.

54 SUSAN STEBBING

ideas, which was not so clear on clarity as one would have wished. One often gets the impression that among the early moderns a certain kind of acquaintance (in Russell's sense) with the experience of clarity of one's ideas is simply assumed.[4]

Peirce revived the notion that clarity is a quality of one's ideas or, as shall be clear from what follows, one's conception. Peirce's major contribution to the subject is not so much to explain what clarity is but to restart discussion of how we can attain it, although these are not entirely distinct for him. For he proposed the following "rule" (known as a precursor to the pragmatic maxim) to attain clarity: "Consider what effects, that might conceivably have practical bearings, we conceive the object of our conception to have. Then, our conception of these effects is the whole of our conception of the object" (Peirce 1878, 293).

Clarity, then, for Peirce is in the first instance not so much a particular quality of our ideas but more akin to a kind of second order effect of a proper conception, which is, in turn, the effect of a successful kind of enquiry. This proper conception itself is attained by a species of verification; if that is too misleading and too anachronistic here, substitute for "verification" a practical understanding of what one may do with such a conception. Once one has completed the verification or survey of the effects of the conception one is exploring then one attains clarity about the conception.

I doubt Peirce's approach to clarity influenced clarity's high status in early analytic philosophy, but Stebbing was familiar with it.[5] As I argue in the next section in more detail, Peirce anticipates something of the structure or form of thought about clarity among early analytic philosophers. By this I do not mean the adoption of verificationism in Vienna or a kind of pragmatism that runs through (say) early Wittgenstein and Frank Ramsey. But rather he anticipates the idea that a certain process of investigation/enquiry leads to clarity. That is, clarity is the fruits of analysis.

---

[4] It's tempting to say that "clarity" was taken to be a primitive, un-analyzed notion within the way of ideas. But this is not true. All of the thinkers say something about it such that one can often say quite a bit about what they *would* say about clarity if pressed.

[5] Stebbing 1936, 117, mentions the essay explicitly when she reviewed some of Peirce's *Collected Papers*. She notes that "pragmaticism" is the "doctrine Peirce regarded as essentially a method for making our ideas clear." She also praises Peirce's "unusually penetrating apprehension of the fact that muddled thinking and the unclear use of language go together; that to clarify thought we must pay attention to language, and that in so doing we shall be led to a theory of signs." I thank Michael Kremer for alerting me to this review.

2 The Standard Conception of Clarity in Early Analytic Philosophy

It is uncontroversial that from its start, analytic philosophy presupposes that, to quote from a well-known lecture by G. E. Moore, "It helps you to be clear, (the desirability of clarity being assumed)" (Moore and Masterman 1934, 29). This was published in the second issue of *Analysis*, a journal Stebbing helped found (and her name is listed as one of its co-editors on the masthead). It's natural to assume, and not wholly wrong, that "clarity" here refers to presentational clarity. What follows is not intended to deny the significance of a commitment to presentational clarity to the development of early analytic philosophy. But I argue that this was not what was thought distinctive of the movement, nor what early critics of the enterprise complained about.[6]

By 1945, H. H. Price summarized a whole range of *criticisms* of analytic philosophy with the slogan "Clarity Is Not Enough" (the title of Price's lecture and also a 1963 volume edited by H. D. Lewis that leads with a reprint of this lecture). It's less clear, however, what clarity amounts to. For example, in Price the *standard* conception of clarity just is the *fruits* or *effect* of analysis. He writes: "I propose to use the words 'clarification' and 'analysis' (both of which are metaphors after all) as if they were synonymous" (Price 1945, 3). But, unfortunately, he does not unpack the metaphors.[7] So, analysis aims at clarity, or analysis clarifies.[8] But this raises the question of what clarity is and to say so *not* by way of negative ostension or contrasting example—say, "British/absolute idealism" (back then), "continental philosophy" (more recently)—but concretely.

---

[6] I have defended the claim that "analytic philosophy" gets baptized in the modern sense by Ernest Nagel (1936a and 1936b) in Schliesser 2013. Ayer 1936, p. 53, describes the British variant as a "movement."

[7] I use "standard" because Price himself also offers a new, additional conception of clarity, what he calls "synoptic" clarity which is the effect of "a conceptual scheme which brings out certain systematic relationships between the [known] matters of fact" (Price 1945, 29). See also my treatment of Stebbing on analytic clarification of a concept and Quine's views in section 3 below.

[8] In fact, this is one of the evident commitments of Moore back in 1934: "That philosophic analysis will make us clearer *when we are doing philosophy*, i.e. *philosophy* is worth doing for its own sake. (a) When you are understanding the analysis itself, because this understanding sometimes produces a specific kind of clearness which is worth having for its own sake. (b) When understanding an analysis helps you to answer other philosophic questions" (Moore and Masterman 1934, 29).

56   SUSAN STEBBING

I do not mean to suggest that treating clarity as the fruits of analysis itself is idiosyncratic in the early analytic tradition.[9] For example, it clearly echoes a famous passage in Wittgenstein's *Tractatus* (in Ogden's translation):

> The object of philosophy is the logical clarification of thoughts.
> Philosophy is not a theory but an activity.
> A philosophical work consists essentially of elucidations.
> The result of philosophy is not a number of "philosophical propositions,"
>   but to make propositions clear.
> Philosophy should make clear and delimit sharply the thoughts which
>   otherwise are, as it were, opaque and blurred.—4.112

In his "Introduction" to the *Tractatus*, Russell called attention to this very passage (and the material leading up 4.16), that on Wittgenstein's conception "The result of philosophy is not a number of 'philosophical propositions,' but to make propositions clear." On the combined authority of Russell and Wittgenstein, then, the claim that philosophical analysis generates clarity will be, henceforth, dubbed "the standard conception" of clarity.

However, in the quoted material in Wittgenstein's *Tractatus* there is an oscillation between propositions and thoughts. And in both cases (thoughts and propositions) there is something of a mystery how they could be more or less clear and, say, remain the same entity. Once one starts pressing on what propositions are supposed to be matters do not get easier. For, at one point Wittgenstein claims, explicitly following Frege and Russell, that a proposition just is "a function of the expressions contained in it" (3.318). Understanding such functions is the road toward clarity, and so on.

I am, then, suggesting that the details of what a particular conception of analysis is about and the tools used in it are going to matter quite a bit in constraining how one conceives of clarity. Not to put too fine a point on it, but it is the nature of one's analysis that explains the kind of clarity one ends up with on the standard conception.

For example, at a suitable level of generality (and vagueness), it is natural to understand Frege, Russell, and Wittgenstein as agreeing that one can design a logical symbolism or formal language to supply the means

---

[9] Near the start of his lecture, Price notes correctly that "the word 'analysis,' it is true, was sometimes associated with a particular school of philosophers, the so-called Cambridge school. But many Philosophers who did not subscribe to all the tenets and methods of that school would have agreed with this conception" (Price 1945, 3).

of analysis. What is clarified thereby is the language or linguistic structure (of, say, mathematics—now stipulating with Paul Samuelson that it is a language) analyzed. (See also Khan 1993, which draws on Wittgenstein.) Wittgenstein also thought that analysis could be applied to the way logical symbolism is used in one's analysis. One could thereby learn to avoid, say, not merely equivocations and ambiguity of the language analyzed but also avoid confusions about language caused by one's symbolic language of analysis, including the specialist one(s) deployed by the analysist.[10]

Notice that in addition to thoughts and propositions (and functions), I have now somewhat cavalierly suggested that language or at least language-use can be clarified, too. That is, to repeat, the details of the kind of analysis one uses matters to the kind of clarity one can achieve in the standard conception of clarity.

It is worth noting that in her lecture, "Logical Positivism and Analysis," Stebbing understands the very same material in Wittgenstein just discussed as follows: "that to clarify our thought we must understand the logic of our language." And she goes on to claim that this "understanding is achieved when we have discerned the principles of symbolism and can thus answer the question how it is that sentences mean" (Stebbing 1933, 10). My interest here is not to contest Stebbing's reading of Wittgenstein (whom she treats as a kind of verificationist of the sort commonly associated with a naïve strand of logical positivism—she clearly relies on Schlick's reading of Wittgenstein). But here clarity involves a kind of semantic understanding that allows one to *do* certain things: according to her Wittgenstein "is thus concerned to lay down certain principles in accordance with which language can be so used as to construct significant propositions" (Stebbing 1933, 11). That is, semantic understanding is the basis for a certain know-how. I mention this not because I agree with Stebbing's reading of the *Tractatus* but to note that even Wittgenstein's presentational clarity can give rise to many kinds of informed interpretations of what he thinks clarification really is. Part of the issue lurking here is that presentational clarity is not just a feature of one's prose but also an interaction with the audience's expectations and knowledge.

Be that as it may, on the standard position, clarity is the fruits of analysis. This is best understood not so much as a quality of ideas or propositions but more a second order effect on the conception of the analyst of the matter analyzed (that is, the analysandum). Of course, what is analyzed and the

---

[10] This whole paragraph is indebted to Kremer 2013.

58 SUSAN STEBBING

manner of analysis may well change the nature of this second order of effect. So, lurking in the standard position, which uniformly treats clarity as the effect and desideratum of (successful) analysis, is a possible equivocation about what is fundamentally achieved. I explore the ramifications of this in the next section.

3 Stebbing on Analytic Clarification

If clarity is the effect of analysis (the "standard conception"), then its character is, at least in part, determined by the nature of analysis. By the 1930s it was sufficiently clear that different kinds of analysis were being practiced alongside each other. In fact, in her "Logical Positivism and Analysis," Stebbing made this very point explicit: "there are various kinds of analysis." She lists "four different kinds," although in context it's possible she thinks there are more. "These four kinds are: (1) analytic definition of a symbolic expression; (2) analytic clarification of a concept; (3) postulational analysis; (4) directional analysis" (Stebbing 1933, 29). At the First International Congress for the Unity of Science (1936), Ayer called attention to this passage and helps explain its polemical significance; that in her "pamphlet," Stebbing charges that "the logical positivists have confused the first three" (Ayer 1936, 58).

On the standard conception of clarity, each of these kinds of analysis generates a clarity proper to it. In all cases this should involve a better understanding of the analysandum, including disambiguation, removal of equivocation, and/or the re-formulation in a more precise language (of symbolic logic). Of course, it's possible that the kind of fruit borne by these four kinds of analysis belongs to the same genus, but one cannot simply assume it, and Stebbing (rightly) does not. For Stebbing thinks that "the analytic clarification of a concept differs considerably from the other three kinds of analysis" (Stebbing 1933, 29). In this section I explain the significance of this remark.

While Stebbing's views on and practice of postulational and directional— which she sometimes calls "metaphysical"—analysis have received considerable and increasing attention,[11] her views on analytic clarification have been much less reviewed, even in some of the best work on Stebbing.[12] What she

---

[11] For recent careful work on Stebbing's views on directional/metaphysical analysis, see Coliva 2021 and Douglas and Nassim 2021.

[12] For example, Beaney assimilates Stebbing's idea of "analytic clarification of a concept" to Russell's "paradigm" of analysis: "I might say 'It is false that the present King of France is bald,' and

STEBBING ON CLARITY 59

means by "analytic clarification of a concept" has not been understood properly with the possible exception of Ayer.

In his review of the Schilpp volume on Moore, Ernest Nagel highlights Stebbing's paper and mentions her judgment that "Moore's lasting influence is to be found in the 'same level analysis' of common-sense propositions he has stimulated 'in the analytic definition of expressions and in the analytic clarification of concepts' rather than in his 'directional' or 'new level analysis' of them" (Nagel 1944, 71; Nagel is quoting Stebbing 1942, 528). Nagel does not elaborate on this (or the terms). The phrase "analytic clarification" seems, in fact—despite its seeming familiarity—not much used in Stebbing's lifetime. I have not found analytic clarification connected to a concept in the literature outside her writings.[13]

At first sight, it is no surprise that Stebbing's analytic clarification of a concept has received little attention. For in 1933 she introduces us to it by saying that it "consists in the elimination of elements supposed to be referred to whenever we use a symbol "S", but which are not such that these elements must be referred to whenever we so use a sentence containing "S" that the sentence says what is true" (Stebbing 1933, 30). It is no surprise that in order to make sense of this remark some have connected it to Russell's paradigmatic account of analysis despite her warning that it is very different from the usual kind of analysis.[14]

In fact, she goes on to say that such analysis "is due to the fact that we often manage to say something which is true although in so saying we believe ourselves to be referring to what is not in fact the case, and are thus also saying something false" (Stebbing 1933, 30). As stated, this seems unpromising and has the air of paradox without having the clarity of the more familiar paradox of analysis.[15]

---

take myself (as Meinong and the early Russell did) to be referring to some subsistent (as opposed to existent) object. According to Russell's theory of descriptions, I am saying something true, despite my confusion as to what I am referring. What we have, then, is also paraphrastic analysis—the aim being here, though, to 'analyse away' a problematic expression" (Beaney 2003, 343–344). In Beaney 2006, he simply skips discussing the analytic clarification of a concept after mentioning its existence. In Beaney and Chapman 2022, it also goes unmentioned.

More recently, Egerton 2021, also assimilates "analytic clarification" to paradigmatic analysis but is not much interested in exploring it.

[13] Cf. Nagel 1936a, 16, where it is connected to clarification of "ideas" and Stace 1943, 120, where it is connected to clarification of "meaning."
[14] Recall Beaney (2003) and Egerton (2021).
[15] On Stebbing's views on the paradox of analysis, see Janssen-Lauret 2022, 61.

60 SUSAN STEBBING

Ayer 1936, 58, however, treats analytic clarification of concepts as significant and had alerted his audience, correctly, that on Stebbing's view, Einstein's treatment of simultaneity is a paradigmatic instance of it.[16] What Stebbing has in mind when discussing analytic clarification of a concept is made evident in the discussion of what follows. For she introduces the very idea of an analytic clarification of a concept in order to handle instances where a previously relatively successful scientific theory requires non-trivial revision after what we would now call a "paradigm change." Her examples are, in fact, "mass," "force," and "simultaneity" with explicit reference to Newton and, as Ayer had noted, Einstein. Here's what she writes. It is terse, and she acknowledges she lacks time to develop it in context:

> Examples of concepts which have been thus clarified are mass, force, simultaneity. The need for such analytic clarification is due to the fact that we often manage to say something which is true although in so saying we believe ourselves to be referring to what is not in fact the case, and are thus also saying something false. This happens when we understand to some extent what we are saying but do not understand clearly exactly what we are saying; hence, we suppose something to be essential to the truth of what we say which is, however, not essential. Certainly Newton did not clearly understand what he was referring to when he spoke of "force," but he often said what was nevertheless true when he used sentences containing "force." A striking example is provided by the concept of simultaneity. Before Einstein had asked the question how we determine whether two events are simultaneous, we thought we knew quite well what was meant by saying "happening at the same time in London and New York." Einstein has made us see that we did not know quite well what we meant; we now understand that what we thought to be essential is not so. This analytic clarification of a concept cannot be made quite tidy. It involves a change in the significance of all statements in which the concept occurs. (Stebbing 1933, 30)

Ever since Kuhn, we tend to discuss examples like this in terms of incommensurability and paradigm shifts. Here I use some of that vocabulary (and also that of Sellars) to elucidate what Stebbing is getting at. But the first thing to note is that analytic clarification is the *effect* of scientific development. The

---

[16] One of the eye-opening claims in Janssen-Lauret 2022, 32, is that "much of Stebbing's published work focused on the philosophy of science and especially on the philosophy of physics." This alerted me to the significance of the passage to be discussed.

clarity achieved is the product of the growth in science ("Einstein has made us see . . ."). "Analytic clarification of a concept" may be in the running for the worst philosophical coinage for failure to convey what it is trying to describe!

Despite Ayer's claim that according to Stebbing it is Einstein's treatment of simultaneity that clarified the concept, in the quoted passage from Stebbing it is left a bit vague who does the clarification in analytic clarification (notice the repeated use of "we"/'us'). As recent scholarship on Stebbing has noted, in her philosophy of science Stebbing tends to treat science as a social, situated activity (Janssen-Lauret 2022, 33ff.). As she puts it a few years later, "Science is the work of scientists, who, profiting by each other's labours, come gradually to achieve an agreed body of knowledge, and in the course of this achievement continually develop new and more powerful technical methods" (Stebbing 1958 (1937), 69).[17] So, I read her as claiming that Einstein triggered a social process of analytic clarification of concepts that had previously been taken for granted in science *and* ordinary life.

On Stebbing's view, analytic clarification does not merely impact the scientific image, but it is also induces shifts in the manifest image.[18] It's not just physicists who learned something new through the development of general relativity about the significance of simultaneity; all of us did. This is how I read her claim that "Before Einstein had asked the question how we determine whether two events are simultaneous, *we* thought *we* knew quite well what was meant by saying 'happening at the same time in London and New York'" (emphasis added). The 'we' here in the example is the manifest image.

As an aside, the impact of science on the manifest image is itself due to what we may call, echoing Max Weber, a wider rationalization of the world. Since the rise of modernity many elements of the manifest image have already been infiltrated and shaped by the scientific image. This means that common sense itself can shift like quicksand.[19]

Now, when I first read the quoted passage (with Kuhn and Quine in the back of my mind),[20] I thought that the lack of "tidiness" of analytic clarification was due to a kind of semantic holism of concepts, that the significance of each concept was determined by adjoining concepts in a network. So that

---

[17] The passage is quoted by Körber 2019, 456, and West 2022, 868.

[18] On my reading, Stebbing thinks Eddington's mistake was not that he thought science could shape the manifest image, but rather that he conflated the scientific and manifest images in places where they are better kept separate.

[19] I suspect that Stebbing's sensitivity to this is one of her more important differences with Moore. See also Janssen-Lauret 2022, 36, 52. See also Schliesser 2019a. But for reservations about the implied narrative about modernity see Schliesser 2024.

[20] Janssen-Lauret 2022, 52, situates Stebbing as a transitional figure toward Quine's holism.

62 SUSAN STEBBING

the adjustments that are required when we figure out what simultaneity really means ramifies out to other, adjoining concepts (like identity and place). But Stebbing does not explicitly commit to such holism in the context of analytic clarification.

Rather, the lack of tidiness is on her account due to the fact that the concepts involved are central to the scientific *and* manifest image(s). So that the clarity gained from analytic clarification about the significance of clarified terms has to be fitted to quite a few claims (recall her, "the significance of *all* statements in which the concept occurs," emphasis added). This still involves a holist-friendly thought that the full, changed significance is not evident from a particular use but needs to be inferred from a whole range of potentially subtly different uses (but this holism is more pragmatic than semantic).

I also suspect that part of the lack of tidiness is also due to Stebbing's recognition that science itself is open-ended, perhaps intrinsically so, and that it may discover new uses for the concepts in new statements (predictions, extensions, etc.) or through the new use of technology (recall the passage quoted from *Philosophy and the Physicists* above). The clarity gained here need not be a second order property of any particular individual, who individually may not know of "all statements in which the concept occurs," but can be *distributed* throughout a community even and (this may go beyond Stebbing's own actual commitments) come to be embedded in material objects *of* technology.

Stebbing's views here foreshadow Quine's views in certain respects. Quine had a tendency, as Greg Frost-Arnold has shown, (i) to associate clarity with more general forms of intelligibility. In later years, Quine might argue that (ii) his program (developed in *Word & Object*) of the philosopher regimenting scientific language to exhibit its ontological commitments, may also be aiming at a species of clarity (about the "ontology" of science), alongside systematicity.[21] He also (iii) came to think of clarity as a more epistemic (not semantic) virtue of an intellectual system (Frost-Arnold 2013, 46ff). What is especially pertinent for my present discussion is that Frost-Arnold shows that the leading figures of analytic philosophy of the age had trouble keeping epistemic and semantic notions of clarity distinct. Ayer, that is, was

---

[21] This second Quine-ian notion of clarity is anticipated by Price in the material discussed in a footnote in section 2 above.

STEBBING ON CLARITY   63

right to call attention to Stebbing's criticism of logical positivists' tendency to conflate different kinds of analysis

Be that as it may, in the quoted passage, Stebbing resists the temptation to claim that once successful scientific paradigms were simply false; that what we once thought was true was actually false. Rather, she suggests that one can say true things without fully understanding the concepts one uses: "This happens when we understand to some extent what we are saying but do not understand clearly exactly what we are saying." This particular vantage point is extraordinarily difficult to achieve about one's own (paradigmatic) utterances, but it does become more easily available retrospectively during and after what we now call a "paradigm shift" (hence the significance of Einstein in the passage).

On the view I am attributing to Stebbing, part of the point of the later paradigm, of the growth of knowledge more generally, is to elucidate how we could speak truth before while strictly speaking not always understanding fully our own concepts.[22] Stebbing here alerts us to the role of philosophy, analytic clarification of concepts, *within* science during shifts of the research frontier. (Of course, this is not philosophy's only role.)[23]

There is a wider lesson here about our lives in societies characterized by complex, cognitive division of labor and evolving knowledge. In the quoted passage, Newton represents the human condition in the following way: as through the growth of science and technology the concepts of the scientific image encroach on the manifest image, and as the division of labor within the sciences becomes ever more fine-grained, it is inevitable that at any given time we say true things without understanding the concepts we use even if we are genius level expert on the subject. Somewhat paradoxically then, the clarity that is the effect of analytic clarification grows while science and technology grows; but simultaneously (!) their growth means that we often are in the dark about the truths we utter confidently.

There is, thus, lurking in Stebbing's philosophy a call for a kind of individual humility. In addition, the present section has highlighted Stebbing's alertness to the significance of clarification of specialist language (in the scientific image) to ordinary life (manifest image). Both of these themes link up importantly with her public facing, more political theorizing in *Thinking to*

---

[22] For a more rigorous exploration of ideas in this vicinity, see Stein 2004, especially 164.

[23] My argument converges with Bryan Pickel's chapter "Stebbing on Linguistic Convention," in this volume, when he notes that for Stebbing "definitions may be discovered empirically."

64 SUSAN STEBBING

Some Purpose, which I discuss in the final section. However, in order to situate the distinctness of Stebbing's discussion, I briefly discuss the conception of clarity in some of her contemporaries.

4 Nagel and Carnap

In previous sections I have argued that the standard conception of clarity disguises considerable heterogeneity. I used Stebbing's account of Wittgenstein and her criticism of logical positivism to articulate this fact. In this section I briefly discuss two influential conceptions of clarity in order to prepare to show how distinctive her account in *Thinking to Some Purpose* is.

First, I discuss Carnapian clarity.[24] In Howard Stein's influential presentation—articulated in the context of the Quine-Carnap polemic—the view of Carnap (ca. 1951) is conveyed as follows:

> Quine and I really differ, not concerning a matter of fact, nor any question with cognitive content, but rather in our respective estimates of the most fruitful course for science [*sic*] to follow. Quine is impressed by the continuity between scientific thought and that of daily life—between scientific language and the language of ordinary discourse—and sees no philosophical gain, no gain either in clarity or in fruitfulness, in the construction of distinct formalized languages for science. I concede the continuity, but . . . believe that very important gains in clarity and fruitfulness are to be had from the introduction of such formally constructed languages. This is a difference of opinion which, despite the fact that it does not concern (in my own terms) a matter with cognitive content, is nonetheless in principle susceptible of a kind of rational resolution. In my view, both programs—mine of formalized languages, Quine's of a more freeflowing and casual use of language—ought to be pursued; and I think that if Quine and I could live, say, for two hundred years, it would be possible at the end of that time for us to agree on which of the two programs had proved more successful. (Stein 1992, 270; see also the elaboration in Carus 2007)

---

[24] I use "Carnapian" rather than "Carnap's" because I am not doing an exegesis of Carnap's writings. I leave for another time the extent to which Carnap's account of explication can be thought to develop Stebbing's notion of analytic clarification.

In Stein's report, Carnap presents himself as the advocate of clarity achieved by the use of constructed languages or, as we would say, formal methods. Carnap explicitly treats clarity as distinct from the more consequentialist virtue of fruitfulness. So, while Carnap and his followers undoubtedly also believe that pursuing such clarity has (many) consequentialist pay-offs, there is an independent merit, and (to use Carnapian lingo), an external, optative value, to the pursuit of clarity. I understand this as a kind of aesthetic preference.

Carnapian clarity here is a property or byproduct of formal systems, of constructed languages. Clarity in the hands of Carnap means to capture a kind of demand for transparency in one's inferential practices, one's commitments, and the use of terms. Again, there are all kinds of other (consequentialist) cognitive and epistemic benefits that are meant to follow from the pursuit of such clarity, but these are not primarily aesthetic.

I quoted the report on Carnap's exchange with Quine to note that he explicitly recognizes the viability and legitimacy of alternative projects *within* scientific philosophy broadly conceived. For, while, in principle, anybody can become a formal philosopher or use formal methods, these methods also create, in practice, barriers to intelligibility and understanding to those not in the know. That is, Carnapian clarity is, despite his socialist sympathies, really a second order property of an otherwise esoteric, expert practice.

This point is explicit in "The Fight for Clarity" (Nagel 1938) that was intended partially to (re-)introduce logical empiricism to an American audience while simultaneously defending them from misrepresentation.[25] Nagel argues that the search for clarity is an effect or byproduct of the advanced development and specialization (and, thus, esotericism) of the special sciences. This means that new criteria of intelligibility distinct from those used in ordinary language are required. As he puts it, "the increased abstractness and generality of modern science require a serious reconsideration and a recasting of those relatively simple canons of intelligibility and validity which are sufficient for the needs of every-day discourse and inquiry" (Nagel 1938, 47–48). So, at a first approximation, Nagel's version of clarity involves the canons of intelligibility and validity apt for special sciences.

In fact, Nagel puts a kind of neo-Kantian and proto-Foucaultian spin on the mature/more recent version of logical empiricism: "Indeed the proper

---

[25] I thank Ádám Tuboly for alerting me to the significance of Nagel 1938.

66 SUSAN STEBBING

question is not "what does a statement mean?" but "what are the conditions which empiricists will acknowledge to be necessary for a statement to have meaning?" (Nagel 1938, 51).

But the reason this effort at clarification is a philosophical task is, in part, due to a limitation of the professional scientist within the cognitive division of labor: "most professional scientists are not sufficiently conscious of their own procedures to enlighten us; special studies must be undertaken by men [*sic!*] sensitive to the logical issues involved. Recent methodological studies aim to supply appropriate answers" (Nagel 1938, 48).

However, Nagel is also concerned with the role of clarity in democratic life. Not unlike Stebbing's account of analytic clarification, we see here (Nagel returns to it later in the essay) the germ of Thomas Kuhn's idea that there is a sense in which ordinary scientists may lack proper self-awareness about their own practices. We might say that a lot of scientific activity (calibration, measurement practices, hidden assumption in the math) is "black-boxed" and "taken off-line," say, in the name of cognitive and operational efficiency. To be sure, Nagel is quick to emphasize (and nods to Mach's influence) that interest in the process of clarification, so not just the results, is widespread among "professional scientists" (Nagel 1938, 47, 58). So, it would be more apt to say that for Nagel, clarification is not just developing the canons of intelligibility and validity apt for (esoteric) special sciences but also making transparent the methods and practices of science that generate warranted claims to the scientists themselves.

Nagel seems to mean by "intelligibility" something like showing how and the way terms/concepts (etc.) hang together (he's a holist) and function in a system of knowledge and bodies of ordinary practice. At least this is suggested by remarks like the following, "the task of philosophy lies in the clarification of terms occurring in scientific *and everyday discourse*, by exhibiting their interrelations and function in the contexts in which they occur" (Nagel 1938, 59; emphasis added).

So, finally, on Nagel's view clarification is not just developing the canons of intelligibility and validity apt for (esoteric) special sciences but also making transparent the methods and practices of science that generate warranted claims in part by showing how and the way terms/concepts hang together and function in a system of knowledge *and* forms of ordinary practice. Now, one may think that Nagel here echoes a kind of "(Lockean) under-laborer to the sciences" conception of philosophy. However, he also endorses some of the political aims for clarification by "some" logical empiricists:

STEBBING ON CLARITY   67

One of [logical empiricism's] functions, that of serving as a disinfectant to the thinking of men, would alone justify the continuance and spread of the movement. It rests its case not on an appeal to authority or the emotional needs of men but on an appeal to a persistent effort to think clearly. The movement is an important arm in the interminable warfare against obscurantism and for clarity. (Nagel 1938, 59; this echoes the kind of language we find in Nagel 1936a and 1936b)

For Nagel, government by discussion is not about achieving authoritative consensus, but rather, as his conception of science and democracy reveal, as the ongoing practice of being responsive to reasons and criticisms based on experimentally controlled facts (Schliesser 2022). Our cognitive practices in science and political life are made possible, and developed and improved, by our socially embedded interactions with each other. For Nagel it is clear that "Perhaps no intellectual tendency is more dangerous than that accompanying the claim that knowledge of human affairs is the exclusive property of men endowed with a "higher insight"—which is not subject to the control of well-established experimental methods" (Nagel 1938, 55). The point is not just the egalitarian ideal that anyone can become a scientist, but also for Nagel the cultivation of clarity in the sciences is a contribution to a properly democratic ethos (Schliesser 2022).

5 Stebbing on Democratic Clarity

Stebbing's *Thinking to Some Purpose* (1939) was written for a wide audience (it originally appeared in the Pelican imprint).The official topic of the book is announced in the prologue:

I am convinced of the urgent need for a democratic people to think clearly without the distortions due to unconscious bias and unrecognized ignorance. Our failures in thinking are in part due to faults which we could to some extent overcome were we to see clearly how these faults arise. It is the aim of this book to make a small effort in this direction. ("Preface to the 1939 edition," Stebbing (2022), xxix–xxx)

It's worth noting that "clear" and its cognates are used repeatedly through the book. Clarity here is a property of thought and perception. In what follows,

68 SUSAN STEBBING

I often use "cognition" as shorthand for both. Clarity seems to be a necessary condition for success at thinking (and action guided by it). In particular, clarity is, as the quoted preface makes clear, the absence of distortions in thought and perception caused by bias and ignorance one is not aware of. *Undistorted thought* is what's being aimed at in describing something as "clear." But the suggestion is that known biases and awareness of ignorance are not an obstacle to successful thought presumably because they can knowingly be controlled for. Crucially, clear cognition is a key ingredient for intelligence on Stebbing's view (Stebbing 2022, 22).

Stebbing's interest in unconscious bias is prompted by the significance of political propaganda, demagoguery, and advertising (she groups these together as "rhetorical persuasion") and presumably also reflects the growing stature of Freudianism in the age. For Stebbing, an important example of such unconscious bias is the "concealed contradictions," including racial biases, we acquire as members of a group (Stebbing 2022, 22). Stebbing deserves a place in the literature on implicit bias.

Stebbing treats clarity as a property of thought and perception that is, in principle, widely diffused among ordinary people; she thinks we all have "some capacity to follow an argument" (Stebbing 2022, 21). In a footnote she adds she hopes it's not unduly optimistic to assert this (Stebbing 2022, 26), For Stebbing, clarity is a necessary condition for success at thinking and action guided by it, or what she calls "effective thinking" (Stebbing 2022, 5). I call this position in which clarity is a capacity of ordinary people to think effectively, that is, without distortion, in ordinary life, "democratic clarity."

Now such democratic clarity is an achievement. Or to be precise, Stebbing treats it as a *skill* that can be acquired; one can be "trained to think clearly" (Stebbing 2022, 4; for an excellent account of how Stebbing conceives of it as a skill, see Pickel 2022, 8ff). Such training makes "rational argument and ... reasonable consideration" in democratic life possible (Stebbing 2022: 4; see also p. 79ff, where she introduces the technical term "convince" when she is describing *public* rational argument). The role of *Thinking to Some Purpose* "as one of the first textbooks in critical thinking" is now well understood, In addition, it articulated a deliberative conception of democracy.[26] This skill itself can, once acquired with "effort" also be something that we control; she emphasizes that we have to "wish" to think clearly. (Stebbing 2022, 29, 6) Once

---

[26] The quote is from Dutilh Novaes 2022. Dutilh Novaes treats deliberative democracy as resting on consensus-oriented approaches.

the skill is acquired we are also capable of logically sound argument (Stebbing 2022, 6). Unsurprisingly, teaching awareness and discovery of possible and kinds of fallacies play a prominent role throughout *Thinking to Some Purpose*.

It is worth emphasizing how distinctive Stebbing's account of democratic clarity is. Of the major early analytic philosophers, Stebbing is the *only* one who really thought that clarity is achievable in ordinary life by ordinary people reasoning about things. Again, while I do not want to exaggerate the differences between Nagel and Stebbing—they share in fact a pragmatist sensibility and agree on the significance of proportioning belief to evidence and the important focus of the way we do things with reasonings—it's important to see the contrasting notions of clarity at work here. In Nagel, clarity is something we do with specialist language and practices that, among other functions, can shape and diagnose features in ordinary life; for Stebbing, clarity can be immanent in and part and parcel of ordinary life. Not to put too fine a point on it, Nagel, Carnap, and Quine all share in the idea that there is *some* salient contrast between formal and specialist, regimented languages, on one hand, and ordinary speech, on the other. (How that contrast is characterized and to what degree it is merely a distinction in degree is famously a matter of substantive disagreement among Quine and Carnap.) For most of these philosophers, clarity is not to be found on the side of ordinary talk. Stebbing is the outlier in thinking that clarity is not so restricted, but is available, in principle, to us all in ordinary life.

So far, I have treated Stebbing's take on democratic clarity as *instrumental* to her account of deliberative democracy. But that's not wholly her own view. Stebbing takes

> for granted that to be clear-headed is worth while for its own sake. Without this assumption I should not have wanted to write this book. It is, however, enough if you will admit that muddled thinking ends in bungled doing, so that to think clearly is useful for the sake of achieving even our most practical aims. Unless you admit at least as much as this, there will be no point, so far as you are concerned, in what I have to say. Our points of view would be too different for discussion to be possible. (Stebbing 2022, 34)

So, democratic clarity is not just treated as an instrumental value to democratic deliberative life. Rather, Stebbing values it as a private and presumably highly intellectual virtue or end in itself. (There are shades of Spinoza here and I return to that below.) Fair enough.

70 SUSAN STEBBING

It is a bit peculiar that she thinks her imagined interlocuter or reader must share in the commitment that "to think clearly is useful for the sake of achieving even our most practical aims." Admittedly, it seems odd for anyone to deny this in the most general sense. But it is not wholly unreasonable for such an interlocuter to claim also that clarity of cognition may often (perhaps always) be unnecessary to achieve our most practical aims (because of relying on tradition, faith, instinct, testimony, or expertise/authority of others). And perhaps (one may say, echoing Hume or Nietzsche) it's our biases or overconfidence that help us acquire our most fundamental, practical aims (which are always constrained by time and other resource scarcities). The problem here is not the purported role of democratic clarity in achieving our aims, but in Stebbing's insistence that muddled thinking must lead to muddled doing. This claim has not been established. It's hard to see how it could be established given how much has been achieved in conditions of ignorance and superstition. It's also at odds with her own example of analytic clarification of concepts.

So, what's odd is that in order to have a discussion at all, Stebbing assumes assent on this very point of contention. And the reason it is odd is that in a democratic society we cannot assume or stipulate agreement over such questions or ways of life including those that, to put it exaggeratedly, resist the clarion call of Enlightenment. My point here is not that one cannot help others see how useful democratic clarity might be (Stebbing is wonderfully persuasive on this score), but rather her insistence that democratic clarity must be the common ground rather than the *potential effect* of discussion.

As I noted, there is a whiff of Spinozism in her treatment of clarity. We know she was familiar with Spinoza's system, which she discusses, in passing in her famous (1932) essay "The Method of Analysis in Metaphysics." She deliberately evokes the last sentence of Spinoza's *Ethics* in the last sentence of the "epilogue" of *Thinking to Some Purpose*:

My point of view with regard to this topic can be summed up in the statement: He alone is capable of being tolerant whose conclusions have been thought out and are recognized to be inconsistent with the beliefs of other persons. To be tolerant is not to be indifferent, and is incompatible with ignorance. My conclusions have been reasonably attained insofar as I have been able to discount my prejudices, to allow for the distorting effects of your prejudices, to collect the relevant evidence and to weigh that evidence in accordance with logical principles. The extent to which I can achieve these aims is the measure of my freedom of mind. To be thus free is as difficult as it is rare. (Stebbing 2022, 256)

To avoid confusion, in the quoted paragraph, "logical principles" include deductive and inductive logic. Be that as it may, clarity, then, is a means toward freedom of mind, but also its measure. Democratic clarity clearly comes in degrees for Stebbing.

Now "freedom" is not introduced until the epilogue of *Thinking to Some Purpose*. I quote the key paragraph to give a flavor of Stebbing's use of it:

I believe also that similar strictures could be truly made with regard to polls held recently in Germany and in Austria. Elections in this country are not in this sense unfree. We are proud to consider ourselves a democracy; we claim to have freedom of election, freedom of speech (including freedom of the Press) limited only by the laws of libel, sedition and blasphemy, and freedom in religion. No doubt there are certain qualifications to be made; it is probable that most people would admit that without economic freedom there cannot be political freedom, and that lacking economic security no man can be regarded as economically free. But, even if these admissions be granted, it will be contended that, by and large, we in this country do have institutions that may properly be described as democratic. It is not to my purpose to dispute these contentions. Nor shall I attempt to determine what characteristics are essential to democracy. It is enough if it be granted that it lies in our national temper to dislike obvious governmental restrictions. We like to feel ourselves to be free. In short, we value civil liberties. (Stebbing 2022, 249)

Here "freedom" means something like the "means conducive toward democratic life," including economic, political, and civil means. So, one might think that by a "free mind," Stebbing also means "the mental state conducive, at least in part, toward a democratic life." This is what she does mean (as I show in the next paragraph.) But, somewhat confusingly, Stebbing goes on to write, "I deliberately omit, however, any discussion of such political obstacles to freedom as we may encounter. I am not concerned with politics. My topic is freedom of mind. Unless I can think freely I cannot think effectively" (Stebbing 2022, 250). And so one might think that insofar as a "free mind" has nothing to do with politics—and democratic life is of political

72 SUSAN STEBBING

significance—that by a "free mind" Stebbing means something *essentially* private.

But that would not be the right conclusion, because she immediately goes on to write, "Here 'I' stands for any person. If I want to make up my mind upon any problem of political action, I must be able to deliberate freely. If it were in fact true that we were all politically and economically free, still it would not follow that we were possessed of the freedom of mind without which, in my opinion, no democratic institutions can be satisfactorily maintained" (Stebbing 2022, 250). So, by "politics" on the same page, Stebbing means not "pertaining to political life," but rather something like "subject to existing political controversy" (in the sense of what policy or political measure to support; Stebbing 2022, 254). For, by a "free mind" Stebbing clearly means a key to, or an effective ingredient that makes public deliberation possible and so is conducive to democratic institutions, that is, political life in the wider institutional or existential sense (but not in the humdrum sense of a "subject of political controversy").

So, fundamentally, on Stebbing's view, democratic clarity is a skill conducive to the kinds of agency involved in public deliberation of a sort that maintains democratic institutions or a democratic way of life. And by "democracy" Stebbing means a participatory one that is exercised in voting but also (as her examples throughout the book make clear) in the formation of public opinion of the sort familiar from British parliamentary democracy. As she puts it, "democratic government" is more than just "the consent of the governed"—this she thinks is actual in British political life—but rather it means that "the voice of the people prevails" (Stebbing 2022, 254). However, she denies that the latter kind of democratic society exists as of yet because under then current (and present) conditions, the British populace *lacks* freedom of mind.

Now, as Stebbing notes, her book has emphasized obstacles to such freedom: "the difficulty of freeing our minds from blinkers, the difficulty of resisting propaganda and of being content to be persuaded where we should have striven to be convinced, the difficulties of an audience dominated by an unscrupulous speaker and the difficulties of a speaker who has to address an audience that is lazy and uncritical—in short, the difficulties created by our stupidity and by those who take advantage of that stupidity." But in the epilogue she focuses on "the difficulty of obtaining information—the difficulty of knowing how to discover reliable testimony" (Stebbing 2022, 250). By this she means, in particular, the way the press shapes access to information.

STEBBING ON CLARITY   73

In light of the concentrated ownership of the press and its interests in withholding or shaping such information, and in light of many examples of partial or biased reporting that Stebbing discusses, she concludes:

> I am forced to say this; if my belief in the reliability of the testimony is false, then I am not free to decide. If such information as I have is not to be trusted, then I lack freedom of decision. For this reason, those who control the Press have power to control our minds with regard to our thinking about "all public transactions." A controlled Press is an obstacle to democracy, an obstacle that is the more dangerous in proportion as we are unaware of our lack of freedom. (Stebbing 2022, 253)

The implication is that the British public *seems* to think that they have free minds, but in reality—because they do not reflect on the conditions that shape their access to the information salient to public life and do not seem perturbed by their controlled press—they do not. They "acquiesce" in rule by a narrow elite, "the ruling class," whose decisions "control us" (Stebbing 2022, 254). Empirically, Stebbing echoes, thus, the sociological thesis that one can have elite rule even in functioning parliamentary democracies (cf. Burnham 1943). Unlike the Italian elite school, she deplores this situation.

Now, it is natural to read *Thinking to Some Purpose*, and come away thinking that to think clearly and to become free requires a lot of very time-consuming individual effort at self-betterment. One can certainly cite passages to that effect: "I do seek to convince the reader that it is of great practical importance that we ordinary men and women should think clearly, that there are many obstacles to thinking clearly, and that some of these obstacles can be overcome provided that we wish to overcome them and are willing to make an effort to do so" (Stebbing 2022, 29). She closes the book with the admonition that "I . . . would maintain that it is desirable that we should develop in ourselves a habit of sceptical inquiry" (Stebbing 2022, 255). These are passages where Stebbing, thus, anticipates Arendt's (republican) conception of democratic life.

But as the book unfolds and reaches its crescendo in the epilogue, it is obvious that Stebbing also thinks that there are many structural obstacles to removing all such impediments to clear thinking. Even if one grants that her rhetoric is designed as a kind of call to action (say, to break up the ruling class monopoly on ownership of the popular press), somewhat disappointingly, she does not offer a program of how those obstacles can be removed while

74 SUSAN STEBBING

not undermining the possibility of a democratic life in the deliberative and self-governing sense she advocates.

In fact, it is also not entirely clear on Stebbing's account what to make of a people that does not seem to wish to be free in Stebbing's sense, as she implies of the English: "The vast majority of English people want to be governed peaceably, and want to be free to pursue their own unpolitical interests" (Stebbing 2022, 254).[27] Even if one agrees with Stebbing's diagnoses, the English public need not be irrational here. For it is, in fact, on her account, very hard work to be free in the sense she advocates, and as the concluding paragraph quoted above suggests, she is explicitly aware of this. In addition, given the obstacles to such freedom she diagnoses, it also seems rather fruitless and (ought implies can) not required or unnecessary to be free in the political or democratic sense advocated by Stebbing. To be sure, for many unpolitical pursuits such freedom, clear thought, will be necessary for effective action and within reach. So, I am not suggesting that democratic clarity should be avoided even if it is not very useful in existing political life.

Given the many economic and educational pre-conditions required and the demands on our time and attention that a life of thinking clearly requires on Stebbing's account, it is a bit surprising that she does not explore the psychological, collective, or institutional means required to organize our lives in complex epistemic and political environments. For example, without wishing to defend the English or its ruling class (then or now), if it's true that its "ruling class, [is] educated for political purposes, trained from birth to undertake the responsibilities of ruling" (Stebbing 2022, 254), then this does represent (one might say echoing Schumpeter or Oakeshott) a possible, even rational response to the structural impediments to creating a mass society of free minds in the political sense Stebbing diagnoses (even if it is also a contributing cause to maintaining such political tutelage).

In fact, Stebbing clearly thinks that attachment to a political party is a contributing source of bias and so of not thinking clearly.[28] Throughout *Thinking to Some Purpose*, she often uses politicians as examples to illustrate biased thinking.[29] By varying these examples she tries to be even-handed

---

[27] This echoes Lippmann's (1922) diagnosis of the (American) democratic public. Stebbing ignores colonial and colonized populations.

[28] This is especially clear in chapter 8; see Stebbing 2022, 98ff, on party attachment. This anticipates a lot of handwringing about partisan polarization today.

[29] Cf. Anscombe's judgment on Stebbing in "Mr. Truman's Degree" (1981 [1956], 66).

and entice her readers to discern the structural obstacle(s) to clear thinking she diagnoses.

It does not seem to occur to Stebbing, however, that part of the epistemic or cognitive function of parties may well be to provide useful signals or cues in complex social and political environments for cognitively overburdened agents without sufficient interest in political life.[30] One may well think that one of liberal democracy's fruits is that such a lack of interest in active political life need not be irrational. So, because Stebbing treats democratic clarity as a property of individual minds who must almost possess the virtues of a Spinozistic sage (and inevitably fall short), she misses how in the division of (cognitive and economic) labor, we might well have strategies or heuristics that allow individuals to remain in partial darkness while being part of collectives that can act with sufficient effectiveness.[31]

References

Anscombe, G. E. M. 1981 [1956]. "Mr. Truman's Degree," reprinted in *The Collected Philosophical Papers of G. E. M. Anscombe*, vol. 3, *Ethics, Religion and Politics*. Oxford: Blackwell, Oxford.

Ayer, A. J. 1936. "The Analytic Movement in Contemporary Philosophy." *Actes du Congres International de Philosophie Scientifique*. vol. 7, Paris: Hermann.

Beaney, Michael. 2003. "Susan Stebbing on Cambridge and Vienna Analysis." In F. Stadler, ed., *The Vienna Circle and Logical Empiricism: Re-Evaluation and Future Perspectives*, 339–350. Dordrecht: Kluwer.

Beaney, Michael. 2016. "Susan Stebbing and the Early Reception of Logical Empiricism in Britain." In *Influences on the Aufbau*, 233–256, Cham: Springer.

Beaney, Michael, and Siobhan Chapman. 2022. "Susan Stebbing." In Edward N. Zalta and Uri Nodelman, eds., *The Stanford Encyclopedia of Philosophy* (Fall Edition). https://plato.stanford.edu/archives/fall2022/entries/stebbing/.

Burnham, James. 1943. *The Machiavellians: Defenders of Freedom*. New York: John Day.

Carus, André W. 2007. *Carnap and Twentieth-Century Thought: Explication as Enlightenment*. Cambridge: Cambridge University Press.

Coliva, Annalisa. 2021. "Stebbing, Moore (and Wittgenstein) on Common Sense and Metaphysical Analysis." *British Journal for the History of Philosophy* 29(5): 914–934.

Douglas, Alexander X., and Jonathan Nassim. 2021. "Susan Stebbing's Logical Interventionism." *History and Philosophy of Logic* 42(2): 101–117.

Dutilh Novaes, Catarina. 2022. "Argument and Argumentation." In Edward N. Zalta and Uri Nodelman, eds., *The Stanford Encyclopedia of Philosophy* (Fall Edition). https://plato.stanford.edu/archives/fall2022/entries/argument/.

Egerton, Karl. 2021. "Susan Stebbing and the Truthmaker Approach to Metaphysics." *Logique et Analyse* 256: 403–423.

---

[30] This truism of political science is given a philosophical treatment in Levy 2021.

[31] In Lippmann (1938), her contemporary develops this strategy, laying the groundwork for a research and political program for handling the problems diagnosed by Stebbing (Schliesser 2019b).

76   SUSAN STEBBING

Frost-Arnold, Greg. 2013. *Carnap, Tarski, and Quine at Harvard: Conversations on Logic, Mathematics, and Science.* Chicago, Il.: Open Court.

Janssen-Lauret, Frederique. 2022. *Susan Stebbing: Elements on Women in the History of Philosophy.* Cambridge: Cambridge University Press.

Khan, M. Ali. 1993. "The Irony in/of Economic Theory." *MLN* 108(4): 759–803.

Körber, Silke. 2019. "Thinking About the 'Common Reader': Otto Neurath, L. Susan Stebbing and the (Modern) Picture-Text Style." *Neurath Reconsidered: New Sources and Perspectives,* Boston Studies in the Philosophy and History of Science, vol. 336, 451–470, Cham: Springer.

Kremer, Michael. 2013. "The Whole Meaning of a Book of Nonsense: Reading Wittgenstein's Tractatus." In Michael Beaney, ed., *The Oxford Handbook of The History of Analytic Philosophy,* online ed., Oxford Academic [accessed May 16, 2023] https://doi.org/10.1093/oxfordhb/9780199238842.013.0035.

Levy, Neil. 2021. *Bad Beliefs: Why They Happen to Good People.* Oxford: Oxford University Press.

Lewis, Hywel David, ed. 2016. *Clarity Is Not Enough: Essays in Criticism of Linguistic Philosophy.* London: Routledge.

Lippmann, Walter. 1922. *Public Opinion.* New York: Harcourt, Brace.

Lippman, Walter. 1938. *The Good Society.* Boston: Little, Brown.

McQuillan, J. Colin. 2017. "Clarity and Distinctness in Eighteenth Century Germany." In Manuel Sánchez Rodríguez and Miguel Escribano Cabeza, eds., *Leibniz en Dialogo,* 149–160. Sevilla: Themata.

Moore, G. E., and Margaret Masterman. 1934. "The Justification of Analysis: Notes of a Lecture." *Analysis* 1(2): 28–30.

Nagel, Ernest. 1936a. "Impressions and Appraisals of Analytic Philosophy in Europe. I," *Journal of Philosophy* 33(1): 5–24.

Nagel, Ernest. 1936b. "Impressions and Appraisals of Analytic Philosophy in Europe. II," *Journal of Philosophy* 33(2): 29–53.

Nagel, Ernest. 1938. "The Fight for Clarity: Logical Empiricism." *American Scholar* 8(1): 45–59.

Nagel. Ernest. 1944. "The Philosophy of G. E. Moore by Paul Arthur Schilpp." *Mind,* 53(209) (January): 60–75.

Peirce, Charles Sanders. 1878. "How to Make Our Ideas Clear." *Popular Science Monthly* 12 (January): 286–302.

Pickel, Bryan. 2022. "Susan Stebbing's Intellectualism." *Journal for the History of Analytical Philosophy* 10(4): 1–24.

Price, H. H. 1945. "The Inaugural Address: Clarity Is Not Enough." *Proceedings of the Aristotelian Society, Supplementary Volumes,* 19: 1–31.

Schliesser, Eric. 2013. "Philosophic Prophecy." In *Philosophy and Its History: Aims and Methods in the Study of Early Modern Philosophy.* Oxford: Oxford University Press, 209–235.

Schliesser, Eric. 2019a. "Synthetic Philosophy." *Biology & Philosophy* 34(2): 1–9.

Schliesser, Eric. 2019b. "Walter Lippmann: The Prophet of Liberalism and the Road Not Taken." *Journal of Contextual Economics–Schmollers Jahrbuch* 139(2–4): 349–364.

Schliesser, Eric. 2022. "Philosophy of Science as First Philosophy: The Liberal Polemics of Ernest Nagel." In M. Neuber, and A. T. Tuboly, eds., *Ernest Nagel: Philosophy of Science and the Fight for Clarity.* Logic, Epistemology, and the Unity of Science, vol. 53, 233–253. Cham: Springer.

Schliesser, Eric. 2024. "Synthetic Philosophy: A Restatement." *Proceedings of the Aristotelian Society* 124(3): 229–252. London: Oxford University Press.

Smith, Justin E. H. 2003. "Confused Perception and Corporeal Substance in Leibniz." *Leibniz Review* 13: 45–64.

Stace, W. T. 1943. "Can Speculative Philosophy Be Defended?" *Philosophical Review* 52(2): 116–126.

Stebbing, L. S. 1932. "The Method of Analysis in Metaphysics." *Proceedings of the Aristotelian Society* (33) (January): 65–94.

Stebbing, L. Susan. 1933. "Logical Positivism and Analysis." *Proceedings of the British Academy.* London: H. Milford.

Stebbing, L. Susan. 1936. "Collected Papers of Charles Sanders Peirce, Vol. IV: The Simplest Mathematics; Vol. V: Pragmatism and Pragmaticism. Edited by Charles Hartshorn and Paul Weiss. Cambridge, MA; Harvard University Press; London: Oxford University Press, Humphrey Milford. 1933. Vol. IV. Pp. x+ 601; 1934: Vol. V. Pp. xii+ 455. Price: Vol. IV, 5, 21s." *Philosophy* 11(41): 116–118.

Stebbing, L. Susan. 1958 [1937]. *Philosophy and the Physicists.* London: Dover Books.

Stebbing, Susan. 2022 [1939]. *Thinking to Some Purpose.* With a new foreword by Nigel Warburton and a new introduction by Peter West. London: Routledge.

Stebbing, L. Susan. 1942. "Moore's Influence." In Paul Schilpp, ed., *The Philosophy of GE Moore,* 2nd ed., 517–532. La Salle, IL: Open Court.

Stein, Howard. 1992. "Was Carnap Entirely Wrong, After All?" *Synthese* 93 (1): 275–295.

Stein, Howard. 2004. "The Enterprise of Understanding and the Enterprise of Knowledge." *Synthese* 140 (1–2): 135–176.

West, Peter. 2022. "L. Susan Stebbing Philosophy and the Physicists (1937): A Re-Appraisal." *British Journal for the History of Philosophy* 30(5): 859–873.

Yolton, John. 1956. *John Locke and the Way of Ideas.* Oxford: Clarendon Press.

SECTION II
PUBLIC PHILOSOPHY, SCIENCE, AND COMMON SENSE

Susan Stebbing's Anti-Idealist Philosophy of Physics

Her Rebuttal of Eddington's Argument from Intrinsic Nature

Frederique Janssen-Lauret

1 Introduction: Stebbing's Anti-Idealist Philosophy of Physics and Her Differences from Moore

In her 1937 book *Philosophy and the Physicists*, Susan Stebbing investigated Arthur Eddington's then popular idealist interpretation of modern physics, according to which "All through the physical world runs that unknown content, which must surely be the stuff of our consciousness" (Eddington 1920: 200). Stebbing found Eddington's argument from intrinsic nature, now often considered his master argument, "a complete muddle" (Stebbing 1937: 125). The prevailing interpretation of Stebbing as a Moorean common-sense philosopher (Milkov 2003, Beaney 2003, 2016) would predict Stebbing's rebuttal of Eddington to run along lines similar to Moore's remarks in his *Some Main Problems of Philosophy*. Moore maintained that idealist and panpsychist positions of this sort simply offend against our common-sense tendency to "believe . . . certainly, that to the vast majority of material objects, *no* acts of consciousness are attached" (Moore 1953: 22, his italics). Yet Stebbing made no such objection to Eddington, and indeed never mentioned Moore at all in *Philosophy and the Physicists*. What's more, I argue in this chapter, Stebbing's views on analysis and the philosophy of physics were at odds with that Moorean view. Stebbing's considered position on analysis implied that common-sense based arguments against idealist or panpsychist interpretations of physics are misguided, because they trade on a fallacy.

Stebbing sharply distinguished between "same-level" (that is, linguistic or conceptual) analysis, which is constrained by common sense and ordinary

Frederique Janssen-Lauret, *Susan Stebbing's Anti-Idealist Philosophy of Physics* In: *Susan Stebbing*.
Edited by: Annalisa Coliva and Louis Doulas, Oxford University Press. © Oxford University Press 2025.
DOI: 10.1093/9780197682371.003.0004

82 SUSAN STEBBING

usage, on the one hand and "metaphysical analysis" or "directional analysis," which reveals which constituents in what arrangements the world contains if a given sentence is true, on the other hand. This distinction, combined with her long-standing expertise in the history of philosophy of physics, enabled her to see that the idealist claim, "all matter is conscious," is a potentially viable piece of directional analysis. To say that it offends against common sense is to miscategorize the analyses used in physics and its philosophy as conceptual analyses, which must avoid sounding uncommonsensical. But physics is not bound by the standards of conceptual analysis.

Modern physics is full of analyses that seem to offend against common sense. It says, for example, that matter is mostly empty space at the subatomic level. We cannot declare that analysis false because it apparently offends against common sense. It is fallacious, Stebbing held, to expect micro-physical objects to inherit the distinctive properties of macro-physical objects such as color, hardness, or solidity. Analyses proposed by physicists should, on her view, generally be treated as directional analyses, hypotheses about the ultimate constituents of the world and their arrangement. As a result, "all matter is conscious" cannot be ruled out of court based on common sense, because it is not a piece of conceptual analysis. It must be considered on its merits as a kind of directional analysis in Stebbing's sense, an attempt to uncover an array of basic facts. In *Philosophy and the Physicists*, we see Stebbing giving due consideration to Eddington's proposed idealist analysis but concluding that the case for it is not strong.

Here I will concentrate on Stebbing's response to Eddington's well-known argument from intrinsic nature. In brief, Eddington inferred from the structuralist nature of physical theories, which describe in heavily mathematized language how physical posits relate to each other but do not describe how matter is in itself, the conclusion that matter can and should be ascribed a mental or conscious intrinsic nature. Stebbing, though agreeing that physical theories are structuralist and thus compatible with idealism about the intrinsic nature of matter, felt that Eddington's conclusion did not follow from his premises. His premises established only that it is consistent with modern structuralist theories of physics that matter has an underlying intrinsic nature of consciousness. Stebbing agreed that this was consistent, but she argued that none of Eddington's premises provided a positive reason for favoring an idealist rather than a materialist interpretation of physics. As Eddington's views are currently undergoing a twenty-first-century resurgence, now reinterpreted as a full-blown panpsychism, Stebbing's original counter-arguments to Eddington's views are of contemporary relevance as well.

2 Analytic Philosophy and the Interpretation of Modern Physics: Stebbing's Views

Historians of analytic philosophy often present its early phase as driven primarily by strong opposition to idealism, starting with G. E. Moore's efforts (Moore 1899, Moore 1903) to rebut F. H. Bradley (Hylton 1990, Candlish 2007). A certain kind of reading of Stebbing, as a "Moorean" (Milkov 2003: 355, 358; Beaney 2016: 242, 245–246, 248–250, 253–54; Beaney and Chapman, 2021: §§3–4), or at least "influenced by Moore" and seeking to settle "the competing claims of realism and idealism" (Chapman 2013: 35) in favor of realism, would slot Stebbing very smoothly into this tradition, classifying her as a quintessential follower of Moore's revolt against idealism.

But Stebbing's story is more nuanced than that. So is the story of the origins of analytic philosophy. Stebbing was not a follower of Moore. While Moore bore an influence on her views on the nature of analysis, I will show that Stebbing's work on analysis went beyond Moore's and solved problems that he could not. And early analytic philosophy had other guiding themes besides anti-idealism. Investigation into the nature of analysis itself was, of course, one such theme. Another was the project of finding a philosophy that is compatible with and makes progress in explaining new developments in the sciences.[1] Though a pioneer of conceptual analysis and anti-idealism, Moore was not a major representative of this latter strand of analytic thought. But Stebbing, who published extensively on the philosophy of physics, was.

When we gain an appreciation of Stebbing's contributions to the philosophy of science, it helps us separate her thought from that of her mentor,

---

[1] The canonical analytic philosophers Russell and Whitehead concentrated their efforts in this regard on the mathematical revolution in rigor, which overthrew such intuitive certainties as "parallel lines never meet" and "nothing is the same size as its proper parts" with the introduction of non-Euclidean geometries and Dedekind's definition of an infinite set, and the new physics, where these mathematical models soon found practical application in Einstein's theory of relativity. I have argued that we should also count as part of this strand of the analytic tradition figures such as Welby, de Laguna, and Stout, who argued in favor of novel views in the philosophy of language and metaphysics in order to encompass new developments in evolutionary biology and experimental psychology (Janssen-Lauret 2022a, Janssen-Lauret 2022b).

84 SUSAN STEBBING

Moore.[2] There are several main themes to Stebbing's philosophy of physics which have no counterpart in Moore's thought. Here I will concentrate on two: her theory of perception, which she developed in the 1920s as a result of her engagement with Whitehead and the philosophy of physics, and her application of her theory of directional analysis to the interpretation of physics. Both are relevant to Stebbing's rebuttal of Eddington's idealism.

Even among Stebbing scholars, very little attention is paid to the papers that span the first six years of her career within analytic philosophy. Beaney and Chapman, for example, write, "Her early work focused on logic" (Beaney and Chapman 2021 §1) and that "Stebbing's first significant work, which established her reputation, was *A Modern Introduction to Logic*" (Beaney and Chapman 2021 §2). But *A Modern Introduction to Logic* was published in 1930, six years after the publication of Stebbing's first work on analytic philosophy of science. She was to publish a paper a year on the topic for the rest of the 1920s. Stebbing's reputation must have been reasonably established already, as these works appeared in such venues as the *Journal of Philosophy*, *Mind*, and the *Proceedings of the Aristotelian Society* (Stebbing 1924, 1924–25, 1926, 1927, 1928, 1929).

The content of these papers fits awkwardly with Beaney and Chapman's narrative according to which Stebbing, who had been drawn to idealism as a young woman, "was 'converted' to analytic philosophy when she encountered G. E. Moore" (Beaney and Chapman 2021 §3). It is true that Stebbing herself is in part responsible for this story (Stebbing 1942: 530–531). Yet her conversion narrative may have been as much inspired by her retrospective mood as her health was failing in 1942, her tendency to be modest to a fault at the best of times, and her inclination to be unusually scrupulous about assigning credit to others (Connell and Janssen-Lauret 2023: 242–246). Whatever its origins, the story of a Moorean road-to-Damascus moment is oversimplified. While Stebbing gave up the idealism-inspired views which she initially disagreed with Moore about in 1917 (Stebbing 1916-17, 1917-18), it is misleading to say that she then became a follower of Moorean commonsense philosophy. Her first foray into analytic philosophy focused on A. N. Whitehead's philosophy of the new physics (Stebbing 1924, 1924–25, 1926), followed by Stebbing's original philosophy of the new physics (Stebbing 1927, 1928, 1929).

---

[2] Other works which undermine the "Moorean" reading of Stebbing by tracing parallels with other philosophers in her work or stressing the originality of her philosophy of science include Janssen-Lauret 2017, Coliva 2021, Janssen-Lauret 2022a, 2022b, West 2022.

ANTI-IDEALIST PHILOSOPHY OF PHYSICS   85

Stebbing's engagement with Whitehead's thought in the 1920s throws new light both on her answer to Eddington and on her long-standing but rarely explicitly pressed disagreement with Moore concerning sense-data. Stebbing differed from Whitehead on several pivotal points, too. There is no suggestion here that the prevailing picture of Stebbing as a Moorean ought to be replaced with one of Stebbing as a follower of Whitehead. But Stebbing took a line similar to Whitehead's, and very different from Moore's, on perception and on its role in analysis.

Whitehead's radical and difficult philosophy of science aimed to make sense of modern physics by overcoming the "Bifurcation of Nature" into binary categories such as particular and universal, mind and body, primary and secondary quality (Whitehead 1920). Instead of trusting the grammar of our Indo-European languages, which traps our minds in its subject-predicate straitjacket, we must embrace the new polyadic symbolic logic, able to express complex relational structures. Having abandoned the particular-universal distinction which is an artifact of language, we replace it with a one-category event ontology. Nature consists in a boundless sequence of events, standing in complex relations of overlap, succession, et cetera. Our common-sense humans, dogs, tables, rocks, trees, stars as well as their properties and relations (even those of duration and location) are not, as we previously naïvely supposed, basic, but are abstractions out of said events (Stebbing 1926: 206). Nature presents us with colors, sounds, smells, and tastes just as much as with hardness, solidity, duration, length, breadth, and depth. Allegedly primary and allegedly secondary qualities are on a par, both being an initial level of abstraction out of the events with which we are confronted (Stebbing 1927: 37). When we theorize in a scientific mood, we move from the absolutely specific qualities and relations we discern in a perceptual situation to increasingly abstract categories and increasingly abstract and general hypotheses, generalizing far beyond the here and now, yet testable against the perceptual data. Stebbing found herself in agreement with much of this Whiteheadian worldview, though demurring from Whitehead's subsequent opposition to the distinction between fact and value (Stebbing 1928: 116).

Toward the end of the 1920s Stebbing had come to propose her own original, positive view about the perceptual facts that serve as a point of departure for analysis. Although Stebbing took ordinary observations and our ordinary-language descriptions of them as a point of departure, her positive proposal was notably different from Moorean common-sense philosophy.

86 SUSAN STEBBING

According to Stebbing, both philosophy and the natural sciences start from "perceptual science" (Stebbing 1929: 147), comprising statements such as "I am perceiving a piece of paper," "the piece of paper was here before I saw it," and "others have seen this piece of paper, too." Stebbing's view explicitly applied to physics as well as philosophy. Her perceptual science takes as a given that perceptual objects have a duration—Stebbing agreed with Whitehead that there is no such thing as nature at an instant, or a physical object at an instant (1924–25: 321)—and also that other minds exist and can perceive the same objects. There is no trace of these theses in the theory of perception that Moore held. Unlike Stebbing, Moore allocated a pivotal role in both perception and analysis to sense-data.

Moore had been the first analytic philosopher to attempt to falsify idealism, both Kant's and Bradley's, by means of a theory of perception and cognition which sharply separated the mind from its object of judgment, external to that mind (Moore 1899). Moore turned Kant's and Bradley's modus ponens—if reality does not resemble our thoughts and language, then we cannot represent it correctly, and reality indeed fails to resemble our thoughts and language—on its head, proposing instead a modus tollens: our thoughts and language certainly can represent reality correctly. Therefore, reality does resemble our thoughts. *Contra* idealism, reality divides into discrete, individually cognizable constituents. We know this because our minds can grasp those constituents directly, and our words can name them directly. Moore's views evolved in the 1910s–30s but Moore (and Russell, who had enthusiastically embraced Moore's idea) remained committed to the position that to defeat idealism, we need some constituents of reality which we can refer to directly. Their term for such constituents was "sense-data."

Sense-data, according to Moore, are known to us directly. They are not abstractions out of perceptual situations. Moore did not regard sense-data as necessarily mental, private items. In fact, his personal preference was for a view of sense-data as the perceptible surfaces of objects (Moore 1925: 56). But whether sense-data were physical or mental, Moore contended, material objects are analyzable in terms of them. He wrote, "the analysis of the proposition 'This is a human hand' . . . includes in its analysis a proposition of the form 'This is part of the surface of a human hand.'. . .[T]his proposition also is undoubtedly a proposition about the sense-datum, which I am seeing, which is a sense-datum of my hand" (Moore 1925: 55). Although Moore had stressed frequently that the certain truth of a given piece of commonsense knowledge does not by any means give us certain knowledge of what its

ANTI-IDEALIST PHILOSOPHY OF PHYSICS   87

analysis is—a thesis with which Stebbing agreed (Stebbing 1929, 1932–33)—
he does appear to have had an inclination to rule out idealist analyses on
common-sense grounds. He called the idealist analysis according to which
his hand was a logical construction out of permanent possibilities of sensa-
tion "paradoxical" (Moore 1925: 54). He also wrote,

> Common Sense has, I said, some quite definite views about the way in
> which acts of consciousness in general are related to material objects. . . .
> We believe, then, that acts of consciousness are attached to some material
> objects. But we believe, I think, no less certainly, that to the vast majority
> of material objects, *no* acts of consciousness are attached. . . . We are sure
> too that the sun and moon and stars and earth are not conscious—that no
> conscious acts are attached to them. . . .[A]mong the vast number of ma-
> terial objects in the Universe there are comparatively few to which acts of
> consciousness are attached; in other words, by far the greater number of
> the material objects in the Universe are *unconscious*. (Moore 1953: 19–21,
> all italics his)

Although Stebbing argued against idealism in her rebuttal of Eddington,
her argumentative strategies bore little resemblance to Moore's. Moore never
made any serious study of modern physics. He made no systematic appeal
to physics or generally to the natural or experimental sciences in his case
against idealism. To Moore, it simply seemed certain that common sense was
incompatible with assigning any kind of conscious nature to rocks, planets,
or stars.

By contrast, Stebbing, who had read History at Girton College prior to
switching to Moral Sciences (that is, philosophy), had been steeped from her
undergraduate years in the history of science. Stebbing had a keener understanding than Moore of the scientific method and the role of observation
within it. She was also more alert to philosophical questions concerning the
conclusions about the real nature of material objects, and whether either observation and experiment, or indeed common sense, really supports such
conclusions. Stebbing had long emphasized the conceptual gulf between
what she called "modern physics"—the physics of Einstein, Eddington,
Rutherford, Heisenberg, Planck, Bohr—and the physics she ascribed to
Kelvin and Tait though not Maxwell (Stebbing 1927: 28 fn.1), typical of
the nineteenth century. Modern physics offered a starkly different way of
thinking about matter from what she described as "the nineteenth-century

88   SUSAN STEBBING

view of the ultra-microscopic world as consisting of solid, absolutely hard, indivisible billiard-ball-like atoms, which were assumed to be solid and hard in a perfectly straight-forward sense of the words 'solid' and 'hard'" (Stebbing 1937: 54).

Practically nothing of that nineteenth-century picture survived into the twentieth. Rutherford split the atom and found it to be mostly empty space. The laws governing their constituent subatomic particles turned out to be probabilistic rather than the deterministic kind apposite to tiny billiard balls. Most importantly for Eddington's argument from intrinsic nature, physics ceased to pronounce on what atoms, or other physical posits, were like in themselves. The basic objects posited by physical theories, the things modern physics said were ultimately there, had largely become unobservables: things that cannot be directly perceived so have to be discovered by other means— on my reading of Stebbing, a combination of inference to the best explanation, same-level analyses such as definitions and directional analysis to reveal what basic entities there are and in what arrangements they occur in the world. Stebbing stressed that due to their size relative to visible light waves, we cannot directly perceive electrons and therefore cannot have sense data of them (Stebbing 1937: 181). What we know about electrons is not due to our awareness of properties or surfaces directly perceived by us. We know about them through descriptions inferred from how our physical theory says they stand with respect to the other posits of the theory. So the properties ascribed to physical posits by modern physics, unlike those ascribed by nineteenth-century physics, were extrinsic, not intrinsic. Eddington was to deploy the contrast between this crude nineteenth-century materialism and modern physics to defend an idealist position according to which the intrinsic nature of matter is consciousness. But Stebbing deployed it to show that "both idealism and materialism . . . are out of date" (Stebbing 1937: 42) and also, obliquely, to indicate that the analysis used to reveal the posits of physical theory was what she called directional analysis, not merely conceptual or linguistic analysis. Analysis in physics and its philosophy is therefore not, according to Stebbing, curtailed by common sense.

When Stebbing spoke of "common sense," she applied the term sometimes to ordinary-language truisms and sometimes to experience and perceptual judgment. She wrote, for example, that in analysis, "We must not start from sense-data; we must start from the perceptual judgment, made in a given determinate perceptual situation. . . . We must begin with commonsense facts, such as *I see this candle*" (Stebbing 1932–33: 72–74). Common sense pertains

ANTI-IDEALIST PHILOSOPHY OF PHYSICS 89

to our direct experience and our ordinary-language ways of speaking about it. But physics is different. Physics "is not, in fact, concerned with tables" (Stebbing 1937: 54). It does not pertain to the level of everyday discourse and experience. Physics aims to find the base level: the smallest constituents of the world that exist if our discourse about physical objects is true. Physicists in their more metaphysical moods, and philosophers of physics, theorize about the nature of the constituents of basic facts posited by physical theory. As Stebbing put it,

> the physicist starts from the familiar world of tables, stars, and eclipses, aims at constructing a complex of metrical symbols which shall symbolize the recurrences in this familiar world, and has found it necessary, in order to fulfil this aim, to introduce symbols that have no exact counterpart in sensible experience and thus cannot be translated into the language of common sense. (Stebbing 1937: 116)

The nineteenth-century physicists, in taking matter incontrovertibly to be solid, hard, impenetrable, perceptible by the senses, and occupying space, seemed to trade on ordinary-language truisms about matter, commonsensical in one sense of the word. But commonsensical truisms about our ordinary experience with matter do not imply any theory about what matter is made of, what basic elements in what arrangement we find upon a full analysis. Although Moore theoretically seemed to affirm this principle in 1925, we saw above that he did not apply it to the case of idealism about physics. Instead, he contended that it is common sense that most matter is not conscious. But Moore's certainty that because rocks, stars, trees, and tables appear to have no perceptual or reasoning states like humans and animals do, it follows that no conscious states are attached to them, assumes that the nature of the whole carries over to the nature of the parts. Stebbing, throughout her career, systematically questioned that assumption: she wrote, for example,

> It has been erroneously supposed that from the two statements *I am sitting on this chair* and *This chair is a logical construction*, it follows that *I am sitting on a logical construction*. . . . The two statements are fundamentally different in logical form. The confusion is as gross as the confusion in supposing that if *men are numerous* and *Socrates is a man*, it would follow that *Socrates is numerous*. (Stebbing 1933: 505)

90 SUSAN STEBBING

The fallacy in question is a case of a *pars pro toto* or *totum pro parte* fallacy: the fallacy of conflating part and whole. Since we cannot in general suppose that parts always inherit the intrinsic nature of the whole or vice versa, Stebbing conceded to the idealist physicists that it was coherent to suppose that micro-physical parts had a radically different nature from the macrophysical whole.

Stebbing did not criticize Moore as she had the nineteenth-century physicists for feeling unduly certain that they knew the intrinsic nature of material objects, but she had the philosophical resources to do so. Her metaphysical method implied that Kelvin and Tait's certainty that atoms, microphysical objects, unproblematically inherit the properties of macro-physical objects—hardness, solidity, being governed by deterministic law—was a *totum pro parte* fallacy. There is no logical necessity that compels parts to be similar in nature to the whole they belong to. The type of analysis that goes in search of the basic constituents and facts referred to by our true statements about matter may uncover basic simples surprisingly different in nature from everyday material objects. This reveals the similarity between Stebbing's "metaphysical" or "directional" analysis and the analysis practiced by physicists. While the metaphysician does not, as a rule, literally take substances apart as the physicist or chemist does, their projects share a goal, namely, "to determine the elements and the mode of combination of those elements to which reference is made when any given true assertion is made" (Stebbing 1932–33: 70). For physics, the goal is restricted to true assertions about the physical world; the fully general statement is what Stebbing describes as "the aim of metaphysical analysis" (Stebbing 1932–33: 70). According to Stebbing, "metaphysics aims at making precise the reference of all true beliefs. For this purpose analysis is indispensable" (Stebbing 1932–33: 70). The physicist's goal is to find out what basic elements in what arrangements are there if our observational claims are true. Although it sounds commonsensical, even like an analytic truth, to say that matter is solid, Rutherford's physical analysis revealed that matter is, at the sub-atomic level, mostly empty space. Common sense cannot overthrow these sorts of results, and therefore cannot by itself overthrow the proposal that matter is, at the subatomic level, conscious.

Stebbing's distinction between directional and same-level (conceptual) analysis implied that being counter-intuitive, even paradoxical-sounding, is no defect in a directional analysis. Directional analysis aims to uncover the

ANTI-IDEALIST PHILOSOPHY OF PHYSICS 91

basic constituents of reality that there are if a given sentence is true. There is no commonsensicality constraint on the basic constituents. What basic constituents there are is a matter of what reality offers up to us. It is, then, a thoroughly *a posteriori* and contingent matter what the basic constituents are. Commonsensicality constraints may apply to conceptual or linguistic analysis, or to Stebbing's 1929 doctrine of perceptual science. We ought not to deny that we can observe outside reality, that others can see the same physical things as we do, et cetera. It is not directional analysis, but same-level analysis, that ought not to be counter-intuitive or paradoxical-sounding. A definition, conceptual analysis, or grammatical analysis that contains utterly unexpected elements is suspect, because these are supposed to be analytically true. But an array of basic constituents of reality is not beholden to our intuitions or common sense. They are discerned in the world by empirical discovery. Statements about them are not logically or analytically true and may therefore be unexpected or surprising (Stebbing 1932–33: 80, 87, 89).

As a result, Stebbing criticized Eddington for inferring from the contrast between the solid table and the tenuous sub-atomic particles "the preposterous nonsense of the 'two tables'" (Stebbing 1937: 54), one "a commonplace object . . . *substantial*" (Eddington 1928: xi), the other "my scientific table [which] is mostly emptiness" (Eddington 1928: xii). On Stebbing's view, the table is an "immediate reference" (1932–33: 78) observed in a perceptual situation, while the predicate "mostly emptiness" is properly applied to sub-atomic objects. "No concepts drawn from the level of common sense thinking are appropriate to sub-atomic, i.e. microphysical, phenomena" (Stebbing 1937: 54). Sub-atomic particles are hypothesized to play the role of simple, basic constituents of reality. They are not parallel objects existing alongside the table. They are the resultants of physical analysis, and feature in the basic facts of the directional analysis of philosophy of physics. The table is a construct, composed at the base level of sub-atomic particles (Stebbing 1937: 55). Two up-quarks and a down-quark combine into a proton, which is orbited by an electron to form a hydrogen atom; the hydrogen atom's electron combines with another atom's electron into a cloud to create a chemical bond that holds together a molecule, the water molecule is arranged with other molecules into cells, arranged into cellulose fibers, arranged into planks, arranged into the familiar tabular shape. Atoms do not compose tables just as bricks compose a house, but the correct conclusion to draw from this shift away from nineteenth-century physical theory is more careful analysis, not Eddington's metaphysical supplementation of modern physical theory (Stebbing 1937: 122).

Stebbing's firm rebuttal of the Eddingtonian move that posits the ordinary, solid table of common sense and a scientific, tenuous, non-solid "table" side by side did not rest on any argumentative strategy borrowed from Moore. Moore rarely engaged with modern physics, and when he did, his analyses of it were not as deep and searching as those of Stebbing, who had much greater familiarity with the subject. In a posthumously published lecture, dating from 1928–29, Moore quoted Russell's *ABC of Atoms*, "ordinary matter appears to be continuous.... Science, however, compels us to accept a quite different conception of what we are pleased to call 'solid' matter" (Russell 1923: 1). Moore inferred that science "compels us to hold the view that this surface *is* a number of surfaces with empty space between them .. . the surfaces in question are surfaces of electrons ... the greater part of this area is not really occupied at all" (Moore 1966: 69). Moore then worried that "this surface *seems* to be continuous" which "entails: is not a number of discontinuous surfaces"(Moore 1966: 70).

Moore's response to this philosophical problem was markedly different from Stebbing's. Stebbing made clear that what the surface seems to be pertains to ordinary observation and everyday discourse—which correctly inform us that our trusted writing desks, for example, are continuous—while the spaces between the surfaces of electrons pertain to the basic facts, the termini of analysis, of whose existence physical theory informs us. According to her, while a conceptual analysis or definition of the ordinary-language "continuous" is incompatible with being mostly empty space, there is no problem of the type put forward by Eddington or Russell. At the observational or ordinary-language level, our desk or chair or floor really is continuous, and is not mostly empty space, while at the level of basic facts, discovered by physico-directional analysis pushed as far as it will go, there is no ordinary-language constraint on acceptable levels of empty space.

Moore's approach to the problem did not make the same distinctions as Stebbing's and was less clear and decisive. He did not distinguish either between directional and same-level (conceptual) analysis or between the levels of observation/ordinary language and basic facts. He remained emphatic that what was continuous, or seemed to be continuous, was the "s.d.," short for "sense-datum" (Moore 1966: 70). So Moore's framing of the philosophical question at hand became one of investigating the possibility whether sense-data can, in principle, be other than they seem. How can the continuous

ANTI-IDEALIST PHILOSOPHY OF PHYSICS   93

sense-datum be a collection of surfaces of electrons separated by empty intervals? Moore made various attempts to answer that question, invoking the theory of continuous and compact mathematical series (Moore 1966: 71–74), and the question of continuity for change and motion as compared to continuity of surfaces (Moore 1966: 74–75). He finally proposed as a tentative solution that "our sense-data, many of them, have parts but that they are not identical with any collection of their parts" (Moore 1966: 76). He gestured towards the position that while Russell had suggested that science "compels us to hold the view that this surface *is* a number of surfaces with empty space between them" (Moore 1966: 69), we might say instead that "electrons & nuclei are *contained* in it, not that they are it" (Moore 1966: 76). But Moore left entirely open how a sense-datum, something immediately cognizable by our minds, could contain, in any useful sense of the word "contain," such radically non-observable entities as electrons. As Stebbing pointed out, the surfaces of electrons cannot be sense-data, nor can electrons be directly presented to us by means of mental sense-data, because electrons are smaller than the wavelength of visible light (Stebbing 1937: 181).

Stebbing's decision to allot to perceptual situations the role that Moore gave to sense-data, as a starting point for philosophical analysis, allowed her to sidestep all worries about whether a sense-datum must be as it seems. Moore's proposed solution, on which Stebbing never commented, was informed by sounder philosophical method than Eddington's positing of an ordinary, solid table of common sense alongside a "scientific" table made of mostly empty space. But he did not answer the question in what sense of "contain" a sense-datum contains unobservable physical posits. Stebbing's solution, replacing sense-data with perceptual science and invoking the distinction between directional and conceptual analysis, would have answered that the observable physical surface was analyzable, by successive steps of physico-directional analysis, into basic facts consisting in electrons orbiting protons.

The analysis of physics reveals observable, solid surfaces to be made of atoms in turn revealed to be mostly empty space. Stebbing saw clearly that there is no affront against common sense in this. By parity of reasoning, common sense does not allow us to infer Moore's earlier conclusion that we "believe . . . certainly, that to the vast majority of material objects, *no* acts of consciousness are attached" (Moore 1953: 22, his italics). But, although Stebbing did not take the idealist conclusion to be ruled out by common sense, she dismissed Eddington's argument for it. She maintained that "The

94   SUSAN STEBBING

rejection of the billiard-ball view of matter does not warrant the leap to any form of Idealism" (Stebbing 1937: 285). She was not opposed on common-sense grounds and even called Eddington's idealist proposal "delightful" at one point (Stebbing 1937: 280). Yet she felt that the idealist conclusion could not be derived from the premises Eddington had presented.

3 Eddington's Argument from Intrinsic Nature

In a section of his book called "Limitations of Physical Knowledge," Eddington, like Stebbing, drew attention to the stark contrast between the nineteenth-century certainty about the intrinsic nature of matter—solid, impenetrable, mechanical, deterministic, immediately perceptible, space-occupying—and the discoveries of modern physics.

> The Victorian physicist felt that he knew just what he was talking about when he used such terms as *matter* and *atoms*. Atoms were tiny billiard balls, a crisp statement that was supposed to tell you all about their nature in a way which could never be achieved for transcendental things like con-sciousness, beauty or humour. But now we realise that science has nothing to say as to the intrinsic nature of the atom. The physical atom is, like eve-rything else in physics, a schedule of pointer readings. The schedule is, we agree, attached to some unknown background. Why not then attach it to something of spiritual nature of which a prominent characteristic is *thought*. (Eddington 1928: 259)

This argument, the 1928 version of Eddington's argument from intrinsic nature, is widely quoted, embraced, and applauded by a group of present-day philosophers who describe their view as "panpsychism" (Strawson 2003, Strawson 2006, Seager 2006). Neither Eddington nor Stebbing used that term. Eddington rarely labeled his own view but sometimes said it had an "idealistic tinge" (Eddington 1928: viii). Some twenty-first-century panpsychists consider their view a form of physicalism (e.g., Strawson 2006), but there is no hint of that in either Eddington's own description of his view or Stebbing's reading of him.

What exactly is the form and content of Eddington's argument from in-trinsic nature, and what follows from it? Eddington's way of putting the point in the quotation above tends, for the twenty-first-century philosophically

ANTI-IDEALIST PHILOSOPHY OF PHYSICS   95

literate reader, to obscure his main message due to his insistence on describing physical posits as "a schedule of pointer readings." This nomenclature suggests to us that Eddington regarded physical theories as dealing only in the readings of measuring instruments. From this, we in turn infer that he must be advocating an anti-realist position, a kind of instrumentalism about physics. But Eddington intended his premises about pointer-readings to support an idealistically tinged conclusion, not an instrumentalist one. So our initial impression must be misleading.

At various points in her book, Stebbing criticized Eddington for his inconsistent attitude toward pointer readings, which he sometimes characterized as signs that "describe" (Eddington 1928: 251), sometimes as "intersections of world-lines" (Eddington 1928: 253), and sometimes as that which "supplies the continuous background" (Eddington 1928: 255) of physical theory, contrasted with its content. Stebbing ventured the view that "Intersections of world-lines are surely *events*" (Stebbing 1937: 94). Yet she found that interpretation of Eddington, though just barely able to make sense of his position on macro-physical objects—"an elephant is said to be 'a bundle of pointer-readings' ([Eddington 1928]: 256), and surely this must be interpreted as a bundle of events" (Stebbing 1937: 94)—utterly incompatible with his account of them as descriptions or signs. Neither of these accounts appears to sit well with the interpretation of pointer readings as that which "supplies the continuous background" (Eddington 1928: 255) of physical theory. This is what Stebbing described as assuming that "pointer-readings are indicative of qualities . . . that must be apprehended by the physicist in the process of discovering the physical laws" (Stebbing 1937: 96). It is this account that does the heavy lifting in Eddington's 1928 argument from intrinsic nature.

Eddington's allusion to pointer-readings is best interpreted here as an oblique expression of the structuralist nature of modern physical theory. An earlier, alternative formulation of Eddington's argument is the following:

> In regard to the nature of things, this knowledge [of relativity] is only an empty shell—a form of symbols. It is knowledge of structural form, and not knowledge of content. All through the physical world runs that unknown content, which must surely be the stuff of our consciousness. (Eddington 1920: 200)

The structuralism inherent in modern physics, but not in mainstream nineteenth-century physics, was a key tenet of Eddington's interpretation of physics, and one which Stebbing shared (Stebbing 1933–34: 7). Modern physical theories do not pronounce on the intrinsic natures of their posits, but provide us with a network of mathematised structural and law-like descriptions of the observable properties of things. Eddington moved from this premise to the conclusion that we are entitled to ascribe an intrinsic nature of consciousness to the atom.

Eddington's argument from intrinsic nature would not support the conclusion which is now often called "cosmopsychism," the ancient position, dating back to the Upanisads, that the universe as a whole has consciousness or mental states (Ganeri and Shani 2022).

Eddington attempted to derive the conclusion that the intrinsic nature of the basic constituents, the atoms, is spiritual. If taken to support panpsychism, the view in question would be what is now known as "micropsychism," ascribing a mental nature to the basic constituents of reality.

Eddington's frequently quoted argument on p. 259 of his 1928, then, might be reconstructed as having the following form:

P1. Unlike nineteenth-century theories of physics, which presumed to know the intrinsic nature of matter, modern physics provides us only with structural descriptions of matter, which describe how physical things are by means of saying how those things stand to other things in a network of mathematical and law-like generalizations.

P2. Theories composed of only structural descriptions do not ascribe any intrinsic nature to their objects.

P3. An intrinsic "spiritual nature," characterized by thought or consciousness, can coherently be ascribed to the objects posited by modern physics, such as atoms.

C. Atoms have an intrinsic nature of consciousness.

Eddington's nomenclature of "pointer readings," and his claim that the atom "is a schedule of pointer readings," amount not to instrumentalism but to structuralism. A structuralist science does not lay claim to knowledge of intrinsic nature. But, Eddington contended, the question of intrinsic nature remains pertinent to its interpretation, in the form of asking for the "unknown background": what is it that has the structural properties ascribed to matter by physics? As physicists do not pronounce on the intrinsic nature of matter anymore, having given up on the assumption that micro-physical bits of matter are just as we experience macro-physical objects to be, it is coherent

ANTI-IDEALIST PHILOSOPHY OF PHYSICS   97

to suppose that that which has the structural properties is mental or conscious in nature.

4 Stebbing's Objections

Stebbing's rebuttal of Eddington's argument from intrinsic nature focused not on common sense, but on the obviously invalid form of the argument. The frequently quoted version excerpted above is quite clearly in need of an additional fourth premise. The mere coherence of ascribing consciousness to the atom does not justify the conclusion that the atom truly does have an intrinsic nature of consciousness. Stebbing, we have seen, wholeheartedly endorsed premises 1 and 2. She expressed some hesitation about Eddington's wording of premise 3, in light of his tendency to describe the "unknown background" as an "inscrutable nature" (Eddington 1928: 251, 254, 260), noting that it is "useless to attempt to scrutinize" what is inscrutable (Stebbing 1937: 124). By contrast, Stebbing could happily accept the rendering of premise 3 above: it is coherent to ascribe an intrinsic nature of consciousness to the atom. Stebbing would have affirmed that this is indeed coherent, because there is no contradiction in an idealist analysis of matter even if it does have a paradoxical ring to it. Directional analyses may sound surprising, unexpected, even paradoxical. They are not subject to constraints of commonsensicality. But just because we can coherently analyze matter in idealist terms, it does not follow that we should.

The frequently quoted passage above leaves out the required premise 4, resting content with Eddington's "why not?" Stebbing instead pointed out the need for a reason why. She read Eddington as offering up the following as a fourth premise: "for pointer-readings of my own brain I have an insight which is not limited to the evidence of pointer-readings. That insight shows that they are attached to a background of consciousness" (Eddington 1928: 259). But Stebbing thought premise 4 was fatally flawed. We may have self-knowledge of our own consciousness, she argued, but knowledge of brains is just as much part of structural science as any other physical knowledge. Such "knowledge is nothing but a schedule of pointer-readings" (Stebbing 1937: 125), so it provides no more direct insight into intrinsic nature than any other scientific knowledge. We have no immediate apprehension into the nature of our brains when we think or introspect, much less into the pointer-readings of our brains, but only into our mental states. Stebbing

98 SUSAN STEBBING

concluded, "it is a complete muddle to argue that anyone has the insight that the pointer-readings of his own brain are attached to his own consciousness" (Stebbing 1937: 125).

It is possible that Stebbing meant the rebuttal above to uncover another *totum pro parte* fallacy. Perhaps the workings of our mind might at some point in history turn out to be analyzable into complex physical brain states. Even if this were true, we should have no expectation that the properties of mental states, such as consciousness and being open to introspection, carry over to the basic facts to which truths about mental states ultimately refer, namely, the specific arrangements of the chemical or physical brain states. Although Stebbing does not outright state the above, there is some textual evidence to suggest that she may have had it in mind when she took Eddington to task for speaking of knowing the "carbon in my own brain-mind" (Eddington 1928: 269). Stebbing worried that "Eddington does not seem to regard it as essentially nonsensical to say that there might have been self-knowledge of the carbon in my own brain" (Stebbing 1937: 126); on the *totum pro parte* analysis of the argument, this turns out to be a clear mistake relying on fallacious reasoning.

5 Conclusion

Stebbing's view of directional analysis as a search for the range of entities in some configuration which exist if the sentence is true allows for paradoxical-sounding, idealist, or panpsychist analyses of statements about the physical world. They are no more immediately ruled out than the also paradoxical-sounding "matter is mostly empty space at the subatomic level." I have shown that in *Philosophy and the Physicists*, Stebbing not only never appealed to incompatibility with common sense to rebut Eddington, but such a move would have been at odds with her own view of directional analysis. Instead, we see Stebbing tackle Eddington's proposed analysis of physical posits as having an intrinsic mental nature, their structural descriptions attached to a "background of consciousness," and argue forensically that the analysis is not justified by Eddington's premises. Eddington showed that an idealist interpretation of physics is compatible with contemporary theories of matter, but his positive case that it is a good idea relied on, as Stebbing put it, "a muddle": the muddling up of mind and brain, of symbol and referent. Eddington's view, now frequently labeled "panpsychism" by panpsychists

ANTI-IDEALIST PHILOSOPHY OF PHYSICS 99

(though not so labeled by Eddington) has come back into vogue. Stebbing's original and perceptive objections, concluding that Eddington's idealism rests on a fallacy, are deserving of a similar revival.

References

Beaney, M. 2003. Susan Stebbing on Cambridge and Vienna Analysis. In F. Stadler, ed., 339–350, *The Vienna Circle and Logical Empiricism.* Dordrecht: Springer.

Beaney, M. 2016. Susan Stebbing and the Early Reception of Logical Empiricism in Britain. In F. Stadler, ed., 233–256. *Influences on the Aufbau.* Cham: Springer.

Beaney, M., and S. Chapman 2021. "Susan Stebbing." *Stanford Encyclopedia of Philosophy.* https://plato.stanford.edu/entries/stebbing/.

Candlish, S. 2007. *The Russell-Bradley Dispute.* Basingstoke: Palgrave.

Chapman, S. 2013. *Susan Stebbing and the Language of Common Sense.* Basingstoke: Palgrave.

Coliva, A. 2021. "Stebbing, Moore (and Wittgenstein) on Common Sense and Metaphysical Analysis." *British Journal for the History of Philosophy* 29 (5): 914–934.

Connell, S., and F. Janssen-Lauret. 2023. "'Bad Philosophy' and 'Derivative Philosophy': Labels That Keep Women Out of the Canon." *Metaphilosophy* 54 (2–3): 238–253.

Eddington, A. 1920. *Space, Time, and Gravitation.* Cambridge: Cambridge University Press.

Eddington, A. 1928. *The Nature of the Physical World.* New York: Macmillan.

Ganeri, J., and I. Shani. 2022. "What Is Cosmopsychism?" *The Monist* 105: 1–5.

Hylton, P. 1990. *Russell, Idealism and the Emergence of Analytic Philosophy.* Oxford: Clarendon Press.

Janssen-Lauret, F. 2022a. *Susan Stebbing.* Cambridge: Cambridge University Press.

Janssen-Lauret, F. 2022b. "Susan Stebbing's Metaphysics and the Status of Common-Sense Truths." In J. Peijnenburg and S. Verhaegh, eds., 167–190, *Women in the History of Analytic Philosophy.* Cham: Springer.

Janssen-Lauret, F. 2017. "Susan Stebbing, Incomplete Symbols, and Foundherentist Meta-Ontology." *Journal for the History of Analytical Philosophy* 5: 6–17.

Milkov, N. 2003. "Susan Stebbing's Criticism of Wittgenstein's Tractatus." In F. Stadler, ed., 351–363, *The Vienna Circle and Logical Empiricism.* Dordrecht: Springer.

Moore, G. E. 1899. "The Nature of Judgement." *Mind* 8: 176–193.

Moore, G. E. 1903. "The Refutation of Idealism." *Mind* 12: 433–453.

Moore, G. E. 1925. "A Defence of Common Sense." In J. Muirhead, ed., *Contemporary British Philosophy.* Reprinted in Moore, G. E. 1959. *Philosophical Papers.* London: George Allen and Unwin.

Moore, G. E. 1953. *Some Main Problems of Philosophy.* London: George Allen and Unwin.

Moore, G. E. 1966. *Lectures on Philosophy.* London: George Allen and Unwin.

Russell, B. 1923. *ABC of Atoms.* New York: E. P. Dutton.

Seager, W. 2006. "The 'Intrinsic Nature' Argument for Panpsychism." *Journal of Consciousness Studies* 13: 129–145.

Stebbing, L. S. 1916–17. "Relation and Coherence." *Proceedings of the Aristotelian Society* 17: 459–480.

Stebbing, L. S. 1917–18. "The Philosophical Importance of the Verb 'To Be.'" *Proceedings of the Aristotelian Society* 18: 582–589.

Stebbing, L. S. 1924. "Mind and Nature in Prof. Whitehead's Philosophy." *Mind,* 33: 289–303.

Stebbing, L. S. 1924–25. "Universals and Professor Whitehead's Theory of Objects." *Proceedings of the Aristotelian Society,* 25: 305–330.

Stebbing, L. S. 1926. "Professor Whitehead's 'Perceptual Object.'" *Journal of Philosophy,* 23: 197–213.

100 SUSAN STEBBING

Stebbing, L. S. 1927. "Abstraction and Science." *Journal of Philosophical Studies*, 2: 309–322.

Stebbing, L. S. 1928. "Materialism in the Light of Modern Scientific Thought." *Proceedings of the Aristotelian Society*, Suppl. 8: 112–161.

Stebbing, L. S. 1929. "Realism and Modern Physics." *Proceedings of the Aristotelian Society*, Suppl. 9: 112–161.

Stebbing, L. S. 1930. *A Modern Introduction to Logic*. London: Methuen.

Stebbing, L. S. 1933. *A Modern Introduction to Logic*. 2nd ed. London: Methuen.

Stebbing, L. S. 1932–33. "The Method of Analysis in Metaphysics." *Proceedings of the Aristotelian Society* 33: 65–94.

Stebbing, L. S. 1933–34. "Constructions: The Presidential Address." *Proceedings of the Aristotelian Society* 34: 1–30.

Stebbing, L. S. 1937. *Philosophy and the Physicists*. London: Penguin.

Stebbing, L. S. 1942. "Moore's Influence." In P. Schilpp, ed., 515–532, *The Philosophy of G. E. Moore*. La Salle, IL: Open Court.

Strawson, G. 2003. "Real Materialism." In L. Antony and N. Hornstein, eds., *Chomsky and His Critics*. Oxford: Blackwell.

Strawson, G. 2006. "Realistic Monism: Why Physicalism Entails Panpsychism." *Journal of Consciousness Studies* 13: 3–31.

West, P. 2022. "The Philosopher Versus the Physicist: Susan Stebbing on Eddington and the Passage of Time." *British Journal for the History of Philosophy* 30: 130–151.

Whitehead, A. N. 1920. *The Concept of Nature*. Cambridge: Cambridge University Press.

Making Sense of Stebbing and Moore on Common Sense

Louis Doulas

1 Introduction

Philosophy, for Susan Stebbing, begins with what is known, with common-sense beliefs like *I see this candle* or *there is a table in this room*. "We must begin with commonsense facts," says Stebbing, for we cannot demonstrate that such beliefs are true, "we cannot find premises more certain than the belief itself *from which* it may be *deduced*" (1932–33: 74, 70). In this respect, "common sense needs no defence" (1938–39: 84).

In granting common sense such a central role in her philosophical theorizing, one cannot help but consider the influence of G. E. Moore. Indeed, the philosophical milieu that Stebbing, twelve years Moore's junior, inherited and would ultimately transform in her own distinctive way, was shaped in significant part by Moore's philosophy. By the time Stebbing's remarks above were published, the impact of Moore's anti-idealist attacks (1899, 1903a) and defense of non-naturalistic ethics (1903b) had already been felt and thoroughly absorbed in Cambridge and beyond. His official defense of common sense would arrive in 1925,[1] sealing his fate—for better or for worse—as the arch analytic philosopher of common sense.

Moore's common-sense view seems to have resonated with Stebbing, who registers her solidarity nearly a decade after his famous defense:

> I agree with Prof. Moore in holding that the "Common Sense view of the World," is, in certain fundamental features, *wholly* true. I agree with him

[1] Moore's first explicit articulation of his "Common Sense view of the World" appeared much earlier, in his 1910–11 Morley College lectures, though these were not published until 1953 as *Some Main Problems of Philosophy*.

Louis Doulas, *Making Sense of Stebbing and Moore on Common Sense* In: *Susan Stebbing*. Edited by: Annalisa Coliva and Louis Doulas, Oxford University Press. © Oxford University Press 2025.
DOI: 10.1093/9780197682371.003.0005

102 SUSAN STEBBING

further in believing that we all, plain men and philosophers alike, have held this. For example, I hold (and I venture to think that you also hold) that there have been "very many other human beings, who have had bodies and have lived upon the earth." Again, at this moment, I *know* that this is a table. I also know that there are trees and rocks. (1933–34: 26–27)

While it would be both inaccurate and reductive to characterize Stebbing as a mere follower of Moore—or, in A. J. Ayer's far less charitable words, "very much a disciple of Moore"[2]—Moore's influence on her work during this period (beginning in the late 1920s) seems unquestionable, if not entirely unsurprising. Most commentators would not hesitate to describe Stebbing's philosophical methodology as broadly "Moorean,"[3] while simultaneously acknowledging that she was a philosopher of her own rank, who diverged from Moore in a great many ways.[4]

Yet, it must be acknowledged, as commentators like Frederique Janssen-Lauret (2022a: 172, 174) have noted, that Stebbing's deferential posture toward Moore, coupled with her conspicuous generosity in attributing intellectual credit to him, often had the effect of obscuring the originality of her own contributions. This, along with several other factors—notably, the relative neglect of her work in the philosophy of science (2022a: 172)—may have led scholars to view Stebbing's philosophy through an unduly simplified, if not subtly distorted, lens. The idea here is not that Stebbing anticipated Moore's common-sense view, but rather—perhaps more surprisingly—that she, in fact, "did not rush to endorse it" (2022a: 174). This is particularly striking when considered alongside the passages from Stebbing above. But what such commentators are drawing our attention to is precisely the fact that there is more to these passages than meets the eye: Stebbing's relationship to common sense is considerably more complex than prevailing interpretations would lead us to assume.[5]

---

[2] Ayer (1977: 157). The full sentiment reads: "Philosophically [Stebbing] was very much a disciple of Moore and she shared his impatience with sloppy or pretentious thinking. She was quite often brusque but she was never mean. She was one of those persons who make you proud if they think well of you" (157–158). Despite Ayer's minimizing remark about Stebbing's discipleship, as this and other passages in his autobiography suggest, Ayer seemed to have very much admired Stebbing.

[3] See, for example, Ayer (1977), Milkov (2003), Beaney (2003, 2016), Chapman (2013), and Beaney and Chapman (2017).

[4] As Beaney remarks, "Stebbing was far too independent a thinker to be described as a 'disciple' of Moore, although she was undoubtedly influenced by him" (2016: 240).

[5] For challenges to the received reading on this score, see especially Janssen-Lauret (2017; 2022a: 172, 174; 2022b; 2023; chapter in this volume). See also Coliva (2021) and West (2022: 144–147).

I agree. However, I think that what is complex and significant about Stebbing's position is not exactly what these commentators take it to be. I maintain that the reasons offered for *resisting* subsuming Stebbing's position under Moore's common-sense view rest on a popular, albeit oversimplified, conception of Moorean common sense. This oversimplification misleads not only those who seek to distance Stebbing's view from Moore's but also proponents of received readings who take Stebbing's and Moore's positions to be closely aligned. As I see it, then, received readings are too quick to assimilate Moore's common-sense view to Stebbing, whereas alternative readings are too quick to conclude the opposite.

In what follows, I advance a new interpretation that retains elements of both. In keeping with received readings, I show how—given a less familiar conception of Moorean common sense—Stebbing and Moore were, in several important respects, on the same page (section 3 of this chapter). Where they ultimately diverge, I argue, lies in Stebbing's project of *integrating* this common-sense worldview with a scientific one—what I call Stebbing's "unity thesis" (sections 4 and 5). It is in this respect that I align with critics of the received reading: close attention to Stebbing's philosophy of science is crucial to disentangling her position from Moore's. In this sense, my reading converges with alternative readings, such as Janssen-Lauret's. However, whereas Janssen-Lauret, for instance, characterizes Stebbing as a philosopher who, if anything, more closely resembles Whitehead and Russell than Moore,[6] one of the central claims of this chapter is that for Stebbing, common sense and science are not in tension but intimately intertwined. As I will show, Stebbing advances her own distinctive defense of the "common sense view of the world," along with a conception of common-sense knowledge that not only departs from Moore's but is explicitly rejected by him: the view that common-sense knowledge is probabilistic and continuous with scientific knowledge. In this way, I see no tension in describing Stebbing as a figure who resembles both Russell and Whitehead *and* Moore.

2 The Basics of Common Sense

When Stebbing writes above that she agrees with "Prof. Moore in holding that the 'Common Sense view of the World,' is, in certain fundamental

---

[6] Insofar as Stebbing, like Whitehead and Russell, "was also on a quest to find a properly scientific philosophy" (2022a: 182).

104   SUSAN STEBBING

features, *wholly* true," she is referring to the common-sense view of the world as articulated in Moore's "A Defence of Common Sense" (DCS, 1925). Naturally, then, we begin there, with a brief outline of the view Moore sketches in that famous essay, alongside the various ways in which Stebbing signals her agreement, before going on to develop a deeper and more complex account.

In DCS, Moore anticipates the familiar unease provoked by appeals to "common sense": that phrases such as the "Common Sense view of the world" or "Common Sense beliefs" are "extraordinarily vague" (DCS, 119). This vagueness means, as Moore acknowledges, that for all he knows, "there may be many propositions which may be properly called features in 'the Common Sense view of the world' or 'Common Sense beliefs', which are not true." (DCS, 119).

What Moore grants here is that some beliefs included under the category of "common-sense" may well be false—not all such beliefs amount to knowledge. So, which ones do? While neither Moore nor Stebbing left us with any neat and tidy account of common sense,[7] they did attempt to indicate which common-sense beliefs they took to constitute common-sense *knowledge*, and they did this largely by way of example. Here is a familiar selection from Moore, paraphrased from the opening pages of DCS:[8]

- There exists at present a human body which is my body.
- This body was born at a certain time in the past, and has existed continuously ever since, though not without undergoing changes.
- There have existed many other things that have shape and size in three dimensions.
- Many human bodies other than mine have before now lived on the earth.
- Many human beings other than myself have before now perceived, dreamed, and felt.
- The earth has existed for many years past.

Though the truisms above may seem so obvious "as not to be worth stating" (DCS, 106), philosophers are notorious for having denied them, or for

---

[7] To attempt to provide such an account would perhaps be antithetical to the spirit of their respective approaches. As Stebbing remarks in a different context: "It is useless first to *define* 'material thing,' or 'cause,' and then to ask whether the terms so defined are exemplified in the world" (1932–33: 74). The same, we might think, holds for common sense.

[8] Neither the list here, nor Moore's own, is meant to be exhaustive.

STEBBING AND MOORE ON COMMON SENSE   105

having admitted them to be "half-true" or "partially true."[9] As Moore urges, however, such philosophers are "confusing the question [of] whether we understand its meaning (which we all certainly do) with the entirely different question [of] whether ... we are able to *give a correct analysis* of its meaning" (DCS, 106).

This is a crucial point. For Moore, knowing an expression's *meaning* and knowing its *philosophical analysis* are different. (We will touch on the significance of this distinction, and to what is meant by "analysis," in section 3.) *The earth has existed for many years past* is, for example, an expression which, taken in its ordinary and popular sense, "we all understand" (DCS, 111). If we know what "earth," "existed," "years," and "past" mean, then we understand the expression as a whole. Moore's point is that we *do* know what such expressions mean; otherwise, communication within and across communities would hardly be possible (again, even if this means that we do not know how such statements are to be philosophically analyzed).

Writing several years later, Stebbing produces a strikingly similar list. Unlike Moore's target in DCS, however, Stebbing's is not the traditional skeptic or idealist but those philosophers and scientists who think modern physics gives us reason to deny truths like the following:

- I am now seeing a red patch.
- I am now perceiving a piece of blotting paper.
- That is a piece of blotting paper.
- That piece of blotting paper is on the table.
- That piece of blotting paper was on the table before I saw it.
- Other people besides myself have seen that piece of blotting paper.

("Realism and Modern Physics," RMP, 1929)

Like Moore's propositions above, the propositions here, as Stebbing claims, are of the sort that are "believed by the plain man to be true" (RMP, 147). They are "the basis upon which all scientific and philosophical speculation must rest" (RMP, 148). Scientific and philosophical speculation rests upon such facts because, for Stebbing, both disciplines (especially theoretical physics) develop "by the continual modification of common-sense views,"

---

[9] Moore's repeated insistence on this point in DCS is an unmistakable attack on Bradley's claim that truth and judgment, understood as non-absolute qualities, admit degrees. See Bradley (1893: 359, 374–375).

106 SUSAN STEBBING

that is, truisms such as the ones above which Stebbing takes to comprise "perceptual science" (RMP, 148). Denying such truisms, as some scientists and philosophers have done, is to deny theoretical physics itself, for "unless perceptual science is true theoretical physics cannot be true" (RMP, 149).

Although the truisms on Moore's list appear more general and Stebbing's more specific—drawing more explicitly on scientific contexts (a point we will revisit in the coming sections of the chapter)—this should not obscure the fact that Stebbing's list reflects the same underlying commitments as Moore's. For example, the claim that there is a piece of blotting paper on the table serves as an instance of something with shape, size, and three-dimensional existence. Similarly, the claim that this piece of blotting paper was on the table *before I saw it* exemplifies something that, like the earth, has persisted through time independently of my own existence. The claim that other people besides myself have seen the blotting paper clearly captures Moore's claim that many human beings *other than myself* have, before now, perceived things.

So, according to Moore and Stebbing, we possess a great deal of common-sense knowledge. The philosophical task, then, is not to challenge this knowledge but to *analyze* it. As Stebbing emphasizes, we must not ask "*how* we come to know such [common sense facts]" but instead "*what* is their correct analysis" (RMP, 148). Moreover, our inability to specify *how* we know what we know does not (and should not) preclude us from knowing it. We know, for instance, that the earth has existed for many years past, even if, as Moore puts it, "we [might] not know what the evidence was" (DCS, 118). Crucially, then, not knowing how we know the truths of common sense is compatible with knowing them—and knowing them with certainty.

Finally, it is important to emphasize that for both Moore and Stebbing, common-sense beliefs such as the ones above are not true by virtue of being believed by almost everyone—that is, they are not true by virtue of sociology—but because *they are evidentially and obviously true*; all inquiry, meaning, and action must, in some sense, presuppose them.[10] In this respect, common sense for Moore and Stebbing really is *common*:

> But it must be remembered that, according to me, *all* philosophers, without exception, have agreed with me in holding [the truths of Common

---

[10] See Coliva (2010: 16–17) for further discussion.

STEBBING AND MOORE ON COMMON SENSE   107

Sense]: and that the real difference, which is commonly expressed in this way, is only a difference between those philosophers, who have *also* held views inconsistent with these features in "the Common Sense view of the world," and those who have not. (DCS, 118–19)

"*All* philosophers," for Moore, include even those skeptics and idealists who have denied—or who profess to deny—the truths of common sense.[11] Stebbing, in her British Academy Lecture, "Logical Positivism and Analysis" (LPA, 1933), echoes something similar. Criticizing the methodological solipsism she attributes to certain positivist views, she remarks:

I have the best grounds for denying solipsism, namely, that I *know* it to be false. You, who are listening to me, and enable me to speak in the plural, *also* know it to be false. [footnote to Moore's DCS] I suggest that there is something wrong with a theory which, as a consequence of its fundamental principles, involves solipsism in any form. (LPA, 27)

Like Moore, Stebbing maintains that philosophers who deny the existence of other minds, cannot escape talk that seems to presuppose them. Such philosophers, she notes, allow her to "speak in the plural," but in so doing, they fail to acknowledge what they already know—that other minds (including Stebbing's) exist. "The *premises* for an argument leading to solipsism," writes Stebbing, "are invariably derived from knowledge which is inconsistent with solipsism" (LPA, 28).

3 Between Ecumenical and Sectarian Readings

So far, Moore and Stebbing appear largely aligned on a core feature of the common-sense worldview: that the philosophical task is to analyze our common-sense knowledge, not to call it into question. They also appear aligned on several specifics of this worldview: the general type of truisms it comprises and the claim that these truisms are *wholly* true; the idea that such truisms are known without necessarily knowing *how* we know them; and the

---

[11] There is important interpretive work to be done on this passage. See Vanrie (2021) for one recent (and interesting) reading.

108 SUSAN STEBBING

foundational role they play in inquiry and communication. However, one might think this is where they begin to part ways.

The key issue lies in how each philosopher conceives of the limits of analysis with respect to common sense—if any. But first: what kind of analysis is at stake? While Moore is not especially explicit about this in his work, the sense of analysis alluded to in DCS is undoubtedly metaphysical.[12] Moore writes, for example, that "the whole question as to the *nature* of material things obviously depends upon their analysis" (DCS, 127–28), suggesting that by analyzing propositions about material objects such as "This is a human hand" we are to discover their nature. The question of their nature, that is, depends on such analysis.

Stebbing, too, recognizes the metaphysical thrust of Moore's conception of analysis here.[13] However, whereas Moore never developed a systematic account of analysis, Stebbing worked to clarify its nature and articulate its significance.[14] She refers to this metaphysical conception of analysis as *directional analysis*, the aim of which is "making precise the reference of all true beliefs" (1932–33: 70). Directional analysis, on her view, must be distinguished from logico-grammatical (or "same level") analysis.[15] While the latter seeks to replace natural language expressions with more perspicuous language—whether ordinary or logical—the former aims to uncover, level by level, the "ultimate reference of what is expressed" (1932–33: 87).[16] To modify our slogan, then: the job of philosophy, on the Moore-Stebbing view, is not

---

[12] See Preti (2017: 78) who also identifies this metaphysical aspect in Moore's sense of analysis.

[13] Stebbing notes that "[it] is from the writings of Prof. Moore that I have learnt the importance of the method of metaphysical analysis," but she immediately adds a footnote clarifying: "I do not wish to suggest that Moore uses this expression [=metaphysical analysis], nor that he would agree with what I say. But if what I say is correct, then I think it could have been derived from a study of his writings" (1932–33: 76, footnote ˙). Notably, it is Stebbing's careful qualification here—her reluctance to attribute these ideas too directly to Moore—that underscores the originality and importance of her own contribution to debates about analysis.

[14] See especially Stebbing (1932–33; 1934a; 1938–39).

[15] The nature of logico-grammatical analysis is thought to be best captured by Russell's theory of definite descriptions which many take to represent the paradigm of analysis in the 1930s.

[16] Stebbing makes a further distinction between what she calls the "immediate reference" and "ultimate reference" of a proposition. The difference comes down to this. The immediate reference of a proposition is what we ordinarily understand it to assert, while its ultimate reference is something we discover through metaphysical analysis. Importantly, we need not know the ultimate reference of a proposition to know its immediate reference, for the latter, unlike the former, is something that "we already know when we understand the proposition" (1932–33: 78–79). For example, the immediate reference of the proposition, "Every economist is fallible," is the following: *If something is an economist, then it is fallible*. When analyzing a proposition, however, we are interested not merely in discovering its immediate reference, but the "ultimate reference of what is expressed" (1932–33: 87). The ultimate reference of "Every economist is fallible" might, then, take the following form: *Maynard Keynes is fallible and Josiah Stamp is fallible, and so on*.

STEBBING AND MOORE ON COMMON SENSE   109

to challenge common-sense knowledge but to *metaphysically analyze* it. The aim of such analysis is to uncover what makes our common-sense beliefs true.

It is here, however—when we consider what could make such beliefs true by means of metaphysical analysis—that we might be tempted to think Stebbing diverges from Moore. For although she holds that all philosophical and scientific speculation must rest on the common-sense truisms above, she appears only to mean that their *truth* must be respected; how we metaphysically analyze those truths remain open-ended. For example, while Stebbing does not think that modern science demands an idealist interpretation of its theories and formalisms, she nonetheless writes that "it is . . . not impossible to interpret science idealistically" (1928: 128). The fact, then, that *there is a piece of blotting paper on the table* or that *there are trees and rocks* does not, for her, necessarily imply the falsity of idealism. Such facts are, in principle, amenable to analysis in terms of an idealist metaphysics.

The difference might be put this way: realism, for Stebbing, does not seem to imply the negation of idealism. A realist, as Stebbing glosses it, is simply "anyone who believes that such propositions as these [e.g., 'That piece of blotting paper is on the table'] are true" (RMP, 147). Realism on Stebbing's view is committed only to the truth and knowledge of common sense—and nothing more. Let us call this the *ecumenical* reading of common sense.

If this is right, then a stark difference emerges in how Stebbing and Moore conceive of the limits of analysis with respect to common sense. After all, the received reading of Moore's view is not ecumenical, but *sectarian*.[17] That is, Moore's common-sense truisms cannot be analyzed in any way consistent with idealism, as they are not neutral with respect to it—they imply its outright denial. For Moore, unlike Stebbing, a commitment to common sense is not just a commitment to the *truth* of certain propositions, but to what those truths imply: that there are mind-independent things out there in the world. This is how philosophical views like idealism and skepticism are thought to be defeated by common sense in the first place. This apparent difference is one of the main reasons that commentators critical of the received view find it misleading to assimilate Moore's common-sense view to Stebbing.[18]

---

[17] Ranalli and Walker (2025) introduce the ecumenical/sectarian distinction in interpreting Moore's proof of an external world. (Incidentally, they classify Moore's views as sectarian, in line with the received view.) My use of the distinction is inspired by theirs, though our applications may not entirely align.

[18] See especially Janssen-Lauret (2022a: 184) and West (2022: 144–145).

110   SUSAN STEBBING

But where does this sectarian reading of Moore come from? Three places, I suggest. Moore's early 1910–11 Morley College lectures, published as *Some Main Problems of Philosophy* (*SMPP*, 1953); his notorious "Proof of an External World" (PEW, 1939); and "A Reply to My Critics" (RMC, 1942) in the Schilpp volume *The Philosophy of G. E. Moore*. In each of the essays here, Moore seems to endorse an account of common sense that is more sectarian than ecumenical, one that appears eminently incompatible with radical metaphysical views such as idealism. This is perhaps the clearest in *SMPP* where Moore takes issue with Berkeley's idealist analysis of common sense, arguing that "what we mean to assert, when we assert the existence of material objects, is certainly the existence of something which continues to exist even when we are *not* conscious of it" (*SMPP*, 21). According to this Moore, Berkeley's view is wholly at odds with the common-sense view of the world:

> I think, then, it may fairly be said that Berkeley denies the existence of any material objects, in the sense in which common sense asserts their existence. *This is the way in which he contradicts common sense.* (*SMPP*, 21, emphasis added)

While Moore is not as explicit in PEW or RMC as he is here, both texts are read as continuous with *SMPP*. For example, while "common sense" is not mentioned once in PEW, commentators have long interpreted Moore as taking "here are two hands" to be synonymous with "there are at least two external things." Similarly in RMC, Moore seems to treat "material thing" as synonymous with "external thing" (RMC, 668–70). In both cases, the existence of external things is taken to be commonsensical for Moore, *implied* by the existence of material things such as hands.

Let us grant that such readings are sound. What I want to argue here is that Moore's conception of common sense is not as monolithic and resolute as commentators have assumed, and that this has important implications for how we understand the direction of influence between Stebbing and Moore with respect to their conceptions of common sense.

We can begin by noting that starting roughly from the late 1920s onward, Stebbing repeatedly refers to Moore's DCS.[19] In LPA, her 1933 British

---

[19] See Stebbing (1926: 194; 1932–33: 73–74, 76; 1933–34: 26–27; 1933: 7, 27; 1938–39, 70–71, 73).

STEBBING AND MOORE ON COMMON SENSE   111

Academy lecture, Stebbing also references a long passage from an even earlier paper by Moore, "The Nature and Reality of Objects of Perception" (NROP, [1905–6] 1922). Stebbing takes this passage (reproduced below) to be central to her philosophical stance. She writes that it is "futile for philosophers to dispute the truth of commonsense statements merely on the ground that the analysis of these statements cannot be given, *or on the ground that if an analysis were given, it would be shocking to common sense*" (1933: 8–9, emphasis added). In her 1942 contribution to the Schilpp volume on Moore, she refers to NROP once again, noting that it has not received the attention she believes it deserves (1942: 524).[20]

Now, what is striking about both of these papers by Moore—NROP and DCS—is the contrast that emerges when they are set alongside *SMPP*, PEW, and RMC; indeed, many readers may find Moore's views about common sense here surprisingly ecumenical. Consider the lengthy passage from NROP which Stebbing reproduces in her British Academy lecture. With respect to the proposition, "Hens' eggs are generally laid by hens," we find Moore writing this (following Stebbing, I believe it is important to quote the passage in full):

I am quite willing to allow for the moment that if it is true at all, we must understand by "hens" and "eggs," objects very unlike that which we directly observe, when we see a hen in a yard, or an egg on the breakfast-table. I am willing to allow the possibility that, as some Idealists would say, the proposition: "Hens lay eggs" is false, unless we mean by it: A certain kind of collection of spirits or monads sometimes has a certain intelligible relation to another kind of collection of spirits or monads. I am willing to allow the possibility that, as Reid and some scientists would say, the proposition "Hens lay eggs" is false, if we mean by it anything more than that: Certain configurations of invisible material particles sometimes have a certain spatio-temporal relation to another kind of configuration of invisible material particles. Or again I am willing to allow, with certain other philosophers, that we must, if it is to be true, interpret this proposition as meaning that certain kinds of sensations have to certain

---

[20] This remark could be taken as somewhat exaggerated, given that it was written for the Schilpp volume, which aimed to canonize Moore. The important point, however, is that Stebbing engages with NROP in both her 1933 and 1942 papers in a substantive and non-trivial way.

112 SUSAN STEBBING

other kinds a relation which may be expressed by saying that the one kind of sensations "lay" the other kind. Or again, as other philosophers say, the proposition "Hens lay eggs" may possibly mean: Certain sensations of mind *would*, under certain conditions, have to certain other sensations of mine a relation which may be expressed by saying that the one set would "lay" the other set. But whatever the proposition "Hens' eggs are generally laid by hens" may *mean,* most philosophers would, I think, allow that, in some sense or other, this proposition was true. (NROP, 64–65)

Of course, Moore would oppose most of the revisionary analyses here, but he clearly treats it as an open question how propositions like "Hens' eggs are generally laid by hens" should be philosophically analyzed—even if, as Stebbing says, such analyses might be "shocking to common sense." Indeed, it is this passage that A. J. Ayer refers to when he writes: "I suppose that in later years Moore would have drawn the line at collections of spirits, but his attachment to common sense was always much looser than has generally been assumed" (1977: 117).[21]

Although it would only be a few years later, in 1910–11, that Moore's views would evolve in a more sectarian direction, nearly two decades later—in both DCS and his posthumously published *Lectures on Philosophy* (*LP,* 1966)—he appears to revive his earlier ecumenical stance found in the long passage from NROP above.

In DCS, recall, Moore claims that he is "not at all sceptical as to the truth of . . . propositions which assert the existence of material things" but that he is "*very sceptical* as to what . . . the correct analysis of such propositions is" (DCS, 127, emphasis added). Moore's point is that the reason we do not know with certainty how propositions like "This is a hand" should be analyzed is because it is not obvious what the "principal" or "ultimate" subject of such propositions are *prior* to our analysis of them (DCS, 128). The correct metaphysical analysis of such propositions could, for example, yield something as radical as phenomenalism, an analysis Moore himself seriously entertains, though ultimately rejects, in DCS. Importantly, while the

---

[21] Interestingly, David Armstrong picks up on this as well, though he overstates the point when he claims that Moore was "*always* ready to insist on what we might call the shallowness of truistic or Moorean knowledge" (2006: 160–161, emphasis added).

STEBBING AND MOORE ON COMMON SENSE   113

phenomenalist analysis strikes him as paradoxical-sounding, Moore does not *reject* it on those grounds.[22]

This ecumenical reading of DCS can be bolstered by considering some revealing passages in *LP*. The specific lectures of *LP* that I have in mind were delivered only four years after DCS, in 1928–29, suggesting a plausible continuity of thought.

In these lectures, Moore distinguishes his usage of the term "material thing" from the uses found in other philosophers. Some philosophers, he writes, use "material thing" to mean something that is "independent of perception"—a phrase Moore finds particularly ambiguous. On this view, if there are no things that are independent of perception, then there are no material things: no human bodies, no blackboards, and so on (*LP*, 15–16). Other philosophers, by contrast, use "material thing" so that even if no material things exist, human bodies, blackboards, and the like still exist, albeit conceived as collections of conscious beings or monads (*LP*, 16).

Importantly, Moore subscribes to neither of these usages. He clarifies that he does not take material things to *ipso facto* entail that they are independent of perception: "I say: That is a blackboard, *does* entail 'that's a material thing' but does *not* entail 'that's independent of perception' or 'that's not a colony of monads'" (*LP*, 17).[23] Usages of "material thing" contrary to this, Moore finds "absurd and unjustifiable" (*LP*, 16).

While obviously Moore ultimately thinks material things *are* independent of perception, according to him, it is more "fantastic [and] absurd" to deny the wholesale existence of material things than to analyze them as colonies of mind-dependent monads:

> I don't use "material thing" in such a sense that in saying that a blackboard is a material thing I'm saying that it's not a colony of monads. Of course, I think it isn't: the view that it is seems to me fantastic & absurd. But not

---

[22] He writes that "the true analysis may, for instance, *possibly* be quite as paradoxical as is the third view given above [i.e., phenomenalism]," though, again, he doubts this will be the case in the end (DCS, 133). It is worth noting that Moore also seriously entertains and rejects both direct and indirect realist analyses.

[23] "In saying that there are such senses I am, of course, assuming, what is perhaps disputable, that from 'This is a human body' there does *not* follow 'This is independent of perception': that is to say that the prop. 'This is a human body, but is not independent of perception,' is *not* self-contradictory" (*LP*, 18).

114   SUSAN STEBBING

nearly so fantastic & absurd as the view that there are no material things in *my* sense. (*LP*, 16)

Once more, we see can see from these texts that Moore leaves the metaphysical analysis of the materiality of objects open. While we *know* that human bodies and blackboards exist and that such things are material, it is not obvious how to metaphysically analyze materiality. Analysis could take us in several different directions: material things could turn out to be independent of perception, or they could turn out to be mind-dependent collections of monads. Analysis may reveal metaphysical constructions even more imaginative than these.

While there is no direct evidence that Stebbing read drafts of Moore's lectures here, it is not unlikely that she encountered some of his ideas in correspondence or discussion with him.[24] However, given that strikingly similar views were developed in texts of Moore's that Stebbing *did* read and discuss extensively—namely, NROP and DCS—it is plausible that Stebbing's own ecumenicalism was likely inspired and influenced by the ecumenicalism on display in these texts. If this is right, the difference between Stebbing and Moore with respect to the truths and commitments of common sense is not as stark as commentators claim it is, that (in my words) Stebbing endorsed a more ecumenical account of common sense than Moore. That is one upshot, but another is that we should be cautious in ascribing *one* specific common-sense view to Moore. I would urge something similar with respect to Stebbing as well.[25]

---

[24] The Cambridge University Library holds twenty documented letters from Stebbing to Moore, dated between 1918 and 1942, many of which also include Moore's wife, Dorothy, in the correspondence. These letters reflect both professional and personal dimensions of their relationship, suggesting that Stebbing and Moore were fairly close friends. In addition to their many written exchanges, Stebbing reports that she had "often been present at discussions with [Moore] and [had] occasionally heard him lecture" (1942: 530).

[25] In "Constructions" (1933–34), Stebbing writes that the "external world is the total set of material things (i.e., perceptible objects) in their spatial and temporal relations. . . . [I]t is the world of macroscopic objects, such as tables, trees, water, human bodies, stars" (1933–34: 10). This, however, make it sounds as if common sense implies the falsity of idealism. Something similarly sectarian is indicated elsewhere by Stebbing: "I wish to maintain . . . that there is a fundamental difference between propositions which would ordinarily be said to be propositions about myself, *e.g.*, 'I am tired,' 'I see a chair,' and propositions *made by me*, but not about myself, *e.g.*, 'That is a chair.'" (1934b: 168). Stebbing says that propositions like "That is a chair" are propositions *not about herself*, the implication being that such propositions are not about her mental states, sensations, or sensible qualities, but about *mind-independent* things like chairs.

4 Common-Sense Knowledge as Scientific Knowledge

So where does the real difference lie?

Consider the fact that Moore's discussions of common sense largely revolve around its relationship to philosophy. Can we—should we—ever give up our common-sense beliefs in the face of McTaggart's argument that Time is unreal? What about when confronted with Bradley's infamous regress? Probably not. But then to what extent are our common-sense beliefs capable of revision? Perhaps there is not much room for philosophy to overturn them, but might science be in more capable hands?

Moore never directly addressed such questions in his work.[26] The closest we get to a discussion of the relationship between science and common sense can be found in a few intriguing passages from *LP*. In Lecture III, "Questions of Speculative Philosophy," delivered in 1933–34, we discover a side of Moore that is rarely on display in his more well-known papers:

> Surely it's the business of the mathematicians to decide whether particular mathematical propositions are true? And if so what's the use of the philosopher discussing whether *any* mathematical propositions are true? Suppose he decides they are, can he give better reasons than the mathematicians give? Suppose he decides they aren't. He's contradicting the mathematicians. And aren't they the better judges? (*LP*, 185)[27]

> The sciences *do* say not only p ... but there's *good evidence for p*: and it has happened that *p* belongs to a class of propositions with regard to which philosophers have concluded: We *never* have good evidence for a proposition of that sort. Isn't the fact that the sciences say: Such-and-such *is* good evidence for so-and-so, a reason for saying: It *is* good evidence? (*LP*, 189)

---

[26] Though Moore rarely wrote on mathematics or the sciences, he had a deep respect for them and was not unaware of the significant advances being made in these fields. See, for example, Moore's posthumously published review of Russell's *The Principles of Mathematics* in Moore (2018–19). We should also not forget that from 1911 to 1925, Moore lectured three times a week on psychology for the Moral Sciences Tripos. His discussion of after-images in PEW 151 perhaps reflects this background, as he references both a physiology textbook and psychology manual, along with simple experiments he conducted himself. See Preti (2008, 2022) for discussion of how Moore's early philosophy was shaped by nineteenth-century anti-psychologism about psychology.

[27] Curiously, we find David Lewis echoing something similar in *Parts of Classes*: "I'm moved to laughter at the thought of how *presumptuous* it would be to reject mathematics for philosophical reasons. How would *you* like the job of telling the mathematicians that they must change their ways, and abjure countless errors, now that *philosophy* has discovered that there are no classes?" (1991: 59). The connection here may not be entirely coincidental given Moore's (admittedly unobvious) influence on Lewis's philosophical method. See Nolan (2005: 203) for discussion.

116 SUSAN STEBBING

Though far from decisive, Moore's deference to science in the passages above suggests that his commitment to common sense might not be as entrenched as is typically assumed.[28]

Stebbing, by contrast, was steeped in philosophical debate surrounding the sciences. Developments in modern physics, namely, relativity theory and quantum theory—the "new physics"—led many philosophers and scientists to question realism and materialism; some, both physicists and philosophers alike, even entertained the idea that this new physics supported radical metaphysical views like idealism. While Moore invoked common sense to resist various forms of British Idealism, Stebbing drew it on it to resist idealist interpretations of twentieth-century physics.

Given Stebbing's interest in, knowledge of, and proximity to the sciences, it has been suggested that, compared to Moore, she was likely more cautious about which common-sense judgments she accepted as true.[29] As Stebbing herself remarks, the scientific and mathematical theories of her day reinforced "the fact that the world is infinitely more complex than common sense assumes" (RMP, 147).[30] Taking modern science and mathematics seriously, then, in the way Stebbing did, may have required her to adopt a more critical stance toward common sense than Moore.

This, however, is difficult to square with the overall evidence, which suggests a different picture. Compared to the passages from Moore above, Stebbing seemed to have exercised more caution when it came to calling on science, physics in particular, for philosophical guidance. Indeed, a common theme throughout Stebbing's work in the philosophy of physics is her resistance to naively "reading off" one's metaphysics from one's physics.[31] Moore's attitude toward science, at least as reflected in the passages above, appears more optimistic—one might even be tempted to say more naïve—when compared to Stebbing's, whose attitude was more critical and circumspect.

---

[28] In RMC, Moore suggests that "There are external objects" is an empirical statement, and that "philosophers who say 'There are no external objects' *are* making a false empirical statement" (RMC, 672). However, if this is indeed an empirical statement, then it is subject to verification—and by the same token, to falsification. So perhaps there is a sense in which Moore allows that such statements could, in principle, be falsified.

[29] See, for example, Janssen-Lauret (2022a: 183).

[30] See also Stebbing (1930: 456).

[31] See especially Stebbing (1937). It is not hyperbole to say that Stebbing showed little hesitation in voicing her disagreement with established scientists, most notably, Arthur Eddington, one of the most authoritative voices in physics in the early twentieth century. Reading her work from this period, one gets the sense that while Stebbing maintained a deep respect for physics, she remained unflinchingly cautious about treating it as *the* ultimate authority on the nature of reality—particularly when it was believed to directly contradict common sense, as I will argue here and in section 5.

STEBBING AND MOORE ON COMMON SENSE   117

This point is worth underscoring, as it highlights what is arguably distinctive about Stebbing's contributions to philosophy during this period. Early twentieth-century physics represented a marked departure from the classical picture of physics of the centuries before it. Twentieth-century physics did not just bring about new mathematical formalisms and experimental techniques, but a new *Weltbild* for understanding reality and our place in it. Many philosophers and scientists were tempted to follow physics' lead, using these developments to draw far-reaching metaphysical conclusions. Stebbing stood out for her methodical dismantling of the arguments and assumptions underlying these conclusions, providing a necessary counterpoint to the prevailing, and at times unbridled, enthusiasm surrounding the new physics.

To be sure, this last point is widely acknowledged by commentators. What has tended to escape notice, however, is a fundamental commitment at the core of Stebbing's philosophy of science. This is what I will refer to as her *unity thesis*: the view that common-sense knowledge and scientific knowledge form a continuous, coherent whole. It is this commitment, I suggest, that underlies Stebbing's account of common sense and its relationship to science. And it is this commitment—rather than any ecumenical or sectarian reading of common sense—that most clearly and plausibly distinguishes Stebbing from Moore in this regard. For Stebbing, the upshot of this unity is that, while our common-sense concepts remain open to revision by science (physics especially),[32] there is an important respect in which common sense cannot be overturned wholesale. As Stebbing puts it, "The validity of physics rests upon the assumption that there are external objects, i.e., that propositions such as 'I am now seeing the sun' are *true*" (RMP, 159).

In section 5, we will examine this unity thesis in more detail. In what remains of this section, I want to focus on how Stebbing develops a conception of common-sense knowledge that is decidedly distinct from Moore's—the view that common-sense knowledge constitutes a form of *scientific knowledge*. Somewhat ironically, this account is sketched in Stebbing's paper, "Moore's Influence" (1942). Exploring this account will not only help to better motivate the unity thesis; it will also bring to light an underappreciated instance in which Stebbing's originality is partially obscured by her generosity toward Moore.[33]

---

[32] We will return to this feature of her view at the end of section 5.

[33] This is something that Stebbing herself appears to acknowledge. She writes that she may have "profoundly misunderstood Moore (which is, unfortunately, not at all unlikely)" (1942: 525) and

118   SUSAN STEBBING

In "Moore's Influence," Stebbing writes that one of Moore's greatest philosophical contributions is having shown that "we may have a *reason*, though not a logically *conclusive* reason for certain statements concerning direct observation" (1942: 524). Stebbing understands beliefs based on such reasons—i.e., reasons that are not logically conclusive—as constituting knowledge of a certain kind: namely, probable knowledge. What Stebbing believes Moore has convincingly demonstrated is that probable knowledge is a *genuine* case of knowledge, that it is "no less *knowledge* than *demonstrative* knowledge, although it is not, and cannot claim to be, logically certifiable knowledge" (1942: 526).

Already, we can appreciate the idiosyncrasies of Stebbing's reading of Moore. Nowhere, after all, does Moore characterize knowledge in probabilistic terms. Stebbing's reading, however, is not entirely without textual basis. She draws the above lesson from a passage in Moore's NROP, where he characterizes a "good reason" for belief as one that renders a statement "*positively probable*" (NROP, 41). For Moore, that is, such a reason is not merely one that conforms to "propositions from which the laws of Formal Logic state that the belief could be deduced" (NROP, 40). Instead, Moore takes his use of "good reason" to align with its "wide and popular" sense. To illustrate, he considers the example of forming beliefs based on the testimony of a newspaper generally regarded as reliable. If, say, *The Times* has reported that the king is dead, then this would constitute a "good reason" to believe that he is, in fact, dead. The evidence we get from *The Times*, would, in other words, render our belief that the king is dead positively probable.

Stebbing sees this as one of the central lessons of Moore's common-sense program. Just as the evidence from *The Times* furnishes us with probable knowledge that the king is dead, so too do our perceptual experiences (alongside other conditions) provide us with probable knowledge that the many propositions of common sense are true. Though Stebbing does not put it explicitly this way, the upshot is that common-sense knowledge ultimately amounts to probable knowledge.

Stebbing recognizes that the very idea of "probable knowledge" is a radical one. Philosophical tradition assumes that without a deductive metaphysics of justification—that is, without demonstrative reasons for

---

that "I am afraid that Moore would entirely disagree with these contentions or, more likely, dismiss them as merely absurd" (1942: 528).

belief—we are not rationally entitled to claim knowledge. We might believe that material objects exist, and even judge it probable that they do, but lacking demonstrative reasons, we cannot truly claim to *know* that they exist. But according to Stebbing, this assumption is a "mistake," one that "lies at the base of Hume's criticism of our belief in external objects" (1942: 525). It is also, she suggests, the same mistake that underlies Descartes's method of doubt:

> To begin, as Descartes began, or at any rate tried to begin, by doubting everything and then to conclude by asserting that most of what he had doubted had now been proved to be true is futile. This is no more possible in the case of common sense propositions than in the case of scientific propositions; nor is it more necessary in the case of the former class of propositions than it is in the latter. *The logical character of the evidence for common sense propositions does not differ fundamentally from the logical character of the evidence for scientific propositions.* (1942: 526, emphasis added)

We do not begin where Descartes begins; we do not try to look for logically certifiable, demonstrative knowledge of the external world.[34] We content ourselves to what is probable. And what is probable, Stebbing argues, constitutes a kind of knowledge in its own right: "probable knowledge really *is* knowledge" (1942: 526). Or so urges Stebbing's Moore.

The sentence emphasized in the passage above is particularly striking. Here, Stebbing makes clear that she sees common-sense knowledge as existing on a continuum with scientific knowledge—that the logical character of the evidence of common sense is not fundamentally different from the logical character of the evidence of science. In this way, the propositions of common sense and science are largely interconnected, though neither is beyond revision; for the former, she acknowledges, is just as corrigible as the latter: "just as scientific propositions are not incorrigible, so too are common sense propositions not incorrigible" (1942: 528).

It is, however, precisely in this respect—that our common-sense beliefs are evidentially continuous with our scientific ones—that they form part of a method "not wholly unlike the methods employed in the natural sciences" (1942: 526). On this basis, we may plausibly attribute to Stebbing (or at least to her reading of Moore) the view that common-sense knowledge is a form

---

[34] See also Stebbing (1932–33: 93).

120 SUSAN STEBBING

of scientific knowledge, insofar as it likewise constitutes a form of probable knowledge.

Unsurprisingly, Moore, in his reply to Stebbing, denies all of this. "I do not at all like [Stebbing's] proposal," he writes, "to call the kind of knowledge I have now that I am sitting in a chair 'probable knowledge.'" He continues: "I hold that it is *certain* that I am now sitting in a chair, and to say that I have 'probable knowledge' that I am, seems to me to suggest that it is *not* certain" (RMC, 677).

Unlike Stebbing, Moore, it seems, could not part ways with the old guard. Given his explicit rejection of the views Stebbing attributes to him, I suggest that Stebbing should be understood not so much as advancing a reading of the historical G. E. Moore, but as offering a rational reconstruction of his common-sense program *as it struck her*. Once we subtract Moore from Stebbing's reading, what remains is her own distinctive account of common-sense knowledge: a form of probable knowledge that differs in degree, not in kind, from scientific knowledge. In the next and final section, I will argue that Stebbing's view is not merely an idiosyncratic reading of Moore, but a reflection of deeper commitments within her broader philosophy of science.

5 Stebbing's Unity Thesis

Stebbing's view that common-sense knowledge constitutes a form of scientific knowledge should not be dismissed as an isolated or idiosyncratic interpretation of Moore's philosophy. Rather, it is embedded within a broader systematic ambition: the integration of the common-sense and scientific worldviews. It is this philosophical ambition that distinguishes Stebbing's "common sense view of the world" from Moore's, who neither shared nor pursued such a project. This ambition is captured by what I have referred to in section 4 as Stebbing's *unity thesis*—the view that common-sense knowledge and scientific knowledge form a continuous, coherent whole. It is time now to substantiate this thesis and further develop its role within Stebbing's overall philosophy of science.

To begin, from Stebbing's point of view, the very suggestion that physics could overturn certain features of the common-sense view has a certain incoherence to it—akin to sawing off the very branch on which one is sitting. A physics severed from public sensible facts, such as "I am now seeing the sun" or "That piece of blotting paper is on the table," is something that

STEBBING AND MOORE ON COMMON SENSE   121

Stebbing finds "difficult to believe." As she writes elsewhere: "Every abstract proposition—such as those asserted in physics—are wholly *based upon* knowledge of this kind" (1933–34: 27). The very possibility of physics, then, depends on such facts; if there could be no such facts, there could be no activity we call 'physics':

> I find it difficult to believe that physics would be possible if there were no public sensible facts. My difficulty is increased when I consider that scientific method has developed out of common-sense knowledge by a gradual transition, however much the latest developments of physics may shock the plain man who has not followed the steps by which these results have been achieved. (RMP, 160)

The recognition that the method of science develops out of common-sense knowledge is crucial to Stebbing's view here. For it is our failure to have "followed the steps" of this development that leads us to the mistaken idea that modern physics has somehow rendered the common-sense world illusory. This recognition, however, goes beyond the (unremarkable) point that all inquiry must start somewhere, and that the truisms of common sense are as good as place as any. Rather, it is the recognition that common-sense knowledge does not simply vanish once a certain level of scientific sophistication or ingenuity is reached. Such knowledge remains indispensable to the scientist seeking to explain and elucidate various phenomena,[35] including *illusions* themselves:

> The scientist has a simple method of distinguishing what is illusory from what is not. An illusory object is one that is relative to a given percipient and which can be accounted for in terms of what is common to many percipients. It is in this way that a mirage is *explained*. The validity of this explanation rests upon the assumption that the phenomena of refraction cannot be reduced to private sensa. That not every illusion can be explained is due to the fact that our knowledge of physical laws is incomplete. But these laws are themselves obtained by generalization from experience; they presuppose public data. (RMP, 160)

---

[35] This point is made by Stebbing several times, in several different ways. See especially *PP* 89–90, 223, 244–245, 262–263.

122 SUSAN STEBBING

The very distinction between illusion and reality relies on shared, "public data"—that is, on common-sense knowledge. The scientist explains illusions like mirages by appealing to phenomena that are observable and generalizable across multiple percipients. But to reduce such explanations to private sensa would undermine what is being explained in the first place: how illusions arise. Hence, neglecting the unity between common-sense knowledge and scientific knowledge can lead to drawing faulty inferences and reinforce a distorted, misleading worldview. This is a view that sets the common-sense world and physicist's world in opposition, as if they were two distinct and incompatible realities. But this, Stebbing argues, is a mistake: "The mistake surely lies in this initial setting of two worlds in opposition between which we are forced to choose" (RMP, 152).[36] She identifies the physicist Arthur Eddington (1928) as a key proponent of this mistake—privileging the physicist's world, especially, over the common-sense world—a move she regards as resting on a false dichotomy. We are not forced to choose *either* world.

Part of the problem lies in how philosophers and physicists like Eddington understand the relationship between the symbolic constructions of physics and the common-sense world. Eddington, as Stebbing reads him, tends to speak as if the symbolic construction is either an *imitation* of the common-sense world or somehow more *real* than the common-sense world itself (*PP*, 66). This, however, leads him and others astray, tempted to conclude, for example, that the objects of the common-sense world can be reduced to bundles of pointer-readings (*PP*, 93–94; cf. Eddington 1928, Ch. XII), or—using a more well-worn example—that nothing in the common-sense world is *really* solid in light of the revelations of modern atomic theory (*PP*, 51; cf. Eddington 1928: xiii, 323). This leads philosophers and physicists to asking questions that, for Stebbing, lack sense:

> "Is that floor really solid?" is a sensible question to ask if we are uncertain whether the floor is as solid as it looks or whether perhaps it has got dry rot in it. But it is not a sensible question to ask if we are asking it because we are thinking that physicists have informed us that wood consists of [electrons] so widely spaced that the wood can be said to be "mostly emptiness." In the first context the question has sense and resembles in form the question, "Is

---

[36] Compare this to some of the remarks about "the world of physics" made in Stebbing (1933–34: 9–10).

STEBBING AND MOORE ON COMMON SENSE   123

that really an apple?" asked by someone who thinks he has been offered a medlar or perhaps an "apple" made of soap. In the second context the question is not sensible because no answer could be given to it of an appropriate logical form. The similarity of grammatical form has misled us.[37] ("Some Puzzles about Analysis," 1938–39: 79)

To clarify, the issue is not that the physicist must somehow avoid abstracting from the common-sense world. On the contrary, the physicist is required to work by seeking "a precise answer to a precise question" (*PP*, 93). To facilitate such a process, the physicist *must* abstract, they must isolate elements within the common-sense world. According to Stebbing, it is the business of physics, and the sciences more generally, to proceed in just this fashion.[38] The problem arises when the physicist disregards or ignores the return process, treating their symbolic constructions as complete in themselves, "in isolation from the processes whereby the physicist has been led to construct it" (*PP*, 261). In doing so, the physicist loses their way, forgetting that they "[work] in the world," and that the purpose of their mathematical constructions is to

correlate our sensory experiences, and that, if in this work of correlation mathematical analysis is indispensable, it remains true that the final test of the success of the mathematical construction is in the experiments to which it leads and from which it started. (*PP*, 264)

This is not intended to impose a superficial constraint on physics, but rather to serve as a reminder that "the construction of the symbolic scheme is subsidiary to the task of co-ordinating our experiences and reducing them to order" (*PP*, 264). It is a reminder that physics is a human activity, one that must ultimately elucidate the common-sense world without erasing it in the process.[39]

---

[37] The strategies Stebbing employs in this passage and elsewhere anticipate the kinds of argumentative moves that would later become synonymous with the canonical figures of Ordinary Language Philosophy. See especially Wittgenstein (1953, 1958) and Austin (1962).

[38] Indeed, it is the distinctive way in which the sciences permit the formation of isolates that—importantly, in Stebbing's view—renders moral philosophy "not a science" (1944: 18).

[39] For Stebbing, this is an especially important point for the special sciences: "[The common reader] is ready to insist that the world contains not only moving bodies but also thinkers, artists, and lovers. *These provide data of which the various special sciences must take note; the scientists must not construct elaborate theories which leave no room for these experiences of our daily life.* Finding something witty we are amused. We may then consider wherein wit consists. If we are presented with an analysis of wit that makes it an inexplicable mystery how we could ever be amused by a witty joke, we reject the analysis. The analysis must fit the experience" (*PP*, 223, emphasis added).

124   SUSAN STEBBING

Yet just as physicists must not treat their constructions as complete in themselves, we must also be wary of treating the common-sense world in a similar way: the common-sense view must remain open to revision in light of scientific development. Recall from the previous section that Stebbing maintains that common-sense propositions are just as corrigible as scientific ones (1942: 528).

Although Stebbing is not always explicit about how this revisability operates within her framework, her views on analysis help clarify how her program can accommodate it. Rather than claiming, as Eddington and others do, that no object in the common-sense world is truly solid, the Stebbingsonian interprets modern atomic theory as *clarifying* our common-sense conception of solidity. This is what Stebbing (somewhat misleadingly) calls in LPA the "analytic clarification of a concept" (LPA, 30).[40] While she does not address the concept of *solidity* specifically, she does mention several other concepts—*mass, force,* and *simultaneity*—that she believes physics has clarified in this way.

What physics reveals through this process of "analytic clarification" is that our earlier understandings of such concepts were imprecise (LPA, 30). For instance, although we may have spoken truly in asserting that two events are simultaneous, "Einstein has made us see that we did not know quite well what we meant; we now understand that what we thought to be essential is not so" (LPA, 30). In this way, Stebbing clearly acknowledges that scientific progress can both substantially revise and reshape elements of our common-sense view of the world, and that such revision, moreover, "involves a change in the significance of all statements in which the concept occurs" (LPA, 30). Hence, while Stebbing clearly resists the idea that scientific theory wholly displaces the common-sense view—this, after all, would involve the mistake of positing two worlds between which we are "forced to choose"—she nonetheless affirms that scientific progress can lead to significant revisions of it.[41]

We can understand the view outlined above as comprising Stebbing's own distinctive *defense of common sense*—one that, while sharing certain affinities with Moore's (as the preceding sections have shown), ultimately departs

[40] See Schliesser (chapter in this volume) for further discussion of this in relation to Stebbing's views about clarity.

[41] Stebbing's unity thesis finds a notable echo in Quine (1966), who writes: "Science is not a substitute for common sense, but an extension of it. . . .To disavow the very core of common sense, to require evidence for that which both the physicist and the man in the street accept as platitudinous, is no laudable perfectionism; it is a pompous confusion, a failure to observe the nice distinction between the baby and the bath water" (216–217).

STEBBING AND MOORE ON COMMON SENSE   125

from it in all the important ways witnessed above. Crucially, this defense involves neither a demand that common sense submit to the authority of science, nor a conservative rallying to shield it from the incursions of physics. It is, as we have just seen, far more complex, hinging on a central commitment in Stebbing's philosophy of science: the view that common-sense knowledge and scientific knowledge form a unity. This commitment reflects Stebbing's deep attentiveness to the grounds of scientific practice. When the connection between mathematical abstraction and everyday experience is severed, there arises a risk of mistaking theoretical constructions for reality itself. For Stebbing, this is more than a mere methodological misstep; it reflects a deeper philosophical confusion—one that gives rise to a false dichotomy between the world described by physics and the world of common sense. Stebbing's corrective is to restore a proper sense of continuity between these two worlds, as exemplified by her philosophical vision for reconciliation.

References

Armstrong, D. M. 2006. "The Scope and Limits of Human Knowledge." *Australasian Journal of Philosophy* 84: 159–166.

Austin, J. L. 1962. *Sense and Sensibilia*. Oxford: Oxford University Press.

Ayer, A. J. 1977. *Part of My Life*. Oxford: Oxford University Press.

Baldwin, Thomas, ed. 1993a. *G. E. Moore: Selected Writings*. London: Routledge.

Baldwin, Thomas, ed. 1993b. *Principia Ethica*. Cambridge: Cambridge University Press.

Beaney, Michael, and Siobhan Chapman. 2017. "Susan Stebbing." In Edward N. Zalta ed., *The Stanford Encyclopedia of Philosophy* (Fall 2022 Edition). https://plato.stanford.edu/archi ves/fall2022/entries/stebbing/.

Beaney, Michael. 2003. "Susan Stebbing on Cambridge and Vienna Analysis." In Friedrich Stadler, ed., 339–350, *The Vienna Circle and Logical Empiricism: Re-evaluation and Future Perspectives*. Dordrecht: Springer.

Beaney, Michael. 2016. "Susan Stebbing and the Early Reception of Logical Empiricism in Britain." In Christian Damböck, ed., 233–256, *Influences on the Aufbau*. Cham: Springer.

Bradley, F. H. 1893. *Appearance and Reality*. Oxford: Clarendon Press.

Chapman, Siobhan. 2013. *Susan Stebbing and the Language of Common Sense*. London: Palgrave Macmillan.

Coliva, Annalisa. 2010. *Moore and Wittgenstein: Scepticism, Certainty, and Common Sense*. London: Palgrave Macmillan.

Coliva, Annalisa. 2021. "Stebbing, Moore (and Wittgenstein) on Common Sense and Metaphysical Analysis." *British Journal for the History of Philosophy* 29: 914–934.

Eddington, A. S. 1928. *The Nature of the Physical World*. Cambridge: Cambridge University Press.

Janssen-Lauret, Frederique. 2017. "Susan Stebbing, Incomplete Symbols, and Foundherentist Meta-Ontology." *Journal for the History of Analytical Philosophy* 5: 6–17.

Janssen-Lauret, Frederique. 2022a. "Susan Stebbing's Metaphysics and the Status of Common-Sense Truths." In J. Peijnenburg and S. Verhaegh, eds., 171–190, *Women in the History of Analytic Philosophy*. Cham: Springer.

Janssen-Lauret, Frederique. 2022b. *Susan Stebbing*. Cambridge: Cambridge University Press.

126 SUSAN STEBBING

Janssen-Lauret, Frederique. 2023. "Susan Stebbing on Well-Foundedness." *Dialectica* 77: 1–30.

Lewis, David. 1991. *Parts of Classes*. Oxford: Oxford University Press.

Milkov, Nikolay. 2003. "Susan Stebbing's Critique of Wittgenstein's *Tractatus*." In Friedrich Stadler, ed., 351–363, *The Vienna Circle and Logical Empiricism: Re-evaluation and Future Perspectives*. Dordrecht: Springer.

Moore, G. E. 1899. "The Nature of Judgment." *Mind* 8: 176–193. Page citations from Baldwin 1993a, *G. E. Moore: Selected Writings*.

Moore, G. E. 1903a. "The Refutation of Idealism." *Mind* 12: 433–453. Page citations from Baldwin 1993a, *G. E. Moore: Selected Writings*.

Moore, G. E. 1903b. *Principia Ethica*. Cambridge, UK: Cambridge University Press. Page citations from Baldwin 1993b, *Principia Ethica*.

Moore, G. E. 1905-6. "The Nature and Reality of Objects of Perception." *Proceedings of the Aristotelian Society* 6: 68–127. Page citations from Moore 1922, *Philosophical Studies*.

Moore, G. E. 1922. *Philosophical Studies*. London: Routledge & Kegan Paul.

Moore, G. E. 1925. "A Defence of Common Sense." In his *Philosophical Papers*. New York: Collier Books. Originally published in London by George Allen and Unwin 1959. Page citations from Baldwin 1993a, *G. E. Moore: Selected Writings*.

Moore, G. E. 1939. "Proof of an External World." *Proceedings of the British Academy* 25: 273–300. Page citations from Baldwin 1993a, *G. E. Moore: Selected Writings*.

Moore, G. E. 1942. "A Reply to My Critics." In P. Schilpp ed., 535–677. *The Philosophy of G.E. Moore*. Evanston, IL: Northwestern University Press.

Moore, G. E. [1910–11] 1953. *Some Main Problems of Philosophy*. London: George Allen and Unwin.

Moore, G. E. 1966. *Lectures on Philosophy*. Edited by C. Lewy. London: George Allen and Unwin.

Moore, G. E. 2018-19. "G. E. Moore's Unpublished Review of *The Principles of Mathematics*." *Russell: The Journal of Bertrand Russell Studies* 38: 131–164.

Nolan, Daniel. 2005. *David Lewis*. Chesham: Acumen.

Preti, Consuelo. 2017. "Some Main Problems of Moore Interpretation." In A. Preston, ed., 70–84, *Analytic Philosophy: An Interpretive History*. New York: Routledge.

Preti, Consuelo. 2008. "On the Origins of the Contemporary Notion of Propositional Content: Psychologism in the Nineteenth Century and G. E. Moore's Early Theory of Judgment." *Studies in History and Philosophy of Science (A)* 39: 176–185.

Preti, Consuelo. 2022. *The Metaphysical Basis of Ethics: G. E. Moore and the Origins of Analytic Philosophy*. London: Palgrave Macmillan.

Quine, W. V. O. 1966. *The Ways of Paradox and Other Essays*. New York: Random House.

Ranalli, Chris, and Mark Walker. 2025. "Metaphysical Ecumenicalism and Moore's Proof." *Episteme*: 1–21. doi:10.1017/epi.2024.32.

Russell, Bertrand. 1922. "Introduction to Ludwig Wittgenstein's *Tractatus Logico-Philosophicus*." London: Kegan Paul.

Stebbing, L. S. 1926. "The Nature of Sensible Appearances." *Proceedings of the Aristotelian Society* 6: 190–205.

Stebbing, L. S. 1928. "Materialism in the Light of Modern Scientific Thought." *Proceedings of the Aristotelian Society* 8: 99–142.

Stebbing, L. S. 1929. "Realism and Modern Physics." *Proceedings of the Aristotelian Society* 9: 146–161.

Stebbing, L. S. 1930. *A Modern Introduction to Logic*. London: Methuen.

Stebbing, L. S. 1932-33. "The Method of Analysis in Metaphysics." *Proceedings of the Aristotelian Society* 33: 65–94.

Stebbing, L. S. 1933. "Logical Positivism and Analysis." *Proceedings of the British Academy* 19: 53–87.

Stebbing, L. S. 1933-34. "Constructions." *Proceedings of the Aristotelian Society* 34: 1–30.

Stebbing, L. S. 1934a. "Directional Analysis and Basic Facts." *Analysis* 2: 33–36.

STEBBING AND MOORE ON COMMON SENSE   127

Stebbing, L. S. 1934b. "Communication and Verification." *Proceedings of the Aristotelian Society* 13:159–173.

Stebbing, L. S. 1937. *Philosophy and the Physicists*. London: Methuen.

Stebbing, L. S. 1938–39. "Some Puzzles About Analysis." *Proceedings of the Aristotelian Society* 39: 69–84.

Stebbing, L. S. 1942. "Moore's Influence." In P. Schilpp, ed., 517–532, *The Philosophy of G. E. Moore*. Evanston, IL: Northwestern University Press.

Stebbing, L. S. 1942–1943. "The New Physics and Metaphysical Materialism." *Proceedings of the Aristotelian Society* 43: 167–214.

Stebbing, L. S. 1944. *Men and Moral Principles*. Oxford: Oxford University Press.

Vanrie, Wim. 2021. "What We All Know: Community in Moore's 'Defence of Common Sense.'" *Journal of the History of Philosophy* 59: 629–651.

West, Peter. 2022. "The Philosopher Versus the Physicist: Susan Stebbing on Eddington and the Passage of Time." *British Journal for the History of Philosophy* 30: 130–151.

Wittgenstein, Ludwig. 1921. *Tractatus Logico-Philosophicus*. Oxford: Blackwell.

Wittgenstein, Ludwig. 1953. *Philosophical Investigations*. Edited by G. E. M. Anscombe and R. Rhees; transcribed by G. E. M. Anscombe. Oxford: Blackwell.

Wittgenstein, Ludwig. 1958. *The Blue and Brown Books*. Oxford: Blackwell.

Susan Stebbing's Critique of Popular Science

Guiding or Gatekeeping?

Karl Egerton

1 Introduction

Susan Stebbing's work in early 20th-century philosophy is notable for ranging over both academically-focused and public-facing work. While it may be tempting to see this "public philosophy" work as interesting purely as outreach, Stebbing seemingly saw this part of her work as more consequential, and with good reason. This applies in particular to her critique of what she saw as careless work on the implications of science for philosophical issues, pursued in detail in her 1937 book *Philosophy and the Physicists*. However in light of broad commitments to philosophical naturalism today, one may wonder whether Stebbing's approach is defensible, or if it is unfairly dismissive of scientists' perspectives. In this chapter I re-examine Stebbing's critique of popular science to trace the themes running through it, use this to defend her project against the charge of gatekeeping, and briefly consider possible lessons for contemporary discussion of philosophy and popular science.

We proceed as follows: in §1 I briefly outline the context of Stebbing's contribution to the debate, and sketch the problem this suggests: that in light of the widely accepted naturalistic stance in analytic philosophy today, Stebbing's effort risks being a problematic instance of gatekeeping. In §2 I delve in detail into Stebbing's critique, drawing out and assessing some repeating argumentative themes. In §3 I locate Stebbing's views on popular science within her broader philosophical perspective, appealing to her work on the utility of logic. This helps confirm that Stebbing's approach holds both scientists and philosophers to account for getting seduced into embracing

Karl Egerton, *Susan Stebbing's Critique of Popular Science* In: *Susan Stebbing*. Edited by: Annalisa Coliva and Louis Doulas, Oxford University Press. © Oxford University Press 2025. DOI: 10.1093/9780197682371.003.0006

CRITIQUE OF POPULAR SCIENCE   129

deeply flawed positions by their passion for scientific developments, and thus should be considered guiding, not gatekeeping. Finally in §4 I consider whether Stebbing's approach is relevant to the communication of philosophical and scientific ideas today.

2 The Fear of Gatekeeping

The relationship of science to both ordinary beliefs and philosophical theories is by no means a concern peculiar to twentieth-century philosophy. It has been widely noted that, for instance, Descartes's method of doubt and substance dualism emerge in part from reflection on contemporary scientific developments.[1] However, the early twentieth century is marked by the emergence of distinctive anxieties prompted by developments in physics, particularly the emergence of the theories of relativity and quantum mechanics. For instance, as Alberto Coffa notes, relativity was formative for the logical positivists since "the leaders of Viennese positivism began their philosophical path as neo-Kantians" (1991, 171); but existing concerns about the viability of the synthetic *a priori* became a crisis when the theories of special and general relativity demonstrated (i) that non-Euclidean geometry played an important role in understanding the world, and (ii) that there were serious problems with the notion of the absolute present, fatally undermining the necessity of the spatiotemporal structure of experience. These developments, which seemingly overturned common-sense and long-held scientific theory, inspired bold philosophical projects but also kicked off a longer-lasting determination to respect scientific results in philosophical enquiry.

This interest in according science due respect has produced a range of outcomes, but perhaps the most widespread is the primacy within analytic philosophy of *naturalism*. The history of this idea is complex and it can take multiple forms, but a succinct summary is this: "it is within science itself, and not in some prior philosophy, that reality is to be identified and described" (Quine 1981, 21). Given the centrality of this doctrine, such that introductions to naturalism will note, e.g., that "[t]he great majority of contemporary philosophers would happily accept [naturalism broadly construed]" (Papineau 2009, Introduction), it is striking that Susan Stebbing in the 1930s tussled with prominent science communicators who sought to

---

[1] For discussion of this relationship, see, e.g., Clarke (1992); Bermúdez (1997).

130   SUSAN STEBBING

lay out the implications of scientific developments for our wider thought. In *Philosophy and the Physicists* (1937, henceforth *PP*) Stebbing took her already established aptitude for "popular" philosophical work from the communication of developments in logic[2] to the criticism of others' efforts in popular science. She would go on to write critically about other domains of communication in *Thinking to Some Purpose* (1939) and *Ideals and Illusions* (1941). These works skewered politicians and other public figures for unclear, misleading or duplicitous arguments that both manifested sloppy thinking on the part of the author/speaker and manipulated audiences unprepared to carefully evaluate claims.

However, one might feel unease at an extensive project that seems either a defensive move on philosophers' behalf, arguing that scientists ought to leave certain work to them, or an attempt to school scientists on the significance of their own results. This worry might be compared to David Lewis's incredulity at the prospect of philosophers "overruling" mathematics:

> I'm moved to laughter at the thought of how *presumptuous* it would be to reject mathematics for philosophical reasons. How would *you* like the job of telling the mathematicians that they must change their ways, and abjure countless errors, now that *philosophy* has discovered that there are no classes? Can you tell them, with a straight face, to follow philosophical argument wherever it may lead? (Lewis 1991, 59)

Lewis compares philosophy's sparse list of "results" with the far greater cohesion and progress in science and mathematics. The clear implication is that philosophers should exercise caution with their interventions in these areas.

This challenges us to show how, if at all, Stebbing's critiques can be fitted to her conception of them. Stebbing speaks frequently of guiding—the popularizers she critiques are "not always reliable guides" (*PP*, ix) to what is "among common readers a genuine interest in scientific research, a desire to follow as far as a layman can what is being found and to understand the implications" (*PP*, 5). Her contention is that "our scientific guides . . . have found it easier to mystify the common man than to enlighten him" (*PP*, 6). It is plausible then to treat Stebbing's conception of her contribution as of guiding.

---

[2] (1930), which Janssen-Lauret (2017) describes as "the world's first accessible text on polyadic logic" (9).

CRITIQUE OF POPULAR SCIENCE   131

The challenge we are considering, though, is that rather than a good-faith attempt at more effective *guiding*, Stebbing's book is an exercise in *gatekeeping*. This would not in itself guarantee that the project was problematic: while "gatekeeping" typically has negative associations, not everything that could be thus described is bad. Enforcing the norms excluding women from playing football during the English Football Association's 1921–1971 ban would clearly be objectionable gatekeeping; preventing unqualified individuals from prescribing treatments looks much more like an activity with a useful place in society.

However, in the context we're considering, if Stebbing's activities amount to gatekeeping, then we certainly have a problem. This is both because her opponents had relevant expertise—one would hope that physicists had at least something to offer for reflection on the philosophical implications of physics—and because of the aforementioned trend toward philosophical naturalism. The former would have been obviously pertinent to Stebbing, whereas she could not be expected to predict a then-nascent philosophical development even if, as Janssen-Lauret (2017) argues, she is an important precursor of that development, but both would be problematic for the significance of Stebbing's project now.

To understand Stebbing's project and begin considering whether it was ill- or well-advised, we must look in detail at her critique and draw out some key strands of the project.

3 The Strategies of *Philosophy and the Physicists*

3.1 The Work at a Glance

While there was a general trend in the early twentieth century toward engagement between science and philosophy, including the posing of questions at their intersection, Stebbing starts from specific cases rather than advancing a general charge—her primary targets in *PP* are James Jeans and Arthur Eddington.

James Jeans was a physicist, astronomer, and science popularizer. His name is not especially well remembered today, perhaps because a central part of his contribution was to advance the "steady state" theory of cosmology (e.g., in his 1929 *Astronomy and Cosmogony*), which would later be decisively set aside due to the evidence in favor of the Big Bang theory. Jeans

132 SUSAN STEBBING

wanted to leverage scientific advances to support a worldview with idealist, mystical, and theistic components, which he sought to promote to the public especially through his book *The Mysterious Universe* (1930).

Arthur Eddington's reputation in science, on the other hand, has remained prominent. His involvement in one of the earliest experimental confirmations of the predictions of general relativity helped secure his place in the mythic history of physics, though he also produced significant work on the composition of stars. He also published several popular works— Stebbing draws primarily on *The Nature of the Physical World* (1928) and *New Pathways in Science* (1935)—which stressed the implications of the recent developments for philosophical theory. He too wished to embrace a form of idealism as well as to rescue free will from the threat of determinism, and in general he saw in modern physics a vindication of the first-person perspective, for instance, in his account of time.[3] Eddington is explicit about the developments he sees as crucial:

> Einstein and Minkowski introduced fundamental changes in our ideas of time and space... [and] Rutherford introduced the greatest change in our idea of matter since the time of Democritus. (1928, 1)

PP can seem initially to be presenting a cocktail of criticisms of the scientists, delighting in attacking their maneuvers piecemeal. However, sustained attention brings out important continuities in Stebbing's critique.

3.2 Misled by Metaphor

One immediately obvious thread in *PP* is that Stebbing systematically charges her targets with an over-absorption in metaphor that leads them astray. Early on, Stebbing states that Eddington and Jeans "present their views with an amount of personification and metaphor that reduces them to the level of revivalist preachers" (*PP*, 6). This isn't just a broad accusation, though—Stebbing picks up on certain repeated metaphors that capture her targets' imaginations. Examining these will show how exactly Stebbing thinks metaphor gets them into trouble.

---

[3] See West (2022b) for a detailed examination of Stebbing's criticisms of Eddington on time.

3.2.1 Personification

Given their mention above, metaphors involving personification are an obvious place to start. For instance, Stebbing points out that Eddington describes nature as an entity *trying out* different things, especially when describing space: when intimating that standard lengths are relative to local space he personifies the meter itself as "wondering how large it ought to be" (1928, 143), and through this claims some form of incoherence in the law of gravitation. The meter he claims, is in a state of uncertainty, and the evident ridiculousness of that is used to problematize space despite this being his own imposition—this "obfuscates the common reader whilst pretending to enlighten him" (*PP*, 18).

The charge comes again with Stebbing's discussion of quantum mechanics. It's pointed out that we cannot predict individual microphysical entities' behaviors but only aggregates, through statistical laws. Unlike other statistical laws, however, those governing quantum phenomena don't presuppose underlying determinate causal laws. They are not statistical just because of practicalities but due to the limits of possible measurement. Stebbing disdains a tendency to term this unpredictability as an electron being able to *choose* where to jump, though uncharacteristically she doesn't directly identify who says this. She does, however, pick up directly on how Jeans discusses the matter. From the observation that "Planck's constant sets a natural limit to the accuracy of physical measurement" (*PP*, 182), Jeans infers that "nature abhors accuracy" (1930, 28), but Stebbing points out that even if accurate measurement is impossible this isn't right: our laws determine probabilities with precision. Here the personification of nature enables the problematic inference because we imagine how decision-making works for ourselves. If I am deciding how precisely to, e.g., instruct a class on a craft project, I might say either "Each group should create a handful of designs" or "Each group should create three designs," so the more imprecise instruction indicates an intentional choice. This, however, does not extend to an environment where the presence of a guiding intelligence is unestablished and the imprecision may simply be an unavoidable feature of microphysical measurement.

Stebbing finds many other examples of personification, but the above cases suffice to demonstrate how the metaphor leads to problematic conclusions. Throughout Stebbing is careful to point out how associations generated by personification are not window-dressing but mask unjustified inferences, especially to idealistic conclusions.

134 SUSAN STEBBING

3.2.2 The game of science

Personification evidently enables unjustified inferences, but another metaphor with a distinct impact captures the imagination of Stebbing's targets: *scientific enquiry as a game*.

The metaphor shows most clearly in one of Eddington's distinctive exercises: *world-building* (1928, ch. 11). Eddington presents this as a game we use to construct a world as like our own as possible using as little material as possible—success for him amounts to "the greatness of the contrast between the specialised products of the completed structure and the unspecialised nature of the basal material" (1928, 230). He claims his game requires only relata and relations, but he needs to distinguish the relata by assigning "monomarks" or coordinates of 4 numbers to each individual, and uses "coefficients" of these to completely represent, so he claims, field physics.[4] But, Stebbing points out, the game can only work if we already understand the distinctions it aims to capture. We can assign identifying numbers to individuals we can *already* distinguish, and can retrofit the coefficients so that laws come out right, but both processes must be tethered to our existing knowledge lest we simply fail to track relevant properties. Eddington uses his construction to claim that many laws are mere truisms since they are defined equivalences, but of course his game must produce this result since it builds in existing scientific theory! The situation is comparable to someone drawing lines connecting English and Spanish words, and then remarking on the implications of the *ink* lying just so rather than simply noting that the *writer* is bilingual. Eddington creates the game to depict science *itself* as a kind of game, and then conflates features of his game with features of science, letting his metaphor run riot.

The metaphor recurs when Eddington imagines a future community looking back at reported chess games and attempting to infer the nature of chess. He claims that such people would be unable to discover the nature of the participants or pieces and this he compares to the inscrutability of the world behind scientific enquiry. Yet, Stebbing points out, Eddington has stipulated that someone has (rather, *had*) the missing connection to this historical game—the actual chess player. The later investigators lack knowledge they *could otherwise have had*, rather than being denied it by necessity as

---

[4] This game might look similar to the reductive project of Carnap's *Aufbau* (1928), but there is at least one significant difference: Eddington doesn't take the game especially seriously so doesn't feel the need to show in detail that the notions he is working with can be dispensed with, seeing the mere possibility of a mathematical structure with the right features as sufficient.

CRITIQUE OF POPULAR SCIENCE 135

when butting up against the limits of measurement. Stebbing indicates the general problem here when she says, regarding Eddington's consternation about questions that scientists cannot answer:

That these questions are unanswerable because they are absurd is concealed from Eddington owing to his habit of *thinking in terms of bad metaphorical illustrations which he mistakes for arguments.* (*PP*, 134, emphasis mine)

Stebbing's critique of the game metaphor is notably complemented by a playful demonstration of its use to create a misleading sense of insight, which also serves to introduce our final metaphor. She begins chapter 6 of *PP* with a cryptogram encoding a sentence of Eddington's, then returns to it at the end of the chapter to indicate that Eddington's view is based on problematic assumptions about what his exercises actually demonstrate. To understand the cryptogram one must discover the translation key and recognize the author's intentions but, she jokes, this is hard for her since Eddington habitually neglects to make his meanings clear. The quote encoded in her cryptogram: "Something unknown is doing we don't know what" (Eddington 1928, 291).

Ironically, that quote serves as the title of a highly credulous 2009 documentary investigating various pseudosciences such as clairvoyance, psychokinesis, and psychic healing. One contributor to the documentary, parapsychologist Gary Schwarz, says when discussing spoon-bending,

remember that any object is 99.9 per cent empty space. . . . [S]ince this structure is mostly thin air, with the right intention and the right resonance it is possible to, so to speak, commune with the atoms and therefore get into its resonance so that very little "power" allows for it to become if you would more liquid. . . . [I[t becomes completely plausible once you look at this as a quantum physics phenomenon. (Scheltema 2009)

Though this is undoubtedly an extreme case, the documentary shows that there are plenty of other examples available of how far careless thinking can take the science enthusiast.

3.2.3 The Coded World

Stebbing's cryptogram is not just a wry reference to Eddington's confused games; it also raises another recurring metaphor, of *the world as coded*. This

136 SUSAN STEBBING

is employed toward a number of his arguments, sometimes in ways that seem incompatible—at the same time he sees the world as resistant to enquiry and as being unlocked by mathematical structures. Our helplessness in the face of a mysterious world is overcome only by the arcane-seeming activity of mapping connections between symbols.[5]

One of Eddington's central analogies exploits this metaphor. He speaks of a storyteller in the mind, telling the agent a story about the world:

> We picture the mind like an editor in his sanctum receiving through the nerves scrappy messages from all over the outside world, and making a story of them with, I fear, a good deal of editorial invention. (1928, 100)

This image of the mind is embellished by comparing the nerves to telegraph cables, in that signal and output have an arbitrary connection. For Stebbing this would mean that "[t]he familiar world is an illusion . . . the mind (i.e., the editor) makes for itself under the delusion that it is translating messages sent from the external world" (*PP*, 103), an illusion that Eddington could somehow detect despite being subject to the filter himself. But, Stebbing says, why posit a mental storyteller or editor rather than appealing to my mind itself? Once again, here Stebbing stresses that this isn't an unfair dissection of a colorful analogy; Eddington's arguments rely on it to claim that the mind is the most intimately understood aspect of experience, with all else inferred at some distance. However, the code supposedly used by the "editor" for the messages sent is a very odd one, since, being the only form of information we can receive, the code has no key—or at best, an unknowable one.

The coded world also influences Eddington's claim that current physics shows that we cannot understand the nature of matter since the world of physics is now a world of "pointer readings" (1928, ch. 12), which he sometimes calls a "shadow-world" (109). Physical entities serve, Eddington says, as mere symbols, but of what? The pointer readings again present as a code, though since the nature of that code isn't explained to us, it's hard to see how we navigate between an optimistic view on which the "code" is no more than our theory, and a pessimistic view on which we can never access the system to which the code is connected (while somehow still knowing it is thus

---

[5] Notably, in later work Eddington employed apparently pseudo-scientific methods. He attempted to show that the "fine structure constant" governing the strength of the electromagnetic force between charged subatomic particles had to be exactly $1/136$ for reasons that appeared to be numerological, as described in (Kean, 2010, ch. 18).

CRITIQUE OF POPULAR SCIENCE 137

connected). Thus, either there *is* no problem or it's mysterious how we could get anywhere at all.

The metaphor can also be found in that comment of Eddington's that has retained the most recognition—his "two tables." Eddington thinks scientific enquiry establishes a scientific counterpart to each familiar, material object I encounter. Where my familiar tables and chairs have features like solidity, these scientific objects do not, so they must be divided into two "worlds." The idea of a gap so great as to make it mysterious how the two could be connected is another manifestation of Eddington's preoccupation with the coded status of the world around us. He makes a point of describing the great mystery in the very idea of navigating the world given the forbidding nature of the scientific objects around me:

> to enter a room ... I must shove against an atmosphere pressing with a force of fourteen pounds on every square inch of my body. I must make sure of landing on a plank travelling at twenty miles a second round the sun—a fraction of a second too early or too late, the plank would be miles away.... The plank has no solidity of substance. To step on it is like stepping on a swarm of flies. (1928, 342)

Stebbing finds Eddington's reasoning unpersuasive, and she provides her own competing description of her experience of being in a room, in the process stressing both how terms like "heavy" and "solid" are linked to how we *interact* with our surroundings and the *ordinariness* of the words "real" and "really." The bifurcation Eddington argues for between ordinary and scientific objects and the attendant question of whether one or the other is not "real" both come from excessive commitment to the coded world metaphor with its imagined barriers. Without the metaphor, it would be hard to justify the idea that scientific knowledge generates a problem with simply navigating the world.

Notably, however, Stebbing doesn't reserve this criticism for Eddington alone; a very similar failing is attributed to Bertrand Russell (*PP*, 273–274).[6] He too is prone, she claims, to mistakenly supposing that we don't really

---

[6] Stebbing also attributes the same to the physicist Max Born in his *The Restless Universe* (1935, 106), where he strikingly displays more of the features critiqued by Stebbing: both personification ("the light merely reports ... I have entirely forgotten what happened to me on the journey on which I set out") and the "editorial office" form of the coded world metaphor ("Everything else ... is an unconscious combination by the editorial department (the brain)").

138 SUSAN STEBBING

touch, or see, things because our sensory experiences are indirect—Russell's position on this is well-known as stemming from his sense datum theory, but the similarity to Eddington is striking:

> The one thing we know about [an ordinary table] is that it is not what it seems. . . . Berkeley tells us it is an idea in the mind of God; sober science, scarcely less wonderful, tells us it is a vast collection of electric charges in violent motion. (Russell 1912/1998, 24)

Yet while my seeing does require a kind of "seeming" that may or may not be veridical, for Stebbing this is not a reason to posit some distinctive *barrier* we must struggle to overcome. This is a clear example of Stebbing doing something in *Philosophy and the Physicists* that is often overlooked—targeting philosophers with her criticisms—and its presence throughout the work is important because it demonstrates willingness to find fault not just with the work of scientists but also in the work of philosophers who are too easily impressed by scientific results.

3.3 Evasive Equivocation

Eddington's two tables metaphor is problematic not just because of the metaphor itself but especially because he vacillates between speaking of the scientific table or the familiar table as "real"—he *equivocates*. On the one hand, he says that science has convinced him that the scientific table is the real one; on the other hand, he describes the scientific world as a "shadow" world. Yet Stebbing finds Eddington guilty of equivocation many more times—she takes it to be deeply ingrained in his writing. His equivocation is often entangled with his overcommitment to metaphors, but the two are distinct—one can mistakenly think a vivid metaphor serves as an indicator of truth without genuinely mistaking one sense for another, and equally one can mistake one sense for another without this necessarily being due to preoccupation with some metaphor.

In another example of equivocation, Stebbing points out that Eddington speaks of the mind *deciding* how to build a system from our experiences. But depending on how "decides" is understood, she says, this is either a truism if we understand "decides" as meaning just something like "chooses

CRITIQUE OF POPULAR SCIENCE   139

between available options" (as when I decide what to eat from the options presented on a menu), or nonsense if we understand it as meaning instead "determines how things are" (as when the chef decides the menu, thus fixing the facts about what diners may eat). Here, it is fair to say, Stebbing overstates her case—it isn't "nonsense" to say that my attention determines how things are, though it is profoundly implausible. This equivocation has wide-ranging implications, much as when Eddington equivocates about worlds, speaking of "the familiar world, the external world, the scientific world, the physical world, Nature, the world of physics, the spiritual world" (*PP*, 99). He tries to justify himself by professing an inability to put things in terms acceptable to philosophers without seeing this as concerning, but Stebbing repurposes Eddington's game metaphor in an attempt to show the problem here:

> It may be true that the onlooker sees the best of the game, although he can hardly do so unless he knows the rules observed by the players. However that may be, it is absurd to assume, on the basis of this unsound analogy, that one who is not a philosopher either by training or by inclination is in a privileged position in the discussion of philosophical problems. (*PP*, 99, 8)

Stebbing stresses that she's not neglecting the difficulty of precision or claiming never to err herself; but she claims that her "criticism of Eddington is that he is confused in his thinking, and that, in consequence of this confusion, he uses many different expressions without himself knowing how far, if at all, they are used as synonyms" (*PP*, 111).

However, Eddington is not alone in being accused of equivocation. Jeans is criticized as well—for instance, for using comparisons of size not to clarify scale or get us to appreciate facts about the universe, but simply to scare us. For instance, Jeans describes huge distances as "meaningless," but Stebbing says we should pause and ask what it would mean for small distances to be meaning*ful*. Jeans here seems to equivocate between "meaningless" in the sense of being so great as to be difficult to process (as in "I was told Jeff Bezos' net worth was over $100 billion, but that figure is meaningless to me") and "meaningless" in the sense of being unreasonable (as in "To risk serious harm because of commitment to a conspiracy theory like QAnon would be utterly meaningless").

140 SUSAN STEBBING

3.4 Haziness on History

A final repeating theme in Stebbing's critique is a charge of *historical igno-rance*. This stands a little apart from the charges of reliance on metaphor and equivocation because there is less overlap, but it is important nonetheless.

To return to Jeans, for example, Stebbing points out that he is heavily influenced by Platonism, inspired by the cave allegory—he sees physics as demonstrating that we're not in contact with reality in a way comparable to Plato's contention. It's evident, she thinks, that Jeans is familiar with Plato and Berkeley but hasn't encountered critical engagement with those ideas. (West (2022a, 863–864) points out this complaint that Jeans is "almost proud of his lack of philosophical training," which leads him to naively embrace views that have already been extensively critiqued).

More wide-ranging concerns are raised about Eddington. She compares his account of the "shadow world" of science and the familiar world to Newtonians as criticized by Berkeley, who

> had substituted a theory of optics for a theory of visual perception. The out-come of this mistake is a duplication of worlds—the Image-World, sensibly perceived by men, the Real-World apprehended only by God. (*PP*, 62)

Eddington's "two tables" discourse and his discussion of the "shadow-world" are depicted as re-runs of Newton's claim that sensory qualities are not re-ally there but are only powers to produce certain responses. She notes also that this thinking is what leads C. E. M. Joad to say, of the philosophical consequences of physics, that

> if I never know directly events in the external world, but only their alleged effects on my brain, and if I never know my brain except in terms of its al-leged effects on my brain, I can only reiterate in bewilderment my original questions: "What sort of thing is it that I know?" and "Where is it?" (Joad 1929, 136–137)

Stebbing raises this twice, in chapters 3 and 6 of *PP*. For her it's straightfor-ward: either the mechanisms at my disposal for understanding the world are reliable, in which case knowledge is clearly possible, or the mechanisms are completely misleading, in which case how could I know anything, even the unknowability itself? In a different form we return to the coded world,

CRITIQUE OF POPULAR SCIENCE   141

but when freed from its non-literal padding, we instead see a debate that in Stebbing's view had already played out in the early modern period.

Stebbing goes on to claim that where Jeans has broadly Platonic motivations, Eddington inherits much of his picture from Bertrand Russell.[7] This might initially prompt less concern about historical ignorance, since Eddington is engaging with contemporaries; however, the promise is illusory, as Stebbing accuses Russell too. Interestingly it is here, speaking not of Eddington or Jeans but of Russell and Joad, that Stebbing betrays the clearest impatience with her material. She says, "Mr Joad is merely echoing Bertrand Russell, whilst Eddington once more repeats their mistakes" (*PP*, 130), and then explains:

> I am aware that this statement is extremely dogmatic. But I do not wish to argue once more against a mistake that has surely been often enough exposed. (*PP*, 130)

Stebbing insists that only because we have knowledge of the external world can we posit sense data in Russell's case, or structures based on pointer readings in Eddington's case, at all.

Stebbing raises this charge again in Part III of *PP*, when discussing how quantum mechanics applies to the question of free will. On Stebbing's telling, physical determinism wasn't seen as especially threatening historically because it governed the inanimate, but this changed with the advent of evolutionary theory, with nineteenth-century biologist T. H. Huxley picked out as an example of someone worried by this development. Since life loses its special status once our various properties are depicted as the product of unthinking evolutionary processes, we suddenly move to being well within the remit of controlling physical laws. Huxley's defense of free will is to insist that the laws' governing our behavior isn't sufficient for normative force over us, but only for *describing* what *will* happen. However, he also says we can be described as free only insofar as we have a *feeling* of freedom, and our actions are in fact determined automatically, which makes consciousness look epiphenomenal. Stebbing points out that Huxley's position is inconsistent and contrasts John Stuart Mill (1843, Bk. VI, ch. 2) who tried to offer

---

[7] Eddington does not seem to claim Russell as a central inspiration, though he does cite him approvingly and says of Russell's *Analysis of Matter* that it is "a book with which I do not often seriously disagree" (Eddington 1928, 160 n.).

142 SUSAN STEBBING

a compatibilist account that was clearer in its implications than Huxley's wavering between seeing laws as non-constraining and treating free will as epiphenomenal.

Stebbing's discussion of free will isn't primarily about Huxley, though, since Huxley can't be fairly claimed to ignore the history. Eddington claims that introducing quantum mechanics moves us from despair—deterministic laws that govern our behavior, notwithstanding Huxley's attempted escape—to respite due to the indeterminism of this new theory. The idea is that, despite deterministic laws appearing to capture the vast majority of events beyond the microphysical, quantum indeterminacy is enough to rescue our freedom. However, this would mean replacing the *impossibility* of doing any differently from what the laws dictate with its overwhelming *improbability*, which is uninformative without the supplementary assumption of an immaterial soul that can somehow *control* the indeterminacy. For Stebbing this means that he has failed to appreciate things learned from discussion of Descartes:

> Eddington's difficulty arises, I think, partly from the fact that he first makes a sharp distinction between I, *myself*, a spiritual agent who experiences spiritual struggles, and the material world; then he remembers that all future configurations are determined by past configurations but wants somehow to find *me* in that future configuration. (*PP*, 243)

Eddington is thus a more sophisticated version of the unreflective dualist, and this position means he doesn't feel the need to recognize that each of us is "an embodied mind" (*PP*, 244).

This line of criticism can be summed up in the introduction to one chapter:

> Every scientist works in a context. To serve his special purpose he isolates certain factors present in the field of his investigation and studies these factors intensively. Frequently, and indeed usually, *he isolates his study also from its history*. (*PP*, 253, emphasis mine)

While this approach is useful in its place, Stebbing thinks, we must recognize its limitations and be broader in our thinking where required, and the consideration of the general philosophical upshot of one's theorizing seems an excellent candidate for a context that does require this. The "blunders"

CRITIQUE OF POPULAR SCIENCE   143

brought about may be less immediately problematic than enchantment with metaphor or equivocation, but they also trap us in repeated rehearsals of old arguments.

3.5 Bringing the Strands of Critique Together

As we've seen, Stebbing sees multiple figures as getting trapped by a suite of metaphors, equivocating accidentally, and ignoring the history of the debates they're wading into. These form a unified core showing what makes *Philosophy and the Physicists* a distinctive contribution to the philosophical landscape of the time. They certainly aren't the only features of interest about *PP*, but they help to make the project cohere.

It is important to recognize that *PP* also contains straightforward philosophical disagreements, which can form part of the case against the gatekeeping charge, because where this happens Stebbing simply argues directly that the views expressed are wrong. In each case her arguments are presented as claims that her opponents *take the wrong message from science*, but nevertheless some of her arguments clearly constitute philosophical disagreements. Stebbing is on shakier ground in these cases since she takes herself to be a scientific amateur, among the "common readers [who] are fitted neither to criticize physical theories nor to decide what precisely are their philosophical implications" (*PP*, ix) but the accusation of gatekeeping recedes here since there is certainly nothing strange or problematic about philosophical disagreement! A clear example is her discussion of time, which as Peter West argues, is motivated in part by her commitment to "realism."[8] These parts of the work stand apart from the strands we have drawn out in this section, though it must be conceded that Stebbing doesn't always clearly mark the shifts between them. It would be reasonable, I think, to criticize *PP* for sometimes neglecting to draw attention to the distinction between those ideas Stebbing regards as misformulated "muddles" and those that merely constitute arguments she finds unpersuasive.

Generally, Stebbing's case against her opponents in *PP* can be seen as attributing a kind of motivated thinking generated by overexcited passion

---

[8] On her usage, "realism" amounts to embracing certain propositions that "*must* be accepted as true before one can engage in either science or philosophy" (2022b, 145).

144 SUSAN STEBBING

for science, of being "wrought up to a pitch of emotional excitement, unduly impressed by the strangeness of their discoveries" (*PP*, 5). Importantly, this isn't restricted to physicists; philosophers can make the error too, and as we have seen, she criticizes them accordingly. Russell is the target of a surprising number of criticisms considering that the work is considered a polemic against scientists, but this makes sense when we recognize Russell's place within a generation of philosophers who saw themselves as taking scientific developments especially seriously compared to their forebears. But while philosophers have a responsibility to engage properly with science to avoid clumsy misunderstandings, scientists bear a similar responsibility due to their privileged position relative to the actual results of science. For this reason, Tuboly (2020) places Stebbing alongside C. E. M. Joad and Philipp Frank as philosophers making efforts to push back against a particular kind of misinformation.

4 *Philosophy and the Physicists* in Context

In light of what we have said, how should we think about *PP*'s position within Stebbing's body of work? Is it more helpful to situate it on its own or as part of a broader project? While the former might be tempting, it would then be difficult to make sense of *PP*'s final passage, which states:

> The world is what it is. Whether God or the physicists made it, or whether the language of "making" is wholly inappropriate, does not affect the fact that men are capable of making a hell upon earth even though they can envisage something better. . . . Our limitation is due not to ignorance, not to the "blind forces of Nature," not to the astronomical insignificance of our planet, but to the feebleness of our desires for good. This limitation is not to be removed by the advance of physical knowledge, nor should our hopes be placed in the researches of the physicist. (*PP*, 286)

What are we to make of this final, ominous exhortation?

A simple answer is that *PP*'s publication was during a time of great political foreboding, which would of course soon prove wholly justified. However, briefly considering another angle will help make the case that the gravity of Stebbing's warning isn't a mere symptom of unease but shows clear continuity in Stebbing's worldview.

CRITIQUE OF POPULAR SCIENCE   145

We can demonstrate this by considering the significance of the position articulated in *Thinking to Some Purpose*. Douglas and Nassim (2021) closely examine Stebbing's attempt to articulate a position for the logician as a contributor to public debate, and in their view Stebbing aims to intervene in cases of problematic thinking which

> begin with one thought and end with another following a mere chain of psychological association [where one] thought prompts another through prejudicial association, by poor analogy, using tricks of language, by stirring up purely emotional reactions, etc. (2021, 12–13)

They identify several barriers to her attempt to interpose the logician between unscrupulous disputants and the public, not least that appeals to "logical form" no longer have a reasonable claim to be uncontroversial, but insist that her project is achievable in modest form. One can present a form the argument *could* be taken to have but which looks clearly problematic, with various options then available, such as accept the form but explain why it *is* warranted, weaken the argument to avoid the controversy, or insist that the argument succeeds for reasons beyond what the logician can capture. This doesn't allow the resolution of disputes by waving a logical wand, but it nevertheless clears the ground and holds reasoners more accountable.

As they point out, many of Stebbing's examples are from political figures, e.g., Stanley Baldwin (1939, ch. 1) and Benito Mussolini (1941, ch. 7). Furthermore, Douglas and Nassim's bad moves quoted above resonate closely with the problems we covered in *PP*—"poor analogy" (in *PP* through misleading metaphors), "tricks of language" (in *PP*, equivocation), and "purely emotional reactions" (in *PP* this seems the motivating factor). In *Thinking to Some Purpose* she makes clear the implications of this sort of problematic thinking, saying that

> either we must freely decide to support (or to oppose) this or that political measure, or we must acquiesce in the decisions made by those who control us [but] for deciding freely it is essential to know whatever is relevant to that decision. (1939, 240)

Furthermore, supposing we want to make these choices in an informed way, and therefore freely, we will be frustrated if we are used to being carried along by flawed chains of thought: "[n]o one can act wisely who has never felt

146 SUSAN STEBBING

the need to pause to think about how he is going to act and why he decides to act as he does" (1939, 19). Our tendency to acquiesce in "potted thinking" (1939, ch. 6) is our enemy here, regardless of domain—hence our failure to think critically about science is not just local but can contribute to a general failure to think critically. Stebbing's work thus makes moves that interestingly prefigure what C. Thi Nguyen calls "hostile epistemology" (2021, 229). He distinguishes between the intentional and unintentional hijacking of epistemic weaknesses, and we can see a similar divide in Stebbing. The distinction between *Thinking to Some Purpose* and *Ideals and Illusions*, on the one hand, and *PP*, on the other, looks like that between political figures' attempts to cynically exploit tricks, and scientists' (and others') adopting those tricks and fooling both others and themselves. As we saw above, Stebbing regards Eddington and those like him as victims much like their readers are.

To press this comparison further, Nguyen argues that the phenomenon of "seductive clarity"—an example of a hostile distortion of enquiry—is problematic because "the sense of clarity can bring us to end our inquiries into a topic too early" (2021, 232). Critiquing the premature settlement of enquiry may be crucial for saving us from unfortunate situations caused by our epistemic and cognitive shortcomings. In this respect, again, Stebbing should be taken to be attempting to guide, not gatekeep—she aims to prevent us from being seduced into mistaking limited explorations of science for conclusive analyses.

5 Guiding Without Gatekeeping Today

It is hopefully clear that engaging with these questions remains relevant. The environment of Stebbing's intervention was different from our own but, worryingly, the current environment appears *less* receptive to such interventions, for several reasons. The nascent naturalism hinted at in Stebbing's work is now fully fledged, so the fear of science denialism is more salient. Furthermore, while Eddington is cautious about his ability to contribute, saying that "[f]rom the beginning I have been doubtful whether it was desirable for a scientist to venture so far into extra-scientific territory. . . . I have much to fear from the expert philosophical critic" (2021, preface)), it is more common now for scientists to confidently assert that philosophers have nothing to offer them, even that "philosophy is dead" (Hawking and Mlodinow 2010, p. 5, quoted in Tuboly (2020)).

CRITIQUE OF POPULAR SCIENCE   147

As a result, it is more acceptable to ignore philosophy or attack it outright, confident in the respectability the label of "science" confers on such behavior. This means not just a disappointing loss of philosophical-scientific dialogue, but more risk of hiding from the public the kinds of mistakes Stebbing unearthed. For reasons of space we cannot embark on a detailed exploration of this trend but will content ourselves with a brief example.

Michio Kaku is a theoretical physicist who has contributed to string field theory (Kaku and Kikkawa 1974a,b) and has published a number of textbooks (e.g., Kaku 1993). However, he is also an influential science communicator, having published multiple popular science books and with videos frequently attracting substantial attention on YouTube and elsewhere. We will briefly indicate some notable extracts from his book *The God Equation: The Quest for a Theory of Everything* (2021) that suggest the continued relevance of projects like Stebbing's.

In its first chapter, Kaku claims that there are two ancient projects to which modern theoretical physics is the heir, both ideas propounded by philosophers. One, the familiar doctrine of atomism, he attributes to Democritus; the other, the use of mathematical descriptions to understand the world, he attributes to Pythagoras. It's less clear what Kaku means by the second idea—he states that "the diversity of nature can be described by the mathematics of vibrations" (2021, 9), but it is not obvious whether this vibration aspect is crucial or if it is rather the general idea of a mathematical structure to reality that matters to him. He impresses upon the reader the significance of these ideas recurring far later, and laments that

> with the collapse of classical civilization, these philosophical discussions and debates were lost. The concept that there could be a paradigm explaining the universe was forgotten for almost a thousand years. Darkness spread over the Western world, and scientific inquiry was largely replaced by belief in superstition, magic, and sorcery. (2021, 9)

Such a grossly oversimplified history would be rightly viewed as unacceptable in philosophical scholarship, but here sketchy philosophical framing is seen as an acceptable prelude. The problems should be clear, but we will recap anyway. First, if the ideas mentioned were lost, to believe that those *same* ideas resurfaced, we need a much fuller history. Second, the idea that for a millennium *no one* aimed to offer unifying explanations of the universe is patently false, as a casual glance at any surviving European work

148   SUSAN STEBBING

from between the classical Greek and the Enlightenment eras confirms (to say nothing of world regions that fall outside that supposed collapse). This brief summary seems to simultaneously subscribe to both the outdated image of the "Dark Ages" and the myth of philosophy as exclusively a white European pursuit. Third, Kaku mentions a loss of scientific enquiry from this supposed catastrophe, yet the time he speaks of long pre-dates the establishment of a distinctive scientific method. The idea of an established science being destroyed, like the vivid imagery of the burning of the Library of Alexandria, invokes a powerful and misleading image for the reader. The reader feels appalled at the "collapse of civilization" and the crushing of ideas that could have unlocked the universe, priming them to be inspired by Kaku's later revival—the idea that recent science single-handedly rescued these ancient ideas would clearly be an apt target for Stebbing's charge of historical ignorance.

Another example is a point to which Kaku returns multiple times: that the possibility of representing physical theories simply, and with symmetry, is deeply important. Summarizing, he says:

> The universe is a remarkably beautiful, ordered, and simple place. I find it utterly staggering that all the known laws of the physical universe can be summarized on a single sheet of paper. . . . Given the utter brevity of this sheet of paper, it is hard to avoid the conclusion that this was all planned in advance, that its elegant design shows the hand of a cosmic designer. (Kaku 2021, 188)

This argument strongly resembles both Eddington and Jeans—notably, Kaku doesn't take this as a conclusive argument for theism, instead professing agnosticism, though the strength of feeling suggested here and in the book's title is likely to lead the reader toward theistic interpretations of Kaku's claims. However, we get no detailed exploration at any point of the significance of something being statable briefly, or a demonstration of what he means. Instead, the reader is left to visualize a beautiful formula unlocking the universe—thus the coded world metaphor resurfaces decades after featuring in Eddington's work.

The mystification brought about in the reader here is also not a harmless confusion. We might legitimately worry about eroding one's aptitude for critical thinking through exposure to these cases; and this risk is more pressing when scientists are encouraged to issue vague pronouncements

CRITIQUE OF POPULAR SCIENCE 149

of insight when interpreting their field, and, more worryingly, when stepping outside it.[9] Impressive but nebulous claims about the world are all-too-easily adapted, as unwittingly revealed by Larry Dossey, a proponent of faith healing who in the previously mentioned documentary explains his feelings about Eddington's "something unknown is doing we don't know what" slogan: "I love this comment so much I apply it to all areas of life; it's my favourite explanation for everything" (Scheltema 2009).

A fuller exploration of Kaku's book and similar projects would be valuable—here we have been able only briefly to indicate some concerning aspects of one work of contemporary popular science. However, the presence of similar structural features to those seen in Eddington should serve as a reminder that there remains an important role for work that guides the public on the philosophical implications of science *without* gatekeeping. Stebbing's work provides a valuable blueprint for such work today.

References

Bermúdez, José Luis. 1997. "Scepticism and Science in Descartes." *Philosophy and Phenomenological Research* 57 (4): 743–772.

Born, Max. 1935.*The Restless Universe*. New York: Dover Publications.

Carnap, Rudolf. 1928. *The Logical Structure of the World*. Berlin: Weltkreis-Verlag.

Clarke, Desmond. 1992. "Descartes' Philosophy of Science and the Scientific Revolution." In John Cottingham, ed., *The Cambridge Companion to Descartes*. Cambridge: Cambridge University Press.

Coffa, Alberto. 1991. *The Semantic Tradition from Kant to Carnap: To the Vienna Station*. New York: Cambridge University Press. Edited by Linda Wessels.

Douglas, Alexander, and Jonathan Nassim. 2021. "Susan Stebbing's Logical Interventionism." *History and Philosophy of Logic* 42 (2): 101–117.

Eddington, A. S. 1928. *The Nature of the Physical World*. Cambridge: Cambridge University Press.

Eddington, A. S. 1935. *New Pathways in Science*. Cambridge: Cambridge University Press.

Janssen-Lauret, Frederique. 2017. "Susan Stebbing, Incomplete Symbols, and Foundherentist meta-ontology." *Journal for the History of Analytical Philosophy* 5 (2): 1–17.

Jeans, James. 1929. *Astronomy and Cosmogony*. Cambridge: Cambridge University Press.

Jeans, James. 1930. *The Mysterious Universe*. Cambridge: Cambridge University Press.

Joad, C. E. M. 1929. "Realism and Modern Physics II." *Proceedings of the Aristotelian Society Supplementary Volume* 9, 112–161.

Kaku, Michio. 1993. *Quantum Field Theory: A Modern Introduction*. Oxford: Oxford University Press.

---

[9] A case in point is the controversy caused, culminating in the withdrawal of "humanist of the year" award, after Richard Dawkins waded into discussions about trans rights without relevant expertise (see https://www.theguardian.com/books/2021/apr/20/richard-dawkins-loses-humanist-of-the-year-trans-comments). Even after his attempts to row back the stronger implications of his comments, anti-trans campaigners continue to appeal to his claims and those of similar figures to erroneously claim to be "on the side of science."

150 SUSAN STEBBING

Kaku, Michio. 2021. *The God Equation: The Quest for a Theory of Everything*. Penguin Books.

Kaku, Michio, and K. Kikkawa. 1974a. "Field Theory of Relativistic Strings. I. Trees." *Physical Review D* 10 (4): 1110–1133.

Kaku, Michio, and K. Kikkawa. 1974b. "Field theory of Relativistic Strings. II. Loops and Pomerons." *Physical Review D* 10 (6): 1823–1843.

Kean, Sam. 2010. *The Disappearing Spoon: And Other True Tales of Madness, Love, and the History of the World from the Periodic Table of the Elements*. Little, Brown.

Lewis, David. 1991. *Parts of Classes*. Blackwell.

Mill, John Stuart. 1843. *A System of Logic: Ratiocinative and Inductive, Being a Connected View of the Principles of Evidence, and the Methods of Scientific Investigation*. John W. Parker.

Nguyen, C. Thi. 2021. "The Seductions of Clarity." *Royal Institute of Philosophy Supplement* 89, 227–255.

Papineau, David. 2009. "Naturalism." In Edward N. Zalta, ed., *The Stanford Encyclopedia of Philosophy*. Spring edition.

Quine, W. V. 1981. *Theories and Things*. Cambridge, MA: Harvard University Press.

Russell, Bertrand. 1912/1998. *The Problems of Philosophy*. Oxford: Oxford University Press.

Scheltema, Renee. 2009. "Something Unknown Is Doing We Don't Know What." Telekan (film).

Stebbing, L. Susan. 1930. *A Modern Introduction to Logic*. Methuen

Stebbing, L. Susan. 1937. *Philosophy and the Physicists*. Methuen.

Stebbing, L. Susan. 1939. *Thinking to Some Purpose*. Penguin Books.

Stebbing, L. Susan. 1941. *Ideals and Illusions*. Watts.

Tuboly, Adam Tamas. 2020. "Knowledge Missemination: L. Susan Stebbing, C. E. M. Joad, and Philipp Frank on the Philosophy of the Physicists." *Perspectives on Science* 28 (1): 1–34.

West, Peter. 2022a. "L. Susan Stebbing *Philosophy and the Physicists* (1937): A Reappraisal." *British Journal for the History of Philosophy* 30 (5): 859–873.

West, Peter. 2022b. "The Philosopher Versus the Physicist: Susan Stebbing on Eddington and the Passage of Time." *British Journal for the History of Philosophy* 30 (1): 130–151.

Stebbing's Pelicans

Public Philosophy in *Philosophy and the Physicists* and *Thinking to Some Purpose*

Peter West

Introduction

By the end of the 1930s, Susan Stebbing had served as president of both the Mind Association (1931–32) and the Aristotelian Society (1933–34), co-founded the journal *Analysis* (1933), and, between 1924 and 1939, published at least one article every year in a range of leading philosophy journals (Janssen-Lauret 2021, 4). She was also the first woman in Britain to be promoted to a full professorship in philosophy, at Bedford College (later integrated into Royal Holloway), in 1933. In the last few years of the 30s, however, Stebbing began to move away from writing for an academic audience and instead wrote two books that were designed to be read by non-specialists: *Philosophy and the Physicists* (1937) and *Thinking to Some Purpose* (*TSP*, 1939).[1] Both texts were published as part of the Pelican series; an imprint of Penguin publishing.[2] Allen Lane, the creator of the Pelican series, described it as "another form of education for people like me who'd left school at 16" (McCrum 2013). Pelican books were written for a rising number of autodidacts in Britain: self-educated individuals who were unable to attend university but nonetheless found themselves with a hunger for knowledge. In that sense, as an article celebrating the return of the Pelican series in 2014 put it, they were "a university without walls" (Sutherland 2014). Both of Stebbing's texts were widely read and did for philosophy what other titles in the Pelican series had done for history, literature, and the sciences.

---

[1] 1941 also saw the publication of *Ideals and Illusions*, another text aimed at a public audience.
[2] *Philosophy and the Physicists* was first published by Methuen & Co. Limited in 1937. A later Pelican edition was published in 1944.

Peter West, *Stebbing's Pelicans* In: *Susan Stebbing*. Edited by: Annalisa Coliva and Louis Doulas, Oxford University Press. © Oxford University Press 2025. DOI: 10.1093/9780197682371.003.0007

152 SUSAN STEBBING

In this essay, I compare *Philosophy and the Physicists* and *Thinking to Some Purpose* in order to discern what they can tell us about Stebbing's approach to writing philosophy for a popular audience. The question of how philosophers can, and why they should, engage in public philosophy is very much a live question today and, I will argue, an analysis of Stebbing's approach can inform that debate.[3] On the surface, *Philosophy and the Physicists* and *Thinking to Some Purpose* are very different texts, which presents a prima facie challenge to thinking of them both as part of the same project. The former is a critique of the popular scientific writings of James Jeans and Arthur Eddington; two of the foremost popularizers of science in Britain in the first half of the twentieth century. The subject matter, predominantly, is the latest developments in physics (such as Einstein's theories of relativity and quantum mechanics), the question of how best to communicate these developments to a non-specialist audience, and what (if any) philosophical conclusions can be drawn from them. *Thinking to Some Purpose,* meanwhile, is described on the cover of the original 1939 Pelican edition as "a manual to clear thinking, showing how to detect illogicalities in other peoples' mental processes and how to avoid them in our own." Stebbing begins *Thinking to Some Purpose* with an analysis of political speeches (especially those of the former Conservative prime minister, Stanley Baldwin) and includes further analysis of speeches, newspaper articles, and advertisements. Stebbing's aim here is to show how we can detect fallacies in language used in the world around us every day—and the importance of doing so. While there are seemingly different issues at stake in each text, I will show that they are part of a unified project: that of ensuring that the citizens of a democracy are in a position to *think clearly.* Stebbing's over-arching aim, in other words, is to ensure that each individual knows *how* to think clearly and is not restricted from doing so by bad mental habits or misuses of language.

I begin, in section one, with an outline of both texts, focusing on the audience, the targets, and the aims of each. In section two, I compare the two texts, identifying key similarities and differences—focusing also on Stebbing's motivations for writing on these two subject matters. I explain what unifies the two texts and give an account of Stebbing's over- arching project. Finally, I reconstruct Stebbing's model of public philosophy and compare it with the account of public philosophy endorsed by Betrand Russell. I also examine

---

[3] See, for example, volume 15, issue 1, of *Essays in Philosophy*, which features a series of articles on public philosophy and its aims and purposes. See, in particular, Weinstein 2014, Pigliucci and Finkelman 2014; Chick and LaVine 2014.

STEBBING'S PELICANS   153

how Stebbing's approach might fit into the contemporary landscape of public philosophy. I argue that Stebbing has an egalitarian, democratic account of human reason and believes that the role of public philosophy is to provide each individual with the freedom to think clearly.

1 The Audience, Targets, and Aims of Stebbing's Pelicans

1.1 *Philosophy and the Physicists*

In *Philosophy and the Physicists,* published in 1937, Stebbing explains that she is writing for "[O]ther philosophers *and* for that section of the reading public who buy in large quantities and, no doubt, devour with great earnestness the popular books written by scientists for their enlightenment" (*PP*, ix, my emphasis)

Stebbing thus has two groups of people in mind as her audience: academic philosophers and the kinds of readers who wish to be "enlightened" about what is going on in the sciences (such autodidactic readers were the target audience of the Pelican series more generally (Sutherland 2014)). What both groups have in common, Stebbing explains, is their dependence on popular scientists to keep them up to date on the latest scientific developments. Only scientists themselves can put in the time, effort, and training required to understand the latest developments in science in depth. Most of us are not scientists and so are unable to do so. Thus, if the role of the sciences is to determine the nature of the world we inhabit, *popular* scientists play a crucial role in keeping the rest of us in the loop about what that world is like.

Stebbing acknowledges that philosophers and "the reading public" will engage with popular scientific writings for different reasons. The latter do so, perhaps, simply out of curiosity or a desire to be "enlightened." The former— philosophers (and metaphysicians, in particular)—do so, Stebbing argues, because

[w]e are dependent upon the scientists for an exposition of those developments which—so we find them proclaiming—have important and far-reaching consequences for philosophy. (*PP*, ix)

Working on the assumption that our *metaphysical* attempts to describe reality ought to be informed by (if not always totally consistent with) the latest

154 SUSAN STEBBING

scientific descriptions of reality, it seems that philosophers are dependent on scientists to keep their work up to date. Like the general readers of popular scientific texts, philosophers do not (usually) have the time and leisure to also be experts within a particular field of science. So, if their work is to be informed by science, it will need to rely on that science being "translated" into a form that is accessible to the non-specialist. It is also worth noting, however, that Stebbing suggests there is a tendency for *scientists themselves* to proclaim that their work has important philosophical consequences. Stebbing maintains that an additional role of the philosopher is to confirm (or deny) such claims and thus keep such scientists in check.

The targets of Stebbing's critique in *Philosophy and the Physicists* are Sir James Jeans and Sir Arthur Eddington—two physicists who, while highly accomplished in their field, do *not* leave it to professionally trained philosophers to identify the philosophical implications of modern physics. Stebbing argues that Jeans and Eddington, as the two most widely read popular scientific writers in Britain at the time, have a particular responsibility to ensure they communicate the right kind of information to their readers in the right kind of way. Yet, she argues, "our popular expositors do not always serve us very well" (*PP*, ix). Both writers are guilty of two sins: gratuitous and misleading use of metaphors and anthropomorphism in their writing about nature, and jumping too quickly from theoretical developments in physics to metaphysical conclusions (*PP*, 5). On the first count, Stebbing criticises the fact that Jeans and Eddington try to "convey exact thought in inexact language" (*PP*, 7). As Stebbing puts it, "*exact* thought cannot be *conveyed in inexact language*; at best it can be but partially conveyed, at worst the illusion will be created that it has been conveyed" (*PP*, 7). In other words, these writers are in danger of giving their readers the impression that they have comprehended the whole picture—that they have properly understood this or that particular issue—when in fact they have been given only part of that picture, or worse, the wrong picture entirely. On the second count, of moving from developments in physics to philosophical conclusions, Stebbing has in mind the fact that both Jeans and Eddington argue for idealism (the view that mind is more fundamental than matter) on the basis that, roughly speaking, modern physics tells us that the world is more observer-dependent than was previously appreciated.

When it comes to misleading uses of language, Stebbing points out that Eddington often portrays science as if it were a person; specifically, a woman. By writing in this way, Eddington implies that the role of scientists is to

STEBBING'S PELICANS   155

communicate with this woman, Science, and that, when pursued in the right way, the job of scientists is to get Science to tell us what the world is really like. In using such language, Stebbing claims, Eddington is guilty of committing "the anthropomorphic fallacy" (*PP*, 15). While Eddington "seem[s] to believe in a strange anthropomorphic female" (*PP*, 15), Stebbing herself emphasis that "Science is not a Goddess or a woman. We cannot ask *science*, but only *scientists*" (*PP*, 9). Stebbing's point is that neither science nor nature is a person whom we can communicate with; it is incapable of telling us about itself. When we are presented with a scientific account of things we are not, strictly speaking, coming face-to-face with a set of *facts*. What we are presented with is a *theory*; a set of conclusions arrived at by *scientists*, based on the evidence available.

However, Stebbing's concern is not just that misleading metaphors can lead to misunderstandings about the nature of science but also that they can be used to manipulate readers. Stebbing identifies herself as "common reader" (*PP*, 5) (at least when it comes to physics), rather than an expert, and worries that she and other common readers are in danger of not only being let down by popularizes of science but deliberately misled. For instance, Stebbing claims that (in the work of Jeans and Eddington) "[m]any devices are apparently used for no other purpose than to reduce the reader to a state of abject terror" (*PP*, 10). Having put their readers in this fearful state, such popularizers then exploit their position of authority to promote mystical or religious claims that often do not actually follow from the science they are expositing. Stebbing argues that this is part of a larger trend and that, by using this kind of language,

> [T]hey [Jeans and Eddington] seek to arouse his [i.e., the reader's] emotions, thereby inducing a frame of mind inimical to intellectual discernment. Popularizations of such a kind constitute a grave danger to clear thinking. (*PP*, 5)

Stebbing's point is that writers like Eddington and Jeans are well aware of their status as scientific experts but, unfortunately, use that status to promote their own agenda.[4] Eddington, for instance, having explained to the

---

[4] Indeed, Stebbing is keen to emphasize the prominent role scientists hold in society—which they are able to exploit. She explains that, uniquely to the twentieth century, "theologians hang on to the mantles . . . of the popularizing scientist" and that some people now regard scientists as "the custodians of the spiritual element in the universe" (*PP*, 143–144).

156 SUSAN STEBBING

reader that physics tells us the world is merely a set of symbols, then argues that it is not science but mysticism—and, in turn, religion—that can provide us with answers to questions like "what is real?" Eddington argues that, unlike the entities described by physics, it is possible to have "intimate knowledge" of God through mystical (i.e., not scientifically measurable), religious experiences (*NPW*, 322). For Stebbing, this goes beyond what Eddington's position as a *scientist*—and a popularizer of science—entitles him to do.

To sum up, then, Stebbing's aim in *Philosophy and the Physicists* is to identify (and, in turn, do what she can to remove) the barriers to clear thinking that popular scientific writing, such as that of Jeans and Eddington, present. Part of what it means to think *clearly,* for Stebbing, is to think *freely.*[5] When language is used, from those with a position of power or expertise, that is intended to raise certain emotions—emotions such as fear which can then be manipulated—an audience (in this case, readers of popular science) is *not* thinking freely. Their thought is, quite deliberately as Stebbing sees it, being *coerced* or *led* in a particular direction: toward the desired conclusions of the writer (such as Eddington's view that we must ultimately turn to mysticism or religion to determine "what is real"). We will find that these are the same concerns that Stebbing more explicitly raises, albeit in a wider context than just popular science writing, in *Thinking to Some Purpose.*

1.2 Thinking to Some Purpose

Stebbing sets up *Thinking to Some Purpose* as a very different kind of text than *Philosophy and the Physicists.* The preface makes it clear that the stakes are high, and it is with a strong sense of impending threat that Stebbing lays out her aims:

---

[5] The frontispiece to *Thinking to Some Purpose* is a quote from the notorious eighteenth-century deist and free-thinker Anthony Collins. The quotation, from Collins's *Discourse on Free-thinking,* is his definition of free-thinking as "[Using] our Understandings, in endeavouring to find out the Meaning of any Proposition whatsoever, in considering the nature of the Evidence for or against it, and in judging of it according to the seeming Force or weakness of the evidence, because there is no other way to discover the truth." By giving this reference pride of place at the beginning of the text and suggesting that her readers (the general public) need to learn to think clearly (and helping to provide the means), Stebbing is adding herself to a long line of free-thinking philosophers. Stebbing's commitment to free-thinking also manifested itself in a more formal manner. There is a strong historical and organizational connection between the free-thinking of the Enlightenment era (which continued into the nineteenth and twentieth centuries) and humanism; an ethical movement that emphasizes independent thinking and a secular approach to various aspects of public life, such as education. Stebbing was president of Humanists UK (then known as the Ethical Union) for 1941–42.

I am convinced of the urgent need for a democratic people to think clearly without the distortions due to unconscious bias and unrecognized ignorance. Our failures in thinking are in part due to faults which we could to some extent overcome were we to see clearly how these faults arise. It is the aim of this book to make a small effort in this direction. (*TSP*, 5)

The audience of *Thinking to Some Purpose* is thus "democratic people"— that is, anyone who wishes to continue living in a democratic society and enjoying the freedoms that entails. The text was published a year before the outbreak of the Second World War and political developments in Germany and Russia are referenced throughout. Stebbing believed that instructing the public on how to "think clearly" can play a role in fending off the twin threats of fascism and communism.

Stebbing maintains that the defense of democracy must start at home. Unlike those in *Philosophy and the Physicists*, Stebbing's criticisms in *Thinking to Some Purpose* are not directed at specific figures or texts but at tropes in British political and public discourse—such as political speeches, journalism, and advertisements. In other words, Stebbing criticizes ways of communicating that are common (whether deliberately or not) in the British public sphere. This is not to say that Stebbing does not pick out *any* particular figures for criticism. For example, the "prologue" of the text focuses primarily on excerpts from speeches by Stanley Baldwin (Conservative prime minister in 1923–24, 1924–29, and 1935–37). Nonetheless, the scope of her criticism is broad and the lessons she offers are intended to be universal (and so applicable beyond Britain and, arguably, beyond the 1930s).

Over the course of fifteen chapters (including a prologue and an epilogue), Stebbing identifies a series of bad habits that can be routinely found in public and political discourse. These include habits such as using "emotive" language in place of purely descriptive language (*TSP*, 45–52), which can lead audiences to believe they are being *informed* when in fact they are being *manipulated*, or "potted thinking" (*TSP*, 53–61), where ideas are condensed into an oversimplified form (such as a political slogan) as a substitute for genuine reflection or critical engagement.

Part of Stebbing's aim is to help us to avoid developing these habits ourselves. For example, in line with David Hume's claim that a "wise man proportions his belief to the evidence,"[6] Stebbing argues that "[t]he strength

---

[6] David Hume. *An Enquiry Concerning Human Understanding.* (1777), 11.4, 110.

158   SUSAN STEBBING

with which we hold a belief ought to bear some proportion to the amount of evidence upon which it is based" (*TSP*, 27). Inevitably, however, this is very often *not* the case; we often hold on to beliefs, due to how we *feel* about things, "unquestioningly" (*TSP*, 32). Consequently, Stebbing encourages us to question our most cherished beliefs. In her own words:

> It is a good habit to ask, with regard to our cherished beliefs, 'Now, how did I come to think that?' An honest answer would sometimes be both surprising and enlightening; it could not fail to be useful. (*TSP*, 32)

In other words, we can do our best to make sure that we do not fall into the habit of holding unjustified beliefs by developing the healthier habit of challenging them. It is worth noting, however, that, for Stebbing, there is value in simply becoming *aware* of our bad mental habits, even if we are not able to totally overcome them. There is utility, she claims, in simply answering the question "how did I come to think that?" regardless of whether we are able to *stop* ourselves from doing so.

As in *Philosophy and the Physicists,* Stebbing's approach is to focus on specific excerpts of writing to make wider claims about the use of language, and the extent to which it can be a barrier to clear thinking when misused. For instance, as an example of potted thinking, Stebbing cites a letter to the editor from an issue of *The New Statesman*:

> Twice, in your leading article in last Wednesday's paper, there occur the words 'British cowardice'. One wonders what is the nationality of the man who wrote it, as the combination of these two words, together, is unknown in the English language, or in the tongue of any country in the world. In the present delicate situation in Europe would not the words 'British Diplomacy' be more appropriate?
> I sign myself,
> 'A Britisher', and Proud of it. (*TSP*, 60)

The potted thought here is the idea that "British cowardice" is a contradiction in terms. The author of this letter holds the (most likely, unquestioned) belief that to be British is to be brave. Stebbing's point is that while there might once have been some truth behind the notion that British people are brave—perhaps there are examples of great bravery by British people (the exploits of the British army in the First World War is likely to have been in the public mindset in the 1930s)—this thought has subsequently been "potted." It has been condensed and oversimplified to the point that the author of the letter sees being British and being a coward as contradictory notions.

Again, Stebbing's aim is to identify misuses of language and their connections to bad mental habits and to instruct us on what we can do to rectify them. The heavy lifting, as it was in *Philosophy and the Physicists*, is concentrated on making us aware of such misuses of language, primarily by using examples. This suggests that, for Stebbing, simply being aware that these bad habits exist is at least half the job of fixing them. In the next section, I explain the similarities between *Philosophy and the Physicists* and *Thinking to Some Purpose* in greater depth and make the case for thinking they are part of a unified project.

2 A Unified Project

In this section, I argue that while the aims of *Philosophy and the Physicists* and *Thinking to Some Purpose* appear to diverge from one another, the two texts are part of the same project. Aside from the separate subject matters (discussed in the previous section), one important difference between the two texts is methodological. Stebbing's approach in *Thinking to Some Purpose* is, at least on the surface, "positive." That is, she attempts to contribute to public discourse by producing a "manual" in clear thinking. The text consists of a series of lessons in how we can think clearly and develop the right kinds of mental habits. In other words, Stebbing's aim here is to explain what we *should* be doing and to instruct us in how to do it. In contrast, Stebbing's approach in *Philosophy and the Physicists* is more "negative" in the sense that she is here largely concerned with criticizing the work of two specific thinkers (Jeans and Eddington). In other words, Stebbing's central aim in *Philosophy and the Physicists* is to tell us what is *wrong* with popular science writing.[7] This was emphasized by several early reviews of the text, including one by the Cambridge metaphysician C. D. Broad, who suggests that the main achievement in *Philosophy and the Physicists* is clearing up

---

[7] Elsewhere, I have argued that *Philosophy and the Physicists* offers more than just a critique of Jeans and Eddington. In West (2021b), I argue that Stebbing offers important insights into her philosophy of time and in West (2022) I argue that Stebbing develops an account of scientific progress that, to some extent, pre-empts Thomas Kuhn's attempt to revise the "image of science" in *The Structure of Scientific Revolutions* (1962, 1).

160 SUSAN STEBBING

"the messes made by amateur philosophers" (Broad 1938, 226). As Siobhan Chapman notes in her intellectual biography of Stebbing, this was part of a larger trend and many early reviews were "almost entirely negative in tone" (2013, 116).

However, I hope to have shown in the previous section that, if we dig a little deeper, there are also some important similarities between Stebbing's approach in *Philosophy and the Physicists* and in *Thinking to Some Purpose*. While the latter certainly appears to be a more "positive" text, offering guidance on how we as individuals can learn to think clearly and, in turn, contribute to the preservation of our democratic freedoms, Stebbing often chooses to instruct her readers by picking out specific pieces of writing for criticism. That is, Stebbing often instructs the reader in what they should be doing by *showing* them what they ought *not* to do or what others are doing badly. For instance, she explains how coverage of the Spanish Civil War in the British Press (which, according to Stebbing, was largely sympathetic to the Spanish government) disguises *judgments* behind language that appears to express merely factual statements. For instance, she explains how descriptions of the Spanish government often include terms like "Loyal" and "Anti-Fascist" while descriptions of their opponents include terms like "Revolt," "Insurrection," "Fascist," and "Rebel" (*TSP*, 50). The problem here, Stebbing claims, is not the judgments themselves (it does not matter, at least when it comes to linguistic analysis, which side you are on) but the fact that are they hidden behind apparently descriptive language. This can lead the reader to believe they are being informed of the facts when, in actuality, they are being *convinced* to support one side of the conflict rather than the other. Again, the problem here is that "emotive" language (language with "tied suggestions" designed to make you *feel* a certain way) is being presented as though it were in fact purely descriptive (or "scientific") language (*TSP*, 45–46). As we have seen, this is the same concern that Stebbing has with Jeans and Eddington's writing in *Philosophy and the Physicists*. There, Stebbing objects to the use of emotional manipulation against an audience of "common readers" who want simply to be informed about the latest developments in physics but are instead (as Stebbing sees it) being scared into accepting conclusions about the nature of reality that go well beyond the scope of the physical sciences.[8]

---

[8] One such conclusion is Eddington's claim that "[t]he idea of a universal Mind or Logos would be, I think, a fairly plausible inference from the present state of scientific theory" (*NPW*, 338).

STEBBING'S PELICANS   161

In both texts, then, Stebbing's approach involves close textual analysis of specific examples (from popular science writing in *Philosophy and the Physicists* or political speeches, newspapers, and advertisements in *Thinking to Some Purpose*) and an examination of what has gone wrong. The errors that Stebbing identifies are often improper or misleading uses of language (as in the example above). Thus, it is clear that Stebbing believes the way we use language is crucially important in public discourse; whether that be discussions of the latest developments in science or debates about politics. We might then ask *why* Stebbing believes that using language in the right kind of way is so important. The answer to this question can be found in *Thinking to Some Purpose*, where Stebbing explains that language is a *tool* that we use to communicate with one another: "to express our personal reactions to situations, to stimulate a response in someone else, and for the sake of thinking something out" (*TSP*, 45). When we *mis*use language, however, we are using that tool improperly and such language will fail to "achieve the purpose for which it is used" (*TSP*, 45). This can also have more severe knock-on effects. If I mislead you, Stebbing argues, or even worse "if I mislead myself . . . I shall be unable to think straight" (*TSP*, 47). Thus, bad language usage is one of the barriers to clear thinking that Stebbing believes presents a threat to democracy (*TSP*, 5).

There is evidence that the same concern motivates Stebbing's criticism of popular scientific writing in *Philosophy and the Physicists*. In the first chapter of that text, Stebbing outlines both the *importance* of works of popular science as well as the danger that such works pose to a "common reader" when they are not written in the right kind of way:

> There is among common readers a genuine interest in scientific research, a desire to follow as far as a layman can what is being found and to understand the implications of these findings. . . The writing of such an exposition is undoubtedly difficult. It requires not only great powers of exposition but also an apprehension of the sort of difficulties the layman is likely to find and the skill to surmount them. . . . [T]here are not a few scientists who have written books that satisfy our needs. Unfortunately, however, there are other famous scientists who do not seem to realize that their subject has an intrinsic interest for the common reader, and accordingly they seek to arouse his emotions, thereby inducing a frame of mind inimical to intellectual discernment. Popularizations of such a kind constitute a grave danger to thinking clearly. (*PP*, 5)

162 SUSAN STEBBING

This is one of the few times that Stebbing explicitly mentions "thinking clearly" in *Philosophy and the Physicists*. Nonetheless, she is making the same point as above. When the tool of language is misused—for instance, when it is used to arouse emotions in contexts where it ought to be used simply to inform—our ability to think clearly is hampered. This supports the claim that Stebbing is working on a unified project across both texts and that this project is an attempt to ensure that the public (or at least, those members of the public who engage in public discourse, whether it concerns science or politics) are free to think clearly.

Stebbing's over-arching concerns seems to be that in the course of their daily lives, ordinary people (non-specialists, or what Stebbing calls "ordinary readers" (*PP*, 5) are likely to come across language—whether written or spoken—that threatens their freedom to think clearly. This might simply be part of the course of one's daily routine—for example, when one is reading the newspaper, listening to the radio, or seeing an advertisement. Or it could be in a text that one has chosen to read (such as Jeans's or Eddington's books) for the sake of personal "enlightenment" (*PP*, ix). Across both *Philosophy and the Physicists* and *Thinking to Some Purpose*, Stebbing's aim is to instruct her readers in how to detect this kind of language and how to avoid allowing it to restrict one's freedom to think clearly. While she does offer more general guidance, she evidently believed that the most effective way to guide her readers was to use specific examples. The examples used in *Thinking to Some Purpose* are considerably more wide-ranging than those used in *Philosophy and the Physicists*, but this is perhaps because there is a wider range of improper uses of language (and thus barriers to thinking clearly) in everyday life than in popular science writing.[9]

The aim of these two works of popular philosophy, then, is, at bottom, to prevent improper uses of language (from popular scientists, politicians, journalists, and advertisers) from restricting individual people's freedom to think clearly. I thus suggest that Stebbing saw the aim of *public* philosophy itself as *equipping* non-specialist readers with the ability to preserve their freedom to think clearly. In the next section, I say more about what Stebbing

---

[9] Additionally, Stebbing seems to think *philosophers* are likely to be misled by the likes of Jeans and Eddington (*PP*, ix). She does not seem to think philosophers are as likely to be misled by improper language in newspapers, political speeches, and advertisements. This is perhaps because of the esteem in which scientists are held (*PP*, 143–144) as opposed to the general skepticism directed toward politicians, journalists, and advertisers—and the fact that scientists are experts, while politicians, journalists, and advertisers need not be.

STEBBING'S PELICANS   163

takes thinking clearly to involve and identify what these two texts tell us about Stebbing's approach to public philosophy.

3 Stebbing's Public Philosophy

3.1 Public Philosophy and Thinking Clearly

In this section, I outline Stebbing's approach to public philosophy as exemplified by *Philosophy and the Physicists* and *Thinking to Some Purpose*. I argue that Stebbing adopts what we might call a "skills and training" approach to public philosophy which aims at helping her readers to identify and avoid barriers to clear thinking. I conclude by suggesting that, at a time when there is a lot of pressure for academic philosophers to disseminate philosophy to a broader audience, there is a gap in the market for something like Stebbing's approach to public philosophy.

Stebbing was not alone in promoting philosophy to a broader audience. Bertrand Russell was perhaps the most successful of Stebbing's contemporaries in breaking through to a popular audience, appearing frequently on television in Britain and, in 1950, winning the Nobel Prize for Literature. In "Philosophy for Laymen," first published in 1946 in the pedagogical journal *University Quarterly* (now, *Higher Education Quarterly*), Russell offers a series of incentives for the "layman" (i.e., the non-specialist) to engage with philosophy.[10] Russell claims that philosophy has two broad aims (which are consistent with the traditional distinction between theoretical and practical philosophy). First, "it [is] aimed at a theoretical understanding of the structure of the world" and, second, it aims to "discover and inculcate the best possible way of life" (1950, 23). It's worth noting that many of Russell's claims echo the kind of advice that Stebbing offers in *Thinking to Some Purpose*. For example, he advocates avoiding "emotional bias" in political discourse, examining the sources of our opinions, and questioning even those beliefs "we find it most painful to doubt" (1950, 30). The latter claim, in particular, is very reminiscent of Stebbing's encouragement that we examine our most "cherished beliefs" (*TSP*, 32).

---

[10] References here are to a republication of the essay in Russell's *Unpopular Essays*, published in 1950.

164   SUSAN STEBBING

However, Russell does not limit the benefits of philosophical training to fixing bad habits. He maintains that the advantages of engaging with philosophy are lofty and that philosophy can improve our moral character. Furthermore, Russell argues that if everyone were equipped with philosophical training then, on a societal level, there would be considerably fewer disputes and, on a personal level, we would all lead more peaceful and fulfilling lives. As he puts it:

[Philosophy] supplies an antidote to the anxieties and anguish of the present, and makes possible the nearest approach to serenity that is available to a sensitive mind in our tortured and uncertain world. (1950, 33)

Drawing on the ancient Aristotelian notion of leading a good life by accruing wisdom, Russell promotes philosophy as something of intrinsic personal value—an "intellectual virtue" (1950, 30).

In that sense, Russell's approach to public philosophy is more idealistic than Stebbing's. Unlike Russell, Stebbing presents the tools of philosophical thinking (e.g., detecting fallacies, avoiding inconsistences, proportioning our beliefs to the evidence) as *means to an end*. After all, for Stebbing, all thinking is *thinking to some purpose*. For instance, she argues that thinking clearly is something that will allow us to continue to hold those who speak in public contexts (like politicians) to account and, in turn, enable us to keep living in a genuinely democratic society. As Stebbing explains, politicians are only able to win us over by using emotive language because we allow them too: "We are sometimes too lazy, usually too busy, and often too ignorant to think out what is involved in the statements we so readily accept" (*TSP*, 53). But if we avoid reacting emotionally to politicians' claims and learn to examine them logically, then they will have to start proving things to us on the basis of evidence.

So what is the aim of public philosophy, for Stebbing, if it is not something of intrinsic value? If it is not something that will contribute to an individual's moral or intellectual improvement (as it is for Russell), why should we engage with it? Given the conclusions arrived at in the previous section—and working on the assumption that *Philosophy and the Physicists* and *Thinking to Some Purpose* exemplify Stebbing's views on the aims (and proper methodology) of public philosophy—we can reasonably infer that Stebbing believes that the aim of public philosophy is to ensure that each individual is able to think clearly. That is, for Stebbing, the tools of philosophy should be used to ensure both that members of the public know *what it is* to think clearly and that they are actually able to do so. But thinking clearly is not of *intrinsic* value either; it is not something for which to strive for its own sake. Thinking clearly, for Stebbing, is essential to freedom and to the flourishing of a democratic society.

In this sense, Stebbing's Pelicans are *situated texts*. It is no coincidence that they were published toward the end of the 1930s; Stebbing felt compelled to turn toward a much wider audience than academic philosophers precisely because of the events taking place in the world around her (most notably, the rise of fascism in Germany). I thus think Beaney and Chapman (2021) are right to say that Stebbing's turn toward public philosophy was driven by "her belief that the structures and principles of formal logic need not be seen as a closed, isolated system but rather could profitably be applied to the problems and issues of modern life." Of course, it is much easier to situate *Thinking to Some Purpose* amid the political goings-on of the 1930s but, as I hope to have shown, this is also true of *Philosophy and the Physicists*. People are not free if they not thinking clearly—if, for example, they are being coerced when they believe they are being informed—and freedom, if anything, is to be sought for its own sake.

3.2 A "Skills and Training" Approach to Public Philosophy

I want to conclude this section with some remarks on how Stebbing's approach to public philosophy might fit into the landscape of contemporary public philosophy.

The ability to engage with a public, non-specialist audience has long been a feature of philosophy, as exemplified by the appearance of figures like Russell on the BBC or the celebrity status of another Nobel Prize winner, Henri Bergson, in France in the 1910s (see Herring 2019). As one scholar has argued, given the fact that Socrates engaged in philosophical debates with the "person-in-the-street" in the agora of ancient Athens, some of the best-known and earliest Western philosophy was public philosophy (Weinstein 2014, 35– 36).[11] In the United Kingdom, in particular, the ability to disseminate research (albeit, not just philosophical research) to a wide audience

---

[11] As Weinstein puts it, Aristotle's interlocutors were "slave boys and seers, strangers and playwrights, bullies and drunks, and prominent citizens" (2014, 36).

166 SUSAN STEBBING

is incentivised by what the Research Excellence Framework (the metric by which the research outputs of UK higher education institutions are evaluated) calls "impact"—defined as "an effect on, change or benefit to the economy, society, culture, public policy or services, health, the environment or quality of life, beyond academia."[12] Academic philosophers in Britain thus have a specific motivation to reach out beyond their peers to a popular audience.

Unsurprisingly, then, there are many channels by means of which philosophy is disseminated to non-specialists (both in the UK and elsewhere); whether that be through books, YouTube videos, or podcasts, for example. This has led to some recent debates about who philosophy is for and who is qualified, broadly speaking, to *do philosophy*. Jack Russell Weinstein, for example, raises the question of what constitutes philosophical expertise, citing Brian Leiter's claim that (as he puts it) "It would be odd if any non-philosopher ever came up with an "interesting philosophical insight" (2014, 34).[13] More recently, Timothy Williamson, in a guest post for the widely read philosophy blog *Daily Nous,* argues that while the democratization of knowledge should be encouraged, academic philosophers should nonetheless be seen as "experts" in philosophy to whom deference should be given, when appropriate. For Williamson, philosophy is not something we can all do equally well. Like any other science, it is something one must be trained to do, since it involves adopting highly sophisticated research methods and familiarizing oneself with a considerable amount of both historical and contemporary literature (for further discussion, with relation to Stebbing's popular philosophy, see West 2021a). Given the distinction between philosophical "experts" and "laypeople" (a distinction Russell was clearly also committed to), Weinstein also raises the question of what good (if any) public philosophy actually achieves. For example, he asks, does public philosophy improve the political life—that is, the quality of political debates, for example—of those with access to it (Weinstein 2014, 40)? Weinstein's answer is pessimistic. He concludes that, at best, philosophy serves as a form of entertainment what he calls a "pleasant distraction" (2014, 47). His explanation for this is that most public philosophy outlets, such as public talks or podcast episodes, are isolated incidents within a person's ordinary life. They might

---

[12] https://re.ukri.org/research/ref-impact/.
[13] Leiter's remark is from the podcast *Why? Philosophical Discussions About Everyday Life*, episode 20, (September 20, 2002).

succeed in encouraging someone to reflect on their assumptions about a specific issue within a limited time frame, but they rarely impact on someone's day-to-day thinking.

However, I think this pessimistic approach to the contribution public philosophy can make to public, and especially political, discourse, is perhaps grounded on a particular understanding of how public philosophy *works*. Many public philosophy outlets—books, YouTube videos, podcasts—adopt what we might call a "transfer of knowledge" approach. On this model, the role of the "expert" is to simplify or condense the theories, arguments, and views of philosophers (both contemporary and historical) and present them to a non-specialist audience in a comprehensible manner. The successful *Philosophy Bites* podcast is a case in point. Williamson, for example, argues that popular philosophy should operate in much the same way as popular science. It should involve a specialist in the field communicating their findings to non-specialists in an engaging and informative manner. The upshot, as Stebbing puts it in her own discussion of popular *science*, is some kind of intellectual "enlightenment" (*PP*, ix).

This "transfer of knowledge" approach, however, is not the one that Stebbing adopts, which suggests that it ought not (at least, without further justification) be subject to the same kind of pessimism. Stebbing's approach, which draws on what was, at the time, a burgeoning field of critical thinking,[14] focuses on the *way* we think rather than *what* certain philosophers think or have thought. Her primary aim is to improve public, and especially political, discourse, meaning that what Weinstein calls "political improvement" is not something she hopes to achieve in a roundabout way—it is not a by-product of learning about various philosophers' views. Rather, it is the explicit and central aim of Stebbing's public writings. Stebbing's approach, which can appropriately be described as a "skills and training" approach to public philosophy, does *not* involve educating the public on any specific philosophical theories, arguments, or ideas.[15] In fact, virtually no philosophers (or their

---

[14] For example, Stebbing identifies Robert H. Thouless's *Straight and Crooked Thinking*, published in 1930, as an important influence on her views.

[15] This is not to say that Stebbing's own views are not influenced by specific philosophical ideologies. She is, as figures like J. L. Austin would later be, committed to an analysis of ordinary language. Further, as both Janssen-Lauret (2021) and West (2021b) argue, *Philosophy and the Physicists* can be seen as part of Stebbing's defense of a philosophical position she calls "realism." I have also argued, in West 2022, that *Philosophy and the Physicists,* upon closer inspection, reveals Stebbing's views on the philosophy of science.

168 SUSAN STEBBING

ideas) are mentioned in either *Philosophy and the Physicists* or *Thinking to Some Purpose*.[16]

Does that mean that Stebbing's "skills and training" model is preferable? On the one hand, one might argue that the continued relevance of a text like *Thinking to Some Purpose* today actually attests to the *failure* of Stebbing's method. As Michael Beaney notes, in a recent public philosophy podcast, when reading *Thinking to Some Purpose,* one cannot help but ask: has anything really changed (Forum for Philosophy, 2021)? Public discourse, especially in the age of the internet, is just as likely to provide examples of improper language usage, bad mental habits, and barriers to free thinking today as it was in the 1930s. If Stebbing's work *had* successfully improved public discourse, one might argue, surely we would be able to observe some kind of change. Of course, this kind of criticism would need empirical support—concerning Stebbing's readership for a start. My own view, however, is that Stebbing's "skills and training" approach to public philosophy has the potential to get around some of the concerns raised by commentators like Weinstein. In its favor, and in contrast to "transfer of knowledge" models, Stebbing's approach emphasizes that public philosophy—like any educational endeavor—should be a two-way street. Stebbing writes:

> An educator has two main objects: to impart knowledge and to create those mental habits that will enable his students, or pupils, to seek knowledge and to acquire the ability to form their own independent judgement based upon rational grounds. (*TSP*, 74)

For Stebbing, education is not just an act of "imparting knowledge"; it also involves the process of *training* students (i.e., broadly construed as anyone being educated) to develop the right kind of mental habits. Public philosophy should not, then, resemble a traditional university lecture-style setting, where an "expert" or "master" bestows the fruits of their scholarly labor on a passive audience. Instead, it requires its audience (i.e., the public) to actively engage rather than passively receive information. The consequence, if it is successful, is an audience that is equipped with learning tools (ways of thinking) that are applicable beyond any specific domain of philosophy.

---

[16] Stebbing does discuss Russell in both texts, but in each case it is to criticize him (see, e.g., *PP*, 275, or *TSP*, 117–118).

Ultimately, the case I am making in this chapter does not hinge upon the success or failure of Stebbing's "skills and training" approach to public philosophy (although, as I have suggested, I think it does offer some potential advantage compared to a typical "transfer of knowledge approach"). What I have set out to establish, instead, is that Stebbing does actually have a coherent, unified approach to engaging in public philosophy. Public philosophy, for Stebbing, aims at ensuring that the public are both motivated and equipped to think clearly. This is of vital importance, she believes, if we are to continue to live in a democratic society—that is, a society where free, public debate is something of value.

Conclusion

I have argued that an analysis of the aims and methods of Stebbing's Pelicans (*Philosophy and the Physicists* and *Thinking to Some Purpose*) reveals that she has a unified approach to writing philosophy aimed at a public audience. Taking her leave from other early texts in the field of critical thinking, Stebbing places the emphasis on what philosophy can do for our *ways* of thinking rather than what exactly it is that we believe. The aim of both texts, I have argued, is to ensure that misuses of language—whether they be from popular scientists, politicians, journalists, or advertisers—do not cloud our thinking. But public philosophers cannot do this alone. We (that is, the "common reader"), too, must ensure that we are able to think clearly, Stebbing argues, by developing healthy mental habits, such as challenging our most cherished beliefs, and rooting out bad mental habits, like holding on to "potted thoughts." Philosophy, for Stebbing, is not an end in itself. Nor is thinking clearly. All thinking is *thinking to some purpose*. At the end of the day, Stebbing believes that that purpose is to preserve our individual liberty. Thinking freely requires thinking clearly—and *thinking* freely is crucial to *living* in a free, democratic society.

References

Beaney, Michael, and Siobhan Chapman. 2021. "Susan Stebbing." *The Stanford Encyclopedia of Philosophy* (Summer edition). Edward N. Zalta (ed.). https://plato.stanford.edu/archives/sum2021/entries/stebbing/.

Beaney, Michael, Siobhan Chapman, Clare Moriarty, and Peter West. 2021. "The Philosophers: Susan Stebbing." *Forum for Philosophy* [podcast] [accessed January 2022]. https://blogs.lse.ac.uk/theforum/susan-stebbing/.

Broad, C. D. "Review of Philosophy and the Physicists by L. S. Stebbing." *Philosophy* 13 (1938): 221–226.

Chapman, Siobhan. 2013. *Susan Stebbing and the Language of Common Sense.* Basingstoke: Palgrave.

Chick, Matt, and Matthew Levine. 2014. "The Relevance of Analytic Philosophy to Personal, Public, and Democratic Life." *Essays in Philosophy* 15 (1); 138–155.

Eddington, Arthur. 1928. *The Nature of the Physical World.* New York: Macmillan.

Herring, Emily. 2019. "Henri Bergson: The Philosopher Damned for His Female Fans." *Aeon* [accessed January 2022]. https://aeon.co/essays/henri-bergson-the-philosopher-damned-for-his-female-fans.

Hume, David. 1777 [2007]. *An Enquiry Concerning Human Understanding.* Stephen Buckle (ed.). Cambridge University Press. https://www.cambridge.org/highereducation/books/hume-an-enquiry-concerning-human-understanding/D27B67182E56A6DB47659731C5F03619.

Janssen-Lauret, Frederique. 2021. "Susan Stebbing's Metaphysics and the Status of Common Sense Truths." *Women in the History of Analytic Philosophy.* J. Peijnenburg and S. Verhaegh, eds., *Springer Nature.* References are to a pre-print copy of this paper, available at https://www.research.manchester.ac.uk/portal/files/177729732/StebbingMetaphysicsFinal.pdf.

Kuhn, Thomas. 2012 [1962] *The Structure of Scientific Revolutions.* Chicago: University of Chicago Press.

McCrum, Robert. 2013. "What Would Allen Lane Make of Amazon?" *The Guardian* [accessed January 2022]. https://www.theguardian.com/books/2013/sep/27/allen-lane-amazon-publishing.

Pigliucci, Massimo, and Leonard Finkelman. 2014. "The Value of Public Philosophy to Philosophers." *Essays in Philosophy* 15 (1): 86–102.

Russell, Bertrand. 1950. "Philosophy for Laymen." *Unpopular Essays.* New York: Simon and Schuster, 21–34.

Stebbing, Susan. 1958 [1937]. *Philosophy and the Physicists.* London: Dover Books.

Stebbing, Susan. 1941 [1939]. *Thinking to Some Purpose.* London: Penguin.

Sutherland, John. 2014. "Blue, White, and Read All Over: The Return of Pelican Books." *The New Statesman* [accessed January 2022]. https://www.newstatesman.com/culture/2014/05/blue-white-and-read-all-over-return-pelican-books.

West, Peter. 2021a. "On Susan Stebbing and the Role of Public Philosophy." *Aeon* [accessed January 2022]. https://aeon.co/essays/on-susan-stebbing-and-the-role-of- public-philosophy.

West, Peter. 2021b. "The Philosopher Versus the Physicist: Stebbing on Eddington and the Passage of Time." *British Journal for the History of Philosophy* 30 (1): 130–151.

West, Peter. 2022. "L. Susan Stebbing, *Philosophy and the Physicists* (1937): A Re-Appraisal." *British Journal for the History of Philosophy* 30 (5): 859–873.

Weinstein, Jack Russell. 2014. "What Does Public Philosophy Do? (Hint: It Does Not Make Better Citizens)." *Essays in Philosophy* 15 (1): 33–57.

Williamson, Timothy. 2020. "Popular Philosophy and Populist Philosophy." *Daily Nous* [accessed January 2022]. https://dailynous.com/2020/06/08/popular-philosophy-populist-philosophy-guest-post-timothy-williamson/.

SECTION III
THE LOGIC AND POLITICS
OF EVERYDAY LANGUAGE

Susan Stebbing and Some Poorly Explored Venues of Analytic Philosophy

Nikolay Milkov

> Most people would die sooner than think—in fact, they do so.
>
> Bertrand Russell (1925, p. 166)

Overview

This chapter discusses Susan Stebbing's conception of analytic philosophy as a discipline that can help to achieve clear thinking not only in fields of academic interest but also in public matters. We first explore Stebbing's long road to analytic philosophy, her mature position as an analytic philosopher and her work on developing and in defense of clear thinking. Then we show that this work of Stebbing's is the clearest expression of a side of the early analytic philosophy that is generally neglected. Analytic philosophy, as seen by its founding fathers G. E. Moore and Bertrand Russell, can help us to improve our thinking. As a matter of fact, many of its contemporaries saw it this way. Especially close to Stebbing's understanding of the practical significance of analytic philosophy was Russell. This side of analytic philosophy was not forgotten in the United Kingdom in the first years after the Second World War. Unfortunately, in the 1960s and later it was left behind by what is now called late analytic philosophy.

1 Introduction

Analytic philosophy started with an ambitious program for a revolution in philosophy. In fact, it was a complex project. Its founding fathers, G. E. Moore

---

Nikolay Milkov, *Susan Stebbing and Some Poorly Explored Venues of Analytic Philosophy* In: *Susan Stebbing*. Edited by: Annalisa Coliva and Louis Doulas, Oxford University Press. © Oxford University Press 2025. DOI: 10.1093/9780197682371.003.0008

174   SUSAN STEBBING

and Bertrand Russell, were united in their fight against British Idealism. At the same time, however, they followed effectively different intuitions and had developed virtually different programs. The projects of Moore and Russell had discrete layers that were oriented toward divergent directions. Unfortunately, the philosophical movement—analytic philosophy—they stirred up together developed only some of them, putting others in shadow. So much so that according to some scholars today (Soames 2014/17; Potter 2020), analytic philosophy mainly explores logical forms. Soames, in particular, reads the history of analytic philosophy from Russell to Kripke as a successive step-by-step dismantling of the idea of analyticity.

The claim of this chapter is that such interpretations deliver only a one-sided picture of analytic philosophy. To reveal a more complex view of this project in philosophy and to explicate tendencies in it that have remained "roads less traveled," we shall call for the help of Susan Stebbing, who, like nobody else before or after her, explicated tendencies in analytic philosophy that had remained in shadow until then.

2 Susan Stebbing and Analytic Philosophy

2.1 Stebbing's Progress Toward Analytic Philosophy

Susan Stebbing (1885–1944) needed time to get acquainted with and to embrace analytic philosophy as her own. Starting in 1904, she studied History and Moral Science in Girton College, Cambridge, where she attended logic classes of W. E. Johnson and was supervised by Constance Jones. In 1908, Stebbing moved to King's College, London, where she received her MA degree in 1912 with a thesis titled *Pragmatism and French Voluntarism* published two years later (1914).

Significantly, Stebbing was most influenced in philosophy by reading books, not listening to lectures. In 1907, she read F. H. Bradley's *Appearance and Reality* (1893), which deeply impressed her. Apparently, her interest in Bradley directed her attention to the animated discussion of the "intuitivists" and "intellectualists" on the nature of truth that dominated the philosophical scene in the Anglophone world of the late 1900s. In it, Stebbing sided with Bradley: her first book (1914) was in defense of the "intellectualists" on the theory of truth and criticized the "intuitivists," Bergson and James. The difference between the latter two was that "while M. Bergson condemns the intellect because it *is* pragmatic, the pragmatist condemns any view of the structure of intellect that makes it *not* pragmatic" (p. 136).

Stebbing's fight with these two forms of intuitionism ended with the conclusion that "philosophy is essentially the affair of intellect.... [Philosophy's task is] the development of intellect itself to the full possession of its powers" (pp. 162–163). This, however, was also the position of Moore and Russell.[1] It is a matter of fact that William James characterized all the three philosophers, Bradley, Moore, and Russell, as "intellectualists," setting them against the position on truth of Bergson and Pragmatism. Ironically enough, Stebbing took her first step in the direction of analytic philosophy with the help of their declared opponent—F. H. Bradley.

Stebbing took the next step toward analytic philosophy by reading the works of A. N. Whitehead. She extensively explored his works and also published much on them. For example, through Whitehead she adopted Russell's criticism of seeing in ordinary language a lead in logic. This is especially pernicious when we accept Indo-European languages as our logical guide (1925, p. 313). However, in the late 1920s, Stebbing was estranged by Whitehead's drive to idealism and openly criticized him for that. The "Whitehead chapter" of her development came to an end.

2.2 Stebbing as Analytic Philosopher

Gradually, Stebbing's engagement with works of Bradley and Whitehead brought her to the founding fathers of analytic philosophy, G. E. Moore and Bertrand Russell. She first made direct acquaintance with Moore at the Joint Session of the Aristotelian Society and the Mind Association in 1917 (1942, p. 530). Shortly afterward, they started an extensive correspondence in which Moore fairly tutored Stebbing on problems that he had introduced in philosophy. They also became close privately. Susan often visited Moore's house and also made friends with his wife Dorothy with whom she maintained a private correspondence until the end of her days. In the summer vacation of

---

[1] This is not surprising. It was the position of Hermann Lotze who markedly influenced English philosophy at the end of the nineteenth century—including Bradley, Moore, and Russell (Milkov 2023). Stebbing's tutor in Girton College, Constance Jones, was one of the translators of Lotze's *Mikrokosmus* in English (1885); therefore, it was quite natural that she taught in her classes Lotze's *Logic*. And, it is understandable that in her first book, Stebbing positively referred to Lotze's *Logic* (1914, p. 148).

176　SUSAN STEBBING

1941, Moore's son, Timothy, accompanied Stebbing on a holiday (Chapman 2013, p. 157).

Stebbing's intensive discussions with Moore helped her to reach her final and full-fledged position in analytic philosophy and it found mature expression in her papers: "The Method of Analysis in Metaphysics" (1932) and "Logical Positivism and Analysis" (1933). In them, Stebbing provided a harsh criticism of logical positivism and also of Wittgenstein's *Tractatus*, putting them together and defending Moore's, and partly also Russell's philosophical realism and Moore's vindication of the ordinary language against the pursuit of ideal languages. At the same time, Stebbing criticized the program of logical constructivism of Russell and Carnap as excessively abstract. Her argument was that the objective of Russell's and Carnap's "symbolic (or postulational) analysis" was "the construction of a deductive system" that presented reality in an epistemologically impeccable ("aseptic") way (1933, p. 80). However, we do not need to construct the external world—it is given to us. Stebbing also attacked Russell's and Carnap's method of translating one system of concepts into another, allegedly, *salva veritate*. The point is that this program does not capture the phenomena of experience. The gravest problem of the symbolic analysis, however, is that it leads to solipsism.

Opposing it and partly following John Wisdom (Milkov 2019), Stebbing pursued what she called "directional analysis." Its objective is the *elucidation* of the structure of facts, reaching beyond their surface level. It is not a kind of philosophy of language but is a philosophy of *facts*, of the real world. That is also why it is called *metaphysical* analysis.

For good or for bad, in the second half of the 1930s Stebbing generally lost interest in discussing problems of academic analytic philosophy, in particular, "directional analysis." At the same time, she continued to closely follow the type of analytic philosophy she had adopted around 1933 as a point of orientation. In particular, she followed the ideas of Moore, became fairly critical of Wittgenstein, and rejected at least some ideas of Russell.[2] Following Moore, for example, in *A Modern Elementary Logic* (1930) Stebbing discriminated three types of implication instead of Russell's two—material and formal implication: (i) Russellian "material implication" is a dependence on truth-values; (ii) "necessary implication," or "necessary connexion" or *entailment*, is a logical dependence on content (Stebbing, 1943,

---

[2] In § 4.1 we are going to see, however, that this did not hinder Stebbing and Russell from having related views on meta-philosophical problems.

p. 136); (iii) "relevant connexion" is "a connexion in the *meaning* of the proposition" (p. 138). Of the last type is, for example, "the connexion between *being human* and *erring.*" (p. 144). Already, in *A Modern Introduction to Logic* (1930) Stebbing exposed a confusion over "incomplete symbols" and "logical fictions" in Russell's terminology. Here, she followed a hint, given to her in a letter by G. E. Moore (p. 155), that Russellian "definite descriptions" are not always "incomplete symbols."

For Stebbing, the ultimate objective of analytic philosophy was to obtain a clear and precise grasp of the meaning of words and phrases to improve human *thinking*—in the final reckoning, in order to apprehend how the *facts* were interconnected and how they developed.

3 Susan Stebbing on Thinking and Politics

3.1 Logic and Thinking

Being a student of Constance Jones and W. E. Johnson, and also an attentive reader of F. H. Bradley and A. N. Whitehead, Stebbing was interested in logic from the very beginning. Significantly, in her first book in the area, *A Modern Introduction to Logic* (1930), she provided examples from practical life—its chapter I was dedicated to "Reflective Thinking in Ordinary Life." In fact, already in 1915, Stebbing had written that "logic will undoubtedly benefit by being brought more into touch with practical life—that is, in being shaped with a view to its application to the concrete arguments of science and everyday life" (p. 412). In other words, she was convinced from the beginning that "the structures and principles of formal logic need not be seen as a closed, isolated system, but rather could profitably be applied to the problems and issues of modern life" (Beaney and Chapman 2021). Today, this conception is called "logical interventionism" (Douglas and Nassim 2021).

However, Stebbing made the radical step to connect academic—that is analytic—philosophy with practical life only after she cleared her position in philosophy around 1933. She started to refer to examples from newspapers and political speeches for the first time in her book *Logic in Practice* (1934)—there were no such examples in *A Modern Introduction to Logic* (1930).

Soon, Stebbing's interest turned to the problem of *thinking* which found its first expression in her article published under the same title in (1936).

178   SUSAN STEBBING

Three years later, Stebbing published her bestselling book *Thinking to Some Purpose* (1939). This was a critical epistemological investigation of thinking and of human *rationality* in general. Two years later the book was issued in the "Penguin Pelican" book series. The book was described on its cover as "a manual of first-aid to clear thinking, showing how to detect illogicalities in other people's mental processes and how to avoid them in our own" (1941).

In short, Stebbing's "clear thinking," that is, thinking that is not poor (Stebbing often called poor thinking "muddled"), "draws connections between thoughts [and facts] that are relevant to the problem. [In contrast, the muddled thinking . . .] draws connections that are not relevant to solving their problem" (Pickel 2022, p. 1). Stebbing further maintained that many actions humans perform are done automatically so that "our common daily activities are for the most part carried on without reflection" (1943, p. 2). However, when we think with purpose, or apply "purposive thinking" in order to solve a problem, to face "something unexpected" (1930, p. 3), when we are "puzzled about something, i.e., about a topic" (1939, p. 22), when we are in a "questioning frame of mind" (p. 23), we need purposive thinking.[3] That is why according to Stebbing, "to think logically is to think relevantly to the purpose that initiated the thinking" (1939, p. 10). To be more exact, in such cases we need propositional thinking, i.e., we need proved *information* about *facts*.[4] In other words, clear thinking is achieved in a process of *rational deliberation* to which exact connections between facts are relevant in each particular case.

It is true that, usually, the best qualified individuals in "connecting thoughts that are relevant to a problem" are the scientists and also the experts in particular practical areas. However, their kind of knowledge alone is not enough to achieve clear thinking in all areas and in all situations. In realms that are not immediately susceptible to treatment by specialized experts, philosophy and logic are most helpful. It is especially difficult to achieve clear thinking in politics where there are no hard rules for how to master a situation in an ever changing environment.

As if in order to demonstrate that this conception of clear thinking effectively works also in science, Stebbing first put it on probation in physics. To be more explicit, in her book *Philosophy and the Physicists* (1937), she

---

[3] In Milkov (1992, back cover; p. 92), after a free interpretation of Wittgenstein's philosophy, we find the main problem of philosophy as: "How does our mind respond to a certain tasks?"

[4] This point of Stebbing's logic explains why securing the relevant facts played a central role in her ethics and political philosophy (§ 3.2, below).

VENUES OF ANALYTIC PHILOSOPHY   179

critically discussed the language of the popular works of such exact thinkers as physicists Arthur Eddington, James Jeans, and Max Planck. Stebbing criticized, in particular, Eddington's use of emotive instead of informative language in his effort to put the results of his scientific exploration in popular form. The problem is that "*exact* thought cannot be *conveyed in inexact language*" (p. 14).[5] Inexact language distorts facts.

Very instructive is Stebbing's final judgment that Eddington's "lack of philosophical training . . . has made it possible for him to slip into pitfalls that he might otherwise have learned to avoid" (p. 6). Clearly, Stebbing assumed that physicists *need* philosophy, that is, *analytic* philosophy—especially when they decide to bring their results to the general public. Philosophy is important.

Essential for achieving clear thinking is also human *freedom*. Stebbing firmly believed that "unless I can think freely I cannot think effectively" (1939, p. 235). Otherwise we cannot effectively cope with unexpected turns of events—cannot connect the facts that will lead us to a solution of the problem, or to a decision for acting. Moreover, we also need a *will* for freedom. To be sure,

Our limitation [in judging] is due not to ignorance, not to "blind force of Nature," not to astronomical insignificance of our planet, but to the feebleness of our *desires* for good, [. . . to] our greed, our stupidity and lack of imagination, our apathy. (1937, p. 212; italics added)

3.2 Ethics and Political Philosophy

Starting in 1938, Stebbing discussed the "European situation" with increasing intensity. In that year the civil war in Spain reached its worst phase while the Munich Conference tried to appease Hitler, putting into his hands the fate of Czechoslovakia. At the same time Stebbing fought Marxism. She saw "perhaps the sole element of truth [in Marx] in the Marxian dictum: 'Religion is the opium of the people'" (1939a, p. 38). She was a resolute fighter for idealism and an eloquent defender of realism.

---

[5] Apparently, Stebbing was convinced that ordinary language is exact. After the Second World War, this position was also adopted by the Oxford ordinary language philosophers. Significantly, their champion, J. L. Austin, was also a devoted follower of G. E. Moore (see § 4.2).

180 SUSAN STEBBING

In the same year, Stebbing wrote *Thinking to Some Purpose* (1939) in which she attacked, above all, the tricks of the fascist totalitarian ideology and its propaganda. She was against the use of "muddled language" in politics, in particular, of misleading words and phrases as they lead to "twisted thinking." Ultimately, Stebbing presented her work as an "argumentative book about arguing" (p. 32). And to her, propaganda was just a weak form of argument.

Stebbing insisted that ethics is radically different from science. Morally relevant situations are produced by many different factors that change over time and context. The "ultimate spiritual values" play a primary role in them in the form of ideals. However, ideals are neither "categorical imperatives" nor principles. They are more regulative ideas, a form of relative a priori— that is, ideas that change in time. At the same time they are not nonsensical, as the logical positivists maintain.

Following this conception, Stebbing claimed that "there is no good reason to suppose that one way of life, one clearly stated ideal, is appropriate to all stages of human development and to all sorts and conditions of societies" (1944, p. 27). It explains why philosophers are not sages or prophets, and also why *discussions* in ethics are of prime importance. Ethics has a clearly outlined objective; and it is the *analysis*, or the criticism, of the ways of life in which also the social and political ideals and the political principles get their shape.

The conclusion Stebbing drew from this position is that philosophers are not to lead public affairs. Deliberating on the tasks of philosophy, she inferred that "the business of the philosopher [is simply] critical questioning combined with the resolute conviction that hard intellectual effort can resolve the questions it is worthwhile to ask"[6] (1939b, p. 159). Besides, philosophers have to educate the citizens, the young, in particular. It is their ultimate assignment. Philosophers must "so *train* ... citizens as to make them able to criticise not only rival 'philosophies of life' but also their own; in short, by helping them to think philosophically" (p. 161; italics added).

Stebbing held that politics was a battle of ideals. Social change was not only determined by economic factors, as Marx believed, but also by ideals. The task of *Stebbing's Ideals and Illusions* (1941), in particular, was to outline clear ideals that could lead humanity and make our life worth living.

---

[6] Stebbing's position is clearly close to Socrates's dialectics. In this connection, it deserves notice that two of the *mottoes* in which Stebbing started her ninth chapter on *Insights and Illusions* were from Socrates.

There are true ideals and false ones, and there are also downright deceptive illusions. Religious faith, for example, is not an ideal but a mere an illusion. With this assumption, Stebbing joined moral realism and here she followed Moore again.

Stebbing's political ideal was democracy. Not just economic democracy, though—democracy is not just a materialistic ideal. Nor is the ideal of democracy only political democracy. The latter "merely signifies the machinery, or constitutional forms, through which democracy may be put into effect within the political sphere" (1941, p. 153). To be sure,

> If it were in fact true that we were all politically and economically free, still it would not follow that we were possessed of the freedom of mind without which, in my opinion, no democratic institutions can be satisfactorily maintained. (1939, p. 235)

Stebbing's regulative idea was that "of a community of individuals, each of whom counts, associated together in such a way that 'the free development of each is the condition of the free development of all'" (1941, pp. 144–145). In short, the ideal of democracy is "freedom, respect for other men issuing in tolerance and humanity, respect for truth and delight in knowledge" (p. 151). In other words, "the fundamental principle of democracy [tentatively formulated already by Pericles] is an ethical principle which can be expressed in the form: *all men alike ought to be free and happy*" (p. 155). In contrast, "the ideal of Fascism was power and the glorification of the State" (p. 133). Nevertheless, "to seek to destroy Nazi ideal is not enough; we must put something in its place; we must construct [it]" (p. 144). Clearly, democracy "is not an easy ideal" (p. 129). Being a kind of regulative idea, an ever-changing political a priori, it is to be recurrently transformed in new contexts.

Stebbing directly connected the fight for the democratic ideal and also her teaching in clear thinking with the new analytic philosophy. In her contribution to Schilpp's *Moore* volume, she wrote:

> Anyone who has been able to learn something of Moore's way of thinking, ... could not, I think, succumb to the muddle-headed creed of Fascism or National Socialism. For, to be imbued with his *critical* yet positive *spirit* is to be forearmed against the forces of *irrationalism* (Click here to enter text.1942, pp. 532; italics added).

182   SUSAN STEBBING

4 Early English Analytic Philosophy vis-à-vis
Social and Political Problems

Stebbing's project for creating a better world with the help of philosophy was not just a solitary effort. The very analytic philosophy emerged in Cambridge, England, as a revolution in *thinking*, adopting a form of robust *realism*. Because of its very nature, it could not remain without making an impact on public life. This point was clearly underlined by some of its contemporaries. As Leonard Woolf, Virginia Woolf's husband and a core member of the Bloomsbury Group put it, "suddenly [Moore's philosophy] removed from our eyes an obscuring accumulation of scales, cobwebs and curtains, revealing from the first time to us, so it seemed, the nature of truth and reality, of good and evil and character and conduct" (Woolf 1960, p. 147). Another member of the Bloomsbury Group, J. M. Keynes, reported: Following Moore, "we repudiated entirely customary morals, conventions and traditional wisdom.... We recognized no moral obligations on us, no inner sanctions, to conform or obey. Before heaven we claimed to be our own judge in our own case" (1972, p. 446). These are the vociferous avowals of leading British intellectuals of the time about the power of the Cambridge early analytic philosophy as a school of clear thinking.

In this regard, some authors maintain that we can see Moore's project for "new realism" as an "attempt to reform civilization through his [Moore's] philosophy" (Levy 1979, p. 259). Other interpreters go so far as to claim that "the intellectual climate of Britain and America between the two World Wars would have been quite different if G. E. Moore had not published *Principia Ethica* back in 1903" (Priestley 1970, p. 81). Roughly, the influence of Moore and his friends can be portrayed as accelerating the transition to effective democracy.

This contention can be supported by the fact that in his *The General Theory of Employment, Interest and Money* (1936), one of Moore's devotees, J. M. Keynes, clarified the foundations of the welfare state and prepared the New Deal policy of F. D. Roosevelt. In particular, Keynes fought the classic political economy maintaining that the most important task of scientists today is not to develop new ideas in it but to free the public from old prejudices. Among the latter is Adam Smith's mantra that "the invisible hand of the market" alone can regulate political economy. Arguably, Keynes adopted this approach under the influence of the "common sense philosophy" of G. E. Moore and was also inspired by Wittgenstein (Coates 1996)

VENUES OF ANALYTIC PHILOSOPHY   183

with whom he had had regular discussions in the early 1930s in Cambridge. The latter concerns, in particular, Keynes's claim that in uncertain times, people do not behave as rational actors but rely more on conventions.

An alternative view was presented by Hans-Johann Glock who maintains, against Jonathan Cohen (1986) and Dagfinn Føllesdal (1997), "that analytic philosophy has no monopoly on supporting liberal and democratic values.... [Glock's main argument is that] there have been eminent analytic philosophers who have opposed liberalism, democracy and non-violence" (2008, p. 191). His typical example is Gerhard Genzen who, allegedly, was Nazi *tout court*. The problem with Glock's claim is that Genzen was not an analytic philosopher at all. He was merely a mathematician and also a mathematical logician, assistant of David Hilbert and Paul Bernays in Göttingen. Unfortunately, mathematical logicians are not ipso facto analytic philosophers and even less so in the sense of the Cambridge School of analysis.

Glock's conclusion seems justified only if we adopt a widest conception of analytic philosophy that also includes figures like Jean van Heijenoort, Hilary Putnam, Hartry Field, and Noam Chomsky—but not if we limit our attention to the Cambridge and Oxford schools of analysis from 1900 to approximately 1960. This point is of particular significance since immediately after World War II the Oxford school of analysis, connected with the Cambridge school of analysis, was considered by many to be the analytic philosophy *par excellence*. In these years only a few maintained that the mainstream philosophy in the United States was analytical. Carnap, for example, spoke about the "analytic philosophy in England and . . . the logical empiricism in the United States" (1963, p. 28).

It is true that Frege and Wittgenstein were not supporters of liberal and democratic values. However, despite the fact that they were, without any doubt, analytic philosophers, they did not belong to the Cambridge (and even less to the Oxford) school of analysis—at least, as we see this in § 2, not in the critical eyes of Susan Stebbing.[7] Moreover, as we have just seen, Wittgenstein's later philosophy can be readily interpreted as supporting the liberal criticism of traditional capitalism provided by J. M. Keynes in the 1930s. This is no coincidence, though. Starting with the *Tractatus*, Wittgenstein was concerned with elucidations of human *language* and *thinking*; and, as we know, elucidation of language and thinking was the

---

[7] Again, nobody saw things as clearly as Stebbing did.

184 SUSAN STEBBING

ultimate objective of Stebbing's philosophical, political, and public writings as well. In other words, despite the fact that Wittgenstein himself was not a fighter for democracy and free thinking, apparently his writings can be used in support of their pursuit. This claim can be underpinned by Wittgenstein's avowal made to his student and friend Norman Malcolm in a letter from November 16, 1944:

> What is the use of studying philosophy if all it does for you is to enable you to talk with some plausibility about some abstruse questions of logic, etc. if it does not improve your thinking about the important questions of everyday life, if it does not make you more conscientious than any ... journalist in the use of *dangerous* phrases such people use for their own ends. You see, I know that this is difficult to think *well* about 'certainty,' 'probability,' 'perception,' etc. But it is, if possible, still more difficult to think, or *try* to think, really honestly about your life & other people's lives. (Malcolm 1972, p. 39)

As a matter of fact, Wittgenstein had an avid interest in current public affairs. This is confirmed in his letter to Victor Gollancz from September 4, 1945, in which Wittgenstein praised an article Gollancz had published in *News Chronicle*. At the same time he criticized some points of Gollancz's paper (Monk 1990, pp. 480 f.). Wittgenstein ends his letter with the avowal:

> If you ask me why, instead of criticizing you, I don't write articles myself, I should answer that I lack the knowledge, the facility of expression and the time necessary for any decent and effective journalism. In fact, writing this letter of criticism to a man of your views and your ability is the nearest approach to what is denied me, i.e. to write a good article myself. (1990, p. 482)

Even more questionable is Glock's claim that Russell's "political ruminations do not *uniformly* conform to the high standards of his writings in theoretical philosophy" (p. 192; italics added).[8] The problem is that Russell himself never claimed that *all* judgments of philosophers who adopted the "art of rational conjecture" (see § 4.1) discussing practical matters are true.[9]

---

[8] Glock refers in support of his claim to Ray Monk (2000). Unfortunately, as A. C. Grayling (2000) had noted, Monk, being a brilliant biographer, apparently "loathed" Russell. Clearly, one cannot trust all his judgments about Russell.

[9] For Russell as critical thinker, see Russell (1942), Hare (2001), and Hager (2001).

VENUES OF ANALYTIC PHILOSOPHY   185

It is a matter of degree. Moreover, it is a matter of fact that the rate of Russell's correct judgment by examining states of affairs of social and political life— marriage and morals, the outbreak of the Great War, the peace treaties after it, the theory and practice of Bolshevism, the war in Vietnam—was manifestly high. But we shall more closely discuss this subject in the next section.

4.1 Russell on Rationality and Thinking

The effort to achieve clear thinking was central also to Russell. Russell, who started his career in philosophy together with G. E. Moore as a philosophical *realist*, was interested in facts too, not only in language and symbols. Occasionally, he pleaded for "direct contemplation of facts which discards language" (1921, p. 212). Moreover, similarly to Stebbing, Russell wrote extensively on political and public matters. Furthermore, while Stebbing "believed that the exigencies of the time necessitated her defection from serious to more popular writings" (Chapman 2013, p. 157), Russell maintained, similarly, that the First World War brought him to abandon his work on academic philosophy and start intensively to write on matters of public interest.

Unfortunately, more often than not, Russell's interpreters fail to see relatedness between his technical and popular philosophy. In this they apparently follow the Wittgenstein dictum that

> Russell's books should be bound in two colours: those dealing with mathematical logic in red—and all students of philosophy should read them; those dealing with ethics and politics in blue—and no one should be allowed to read them. (Rhees 1981, p. 112)

Significantly, Russell himself did not see an intimate connection between his logic and philosophy, and his popular writings. In order to compensate this, our objective in this section will be to try to build a *bridge* between these two pursuits of Russell.

First of all, Russell's writings on practical subjects extensively applied the method of *reflective equilibrium* that he developed through explorations in theoretical philosophy.[10] In short, this method is a means of critically

---

[10] Significantly, Russell did this much earlier than John Rawls—allegedly, the term "reflective equilibrium" was introduced by John Rawls in his *Theory of Justice* (1971).

186 SUSAN STEBBING

examining competing propositions and principles with the objective of bringing a reflective equilibrium between them. Recently, Dustin Olson and Nicholas Griffin suitably stated that "readers can observe [the method of reflective equilibrium] in action in much of Russell's philosophy" (2019, p. 301). Russell used to weigh up epistemological foundationalism against coherentism already in his early writings; in this way he built a bridge between them. Over the years, this approach extended to a specific philosophical method. Russell himself used the bridge metaphor in *Human Knowledge*:

> The edifice of knowledge may be compared to a bridge resting on many piers, each of which not only supports the roadway but helps the other piers to stand firm owing to interconnecting girders. (1948, p. 413)

As this passage reveals, Russell rejected the divide between epistemological foundationalism and coherentism and propounded instead a hybrid position that could be termed "epistemic holism."

Second, after Russell finished, together with A. N. Whitehead, *Principia Mathematica* in 1910, his theoretical philosophy experienced a dramatic turn. In short, now Russell deliberately attuned it to discussing practical problems. In more technical terms, this was a transition from looking for certainty in human knowledge, which led Russell to the project of setting up a sound, "perfect" logic, with the help of which human knowledge could be grounded or justified, to search for creative uncertainty that advanced and critically tested alternative hypotheses. In the *Problems of Philosophy* Russell openly declared that "the value of philosophy is, in fact, to be sought largely in its uncertainty" (1912, p. 242).

Arguably, this change of heart was related to the endeavor Russell made after 1910 to connect philosophy with problems of *conditio humana*—with his belief that "the philosopher, by virtue of his more refined philosophical perspective, is able to detect errors that *the ordinary citizen overlooks*" (Schwerin 2019, p. 5; italics added). The new logic, in particular, must "assist *philosophers* in their attempts to clarify and more fundamentally grasp the issues endemic to the puzzles that bedevil ordinary citizens" (p. 15).

In his writings on meta-philosophy of these years, Russell insisted that philosophy was not science but also not "groundless credulity."

> It is something between these two; perhaps it might be called "The art of rational conjecture." According to this definition, philosophy tells us how to

VENUES OF ANALYTIC PHILOSOPHY   187

proceed when we want to find out what may be true, or is *most likely* to be true, where it is impossible to know with certainty what *is* true. (1942, p. 1)

In short, it is the philosopher's task to reach true conclusions based on scattered data. The ultimate objective is to make, with its help, judicious non-demonstrative inferences—and these are not only a problem of philosophy of science.[11] Significantly, this definition of philosophy is closely related to that of Stebbing, as discussed in § 3.1 above.

In another popular paper of these years, "Philosophy for Laymen" (1946), Russell maintained in plain words that philosophy means love for wisdom which "can give a habit of exact and careful thought, not only in mathematics and science, but in questions of large practical import" as well (p. 32). In other words, philosophy has both "a theoretical and a practical aim" (p. 29). Russell further pleaded for "intellectual sobriety [... that] will lead us to scrutinize our beliefs closely, with a view to discovering which of them there is any reason to believe true" (p. 30).

Russell emphasized that wisdom is a kind of skill; it is not a theory.[12] Furthermore, similar to Stebbing, he maintained that the skill in question could be achieved through "*training* in judicial habits of thought" (1956, p. 141; italics added). Similar to Stebbing again, an important element of clear thinking for Russell was a person's willingness to achieve it: "What is needed is not merely intellectual. Widening of sympathy is at least as important" (1953, p. 435). Russell also underlined the importance of liberal and democratic attitude to this purpose.

However, despite all similarities between Stebbing and Russell in relating their philosophy to political and public matters, there were also considerable differences between them. First of all, Stebbing believed, while Russell did not, that formal logic could directly help to solve problems of real life. Furthermore, in her critical studies of practical problems, Stebbing put great emphasis on criticizing the language of politics and science, something that was of no specific interest to Russell. Third, Russell was not thus optimistic about the power of critical thinking to change the world. Be this as it may, the two philosophers were closely united in connecting the achievements of the Cambridge School of Analysis to practical problems.

---

[11] In the late years of his life Russell intensively discussed the non-demonstrative inferences (see 1959, chapter 16).

[12] Russell's student and friend, Wittgenstein, adopted practically the same stance but put it in a different theoretical context: "Philosophy is not a theory but an activity" (1922, 4.112).

188 SUSAN STEBBING

4.2 Stebbing's Project after the Second World War

Despite the fact that Stebbing's project for clear thinking and its applications in life remained in shadow after her death, it was not totally alien to analytic philosophy in England after the Second World War. To start with, the problem of teaching in clear thinking or in "thinking straight" with the help (or under the support) of formal logic was also central to Gilbert Ryle. To be sure, Ryle was not a proponent of "logical interventionism." He simply maintained that routine training in the field of formal logic disciplines thought so that after we had completed it, we could tackle practical problems better. In a similar manner, exercises in geometry help the cartographer, the drill of the soldier later helps him in battle, etc. Training helps in improving certain skills that are later put into practice (Milkov 2003, p. 143).

Apparently, for both Stebbing and Ryle, training in formal logic can help to improve our skills in thinking, which will be advantageous for us when we face problems of public life. In other words, there is a bridge between formal logic and attempts to solve practical problems.

Also Antony Flew, a former student of Gilbert Ryle and core member of the ordinary language philosophy group (Flew 1951–53, 1956), worked on a program for developing clear thinking. A product of these efforts was his book *Thinking About Thinking* (1975)[13] in which he specifically referred to Susan Stebbing's *Thinking to Some Purpose* (1939) as one of his forerunners in this realm. Interestingly enough, Flew also referred to two papers of J. L. Austin as helpful in forming clear thinking, "Other Minds" and "A Plea for Excuses." In this way, he confirmed our claim that Stebbing's program for clear thinking was just a powerful expression of a tendency that was inherent in analytic philosophy as it developed in England in the first sixty years of the twentieth century. Austin, in particular, fought abstract concepts in philosophy which are the results of "bad ideology" and which support overhasty generalizations. Typical examples are concepts such as "sense-data," dichotomies such as between "true" and "false" or between "truth" and "illusion," and parasitic words, such as "directly," that are related to the perception of objects of experience.

Another writer of this period, who referred to Stebbing's *Thinking to Some Purpose*, was the Oxford philosopher of education John Wilson. His book *Thinking with Concepts* (1963) was a manual for clear thinking that followed

---

[13] In later editions the book was also published under the title *How to Think Strait* (1977).

ideas of the Oxford ordinary language philosophy by way of conducting careful conceptual analysis. Specifically, Wilson pleaded for learning how to deal with concepts—it is not an easy task. In the last reckoning, "learning to deal with concepts is essentially a process of becoming more self-conscious in relation to one's normal environment" (p. 15).[14]

5 Stebbing's Project and Late Analytic Philosophy

As already seen (in § 2.2, above), Stebbing roughly outlined two conceptions of analytic philosophy around 1933 (Milkov 2020, pp. 193 ff.). On the one hand, Moore and Russell (before 1912) stuck to one language while, on the other, the "middle Russell" (after 1912) and Carnap oriented themselves to constructing many languages that were intertranslatable *salva veritate*. In the lines above, we have shown that Stebbing with her interest in public discussions adopted exactly the first type of analytic philosophy.

As a matter of fact, under the decisive influence of Carnap and Quine, the second conception of analytic philosophy dominated the scene after the Second World War in North America. Above all, it concentrated its attention on the "ice slopes" of formal logic (Reisch 2005), turning its back to problems of public significance. As a result, the practice of directly pursuing clear thinking was virtually expelled from the curriculum of analytic philosophy.

An important factor in this development was the Cold War. Evolving in its shadow, late analytic philosophy progressed into a new form of scholasticism under the banner of strict professionalism. At the end of the day, this development ensured the cultural isolation of philosophy. One of its implications is that today some historians of analytic philosophy, Scott Soames and Michael Potter among them, define it as an exclusive study of logical forms (§ 1, above).

If compared to this development, prominent in analytic philosophy for more than seventy years now, Susan Stebbing's short but distinguished career as a philosopher demonstrated that early analytic philosophy, the Cambridge school of analysis in particular, was not simply formal philosophy. It also had the power to orient us in problems of public life.

---

[14] In a similar vein, Peter Strawson defined the ordinary language philosophy as an "attempt to describe the complex patterns of logical behavior which the concepts of daily life exhibit" (1967, p. 313).

190 SUSAN STEBBING

6 Epilogue

To reveal, revive, and to further explore the venue of analytic philosophy outlined by Stebbing is a challenging task today, in the era of "fake news," "alternative facts," and disparagement of the truth. The new information revolution of the 2010s, which made social networks increasingly prominent, reinforced the attention to the problem of discriminating "true" from "fake" facts (Milkov 2022). Stebbing's writings on public, political, and scientific matters tried to achieve exactly this: to ensure that public and political discourses refer to confirmed facts that are considered without distortions caused by unbridled emotions, false ideals, or downright illusions.

One can consider the fight against the democratic world's "political establishment" that has been going on for the last fifteen years, for greater "authenticity" in politics, to be in profound disagreement with Stebbing's project. It facilitated the rise of such figures in politics as Vladimir Putin and Jair Bolsonaro. The fact that the West today refers in its fight against illiberalism, authoritarianism, and populism to the "intrinsic values" of the Western liberal democracies is full of suggestion. Values in this sense are nothing but the very "political ideals" that Stebbing extensively discussed. She fought to formulate the "right" ones with boundless energy.

References

Beaney, Michael, and Siobhan Chapman. 2021. "Susan Stebbing." *The Stanford Encyclopedia of Philosophy*, Edward N. Zalta (ed.), https://plato.stanford.edu/archives/sum2021/entries/stebbing/.

Bradley, Francis Herbert. 1893. *Appearance and Reality: A Metaphysical Essay*, London: George Allen & Unwin.

Chapman, Siobhan. 2013. *Susan Stebbing and the Language of Common Sense*. London: Palgrave Macmillan.

Coates, John. 1996. *The Claims of Common Sense: Moore, Wittgenstein, Keynes and the Social Science*. Cambridge: Cambridge University Press.

Cohen, Jonathan. 1986. *The Dialogue of Reason: An Analysis of Analytical Philosophy*. Oxford: Oxford University Press.

Douglas, Alexander, and Jonathan. Nassim. 2021. "Susan Stebbinbg's Logical Interventionism." *History of Philosophy and Logic* 42 (2): 101–117.

Flew, Antony. 1951–53. *Logic and Language*, 2 vols. Oxford: Basil Blackwell.

Flew, Antony. 1956. *Essays in Conceptual Analysis*. London: Macmillan.

Flew, Antony. 1975. *Thinking About Thinking, or, Do I Sincerely Want to Be Right?* London: Fontana; reprinted under the title *Thinking Strait*. Buffalo, NY: Prometheus Books, 1977.

Føllesdal, Dagfinn. 1997. "Analytic Philosophy: What Is It and Why Should One Engage in It" In H.-J. Glock, ed., 193–208. *The Rise of Analytic Philosophy*. Oxford: Blackwell.

Glock, Hans-Johann. 2008. *What Is Analytic Philosophy?* Cambridge: Cambridge University Press.

Grayling, Anthony. 2000. "A Booting for Bertie." *The Guardian* (London) October 28. https://www.theguardian.com/books/2000/oct/28/biography.philosophy.

Hager, Paul. 2001. "Russell's Conception of Critical Thinking: Its Scope and Limits." *Inquiry* 20 (2): 11–19.

Hare, William. 2001. "Bertrand Russell on Critical Thinking." *Journal of Thought* 36 (1): 7–16.

Keynes, J. M. 1972. "Two Memoires." In *The Collected Writings of John Maynard Keynes*, 16 vols. London: Macmillan, vol. 10.

Levy, Paul. 1979. *G. E. Moore*. London: Weidenfeld and Nicolson.

Lotze, Hermann. 1885. *Microcosmus: An Essay Concerning Man and His Relation to the World*. 2 vols. Elizabeth Hamilton and Constance Jones, trans. Edinburgh: T. and T. Clark.

Malcolm, Norman. 1972. *Ludwig Wittgenstein. A Memoir*. Oxford: Oxford University Press.

Milkov, Nikolay. 1992. *Kaleidoscopic Mind: An Essay in Post-Wittgensteinian Philosophy*. Amsterdam–Atlanta, GA: Rodopi.

Milkov, Nikolay. 2003. *A Hundred Years of English Philosophy*. Dordrecht: Kluwer.

Milkov, Nikolay. 2019. "John Wisdom." *Internet Encyclopedia of Philosophy* [accessed January 15, 2023]. https://www.iep.utm.edu/wisdom/.

Milkov, Nikolay. 2020. *Early Analytic Philosophy and the German Philosophical Tradition*. London: Bloomsbury Academic.

Milkov, Nikolay. 2022. "The Brave New World: The Illiberal Turn of 2014–2016, Its Causes and Its Implications." In M. Marinov et al., eds., 37–43, *Transformations and Challenges in the Global World*. Newcastle upon Tyne: Cambridge Scholars Publishing.

Milkov, Nikolay. 2023. *Hermann Lotze's Influence on the Twentieth Century Philosophy*. Berlin: de Gruyter.

Monk, Ray. 1990. *Ludwig Wittgenstein: The Duty of Genius*, 2nd ed. London: Vintage Books.

Monk, Ray. 2000. *Bertrand Russell*, vol. 2, *The Ghost of Madness*. London: Jonathan Cape.

Olson, Dustin, and Nicholas Griffin. 2019. "Russell's Bridge." In R. Wahl, ed., 286–311, *The Bloomsbury Companion to Bertrand Russell*. London: Bloomsbury.

Pickel, Bryan. 2022. "Susan Stebbing's Intellectualism." *Journal of the History of Analytical Philosophy* 10 (4): 10.4-Pickel (3).pdf.

Potter, Michael. 2020. *The Rise of Analytic Philosophy, 1879–1930*. London: Routledge.

Priestley, J. B. 1970. *The Edwardians*. London: Heinemann.

Rawls, John. 1971. *Theory of Justice*. Cambridge, MA: Harvard University Press.

Reisch, George. 2005. *How the Cold War Transformed Philosophy of Science: To the Icy Slopes of Logic*. Cambridge: Cambridge University Press.

Rhees, Rush, ed. 1981. *Ludwig Wittgenstein: Personal Recollections*. Oxford: Basil Blackwell.

Russell, Bertrand. 1912. *The Problems of Philosophy*, 2nd ed. London, T. Butterworth, 1932.

Russell, Bertrand. 1921. *The Analysis of Mind*. London: Georg Allen.

Russell, Bertrand. 1925. *The ABC of Relativity*. New York: Harper and Brothers.

Russell, Bertrand. 1942. *How to Become a Philosopher (The Art of Rational Conjecture)*. "How-To" Series 7. Girard, KS: Haldeman-Julius Publications.

Russell, Bertrand. 1946. "Philosophy for Laymen," In *Unpopular Essays*. New York: Simon and Schuster, 1950, 21–33.

Russell, Bertrand. 1948. *Human Knowledge, Its Scope and Limits*. London: Allen and Unwin.

Russell, Bertrand. 1953. "The Spirit of Inquiry" In George Slater, ed., 432–440. *The Collected Papers of Bertrand Russell*, vol. 11, London: Routledge.

Russell, Bertrand. 1956. *Portraits from Memory*. New York: Simon and Schuster.

Russell, Bertrand. 1959. *My Philosophical Development*. London: Allen and Unwin.

Schwerin, Alan. 2019. "Did Russell Experience an Epiphany in 1911?" *Principia: An International Journal of Epistemology* 23(1): 1–17.

Soames, Scott. 2014–17. *Analytic Tradition in Philosophy*, 2 vols. Princeton: Princeton University Press.

Stebbing, Susan. 1914. *Pragmatism and French Voluntarism*. Cambridge: Cambridge University Press.

192 SUSAN STEBBING

Stebbing, Susan. 1915. "A Reply to Some Charges against Logic." *Science Progress* 10: 406–412.

Stebbing, Susan. 1925. "Universals and Prof. Whitehead's Theory of Objects." *Proceedings of the Aristotelian Society* 25: 305–330.

Stebbing, Susan. 1932. "The Method of Analysis in Metaphysics." *Proceedings of the Aristotelian Society* 33: 65–94.

Stebbing, Susan. 1933. "Logical Positivism and Analysis." *Proceedings of the British Academy* 19: 53–87.

Stebbing, Susan. 1934. *Logic in Practice*. London: Methuen.

Stebbing, Susan. 1936. "Thinking." In C. Day Lewis and L. Susan Stebbing, eds., 14–29, *Imagination and Thinking*. London: British Institute of Adult Education.

Stebbing, Susan. 1937. *Philosophy and the Physicists*, 2nd ed. Harmondsworth: Penguin, 1943.

Stebbing, Susan. 1939. *Thinking to Some Purpose*, 2nd ed. Harmondsworth: Penguin. Harmondsworth: Pelican Books, 1941.

Stebbing, Susan. 1939a. "Ethics and Materialism." *Ethics* 50: 35–44.

Stebbing, Susan. 1939b. "Philosophers and Politics." *Scrutiny* 8: 156–163.

Stebbing, Susan. 1941. *Ideals and Illusions*. London: Watts.

Stebbing, Susan. 1942. "Moore's Influence." In P. Schilpp, ed., 515–532, *The Philosophy of G. E. Moore*. La Salle, IL: Open Court.

Stebbing, S. 1943. *A Modern Elementary Logic*. London: Methuen.

Stebbing, S. 1944. *Men and Moral Principles*. Oxford: Oxford University Press.

Strawson, Peter. 1967. "Analysis, Science and Metaphysics." In R. Rorty, ed., 312–320, *The Linguistic Turn*. Chicago: University of Chicago Press.

West, Peter. 2022. "Introduction." In Susan Stebbing, *Thinking to Some Purpose*. London: Routledge, xv–xxviii.

Wilson, John. 1963. *Thinking with Concepts*. Cambridge: Cambridge University Press.

Wittgenstein, Ludwig. 1922. *Tractatus logico-philosophicus*. F. Ramsey, trans. London: Kegan Paul.

Woolf, Leonard. 1960. *Sowing*. New York: Harcourt.

Susan Stebbing and the Politics of Symbolic Logic

David E. Dunning

1 Introduction

L. Susan Stebbing is increasingly recognized as a central figure in the history of early analytic philosophy in Britain. In 1933 she became the first woman to hold a chair in Philosophy in the United Kingdom, being appointed Professor of Philosophy at Bedford College of the University of London. She helped to found the journal *Analysis* and worked to bring British analytic philosophy into productive conversation with the Vienna Circle. These major contributions to the social and professional infrastructure of analytic philosophy complemented a formidable career as an author first and foremost. As recognition of her importance has recently been growing, two features of her own work have rightly been emphasized.

First, there is a growing and now fairly widespread appreciation of the pivotal role she played in making symbolic logic accessible to an undergraduate audience. Her 1930 *Modern Introduction to Logic* (Stebbing 1942), as Michael Beaney has written, "might be regarded as the first textbook of analytic philosophy" (2013, 43). Second, we see her strong commitment to the everyday importance of clear, logical thinking in a modern democracy. In her best-known work, 1939's popular *Thinking to Some Purpose*, Stebbing stated at the outset, "I am convinced of the urgent need for a democratic people to think clearly without the distortions due to unconscious bias and unrecognized ignorance.... It is the aim of this book to make a small effort in this direction" (1939, 5). In an age when democracy's future seemed precarious, philosophy could not be confined to the academy: logic had an indispensable role to play in public life. This chapter aims to illuminate the precise relationship between these two elements—modern mathematical logic and democratic politics—in her thought.

David E. Dunning, *Susan Stebbing and the Politics of Symbolic Logic* In: *Susan Stebbing*. Edited by: Annalisa Coliva and Louis Doulas, Oxford University Press. © Oxford University Press 2025. DOI: 10.1093/9780197682371.003.0009

194 SUSAN STEBBING

As her biographer Siobhan Chapman has argued, Stebbing placed equal weight on formal and everyday realms of thought and insisted that this integrated vision of logic was urgently relevant to real life. Chapman points out that these aspects of Stebbing's thought undermine portrayals of idealization and ordinary language as opposed ways of doing philosophy in the formative decades of the analytic tradition (2013, 3–7). In Stebbing we find evidence of, in Chapman's words, "an earlier start and a greater continuity throughout analytic philosophy than has previously been envisaged for the serious scrutiny of everyday linguistic usage" (2013, 4).

But how exactly did Stebbing bring the formal and the everyday together in her philosophy, and in what sense did she construe logic as political? Is symbolic logic political in Stebbing's conception only insofar as it is a potential tool to help philosophers understand the informal reasoning that citizens actually deploy in their political lives? Or did she embrace a more thoroughgoing political conception of symbolic logic's worth? Does the mathematical approach to logic, in her rendering, itself have a politics? I propose to read Stebbing as a political thinker, not only in her turn to everyday logic in public life but also in her presentation of symbolic logic. I will proceed by interpreting her formal and informal investigations together, considering first the mathematical exposition in the *Modern Introduction* and then turning to the more overtly political arguments of *Thinking to Some Purpose*. As Alexander X. Douglas and Jonathan Nassim have observed, it is not obvious how to reconcile Stebbing's emphasis on the formal with her endorsement of expert interventions in informal reasoning. They propose that while a logical interventionism based on the logician's expertise in formalizing arguments (which Stebbing at times seems to endorse) would be unpromising, Stebbing's writing also points toward a more modest "dialogical interventionism" in which the logician is a collaborator rather than an umpire (2021; see especially 113–116). Concurring with their reading of Stebbing as modest interlocutor rather than formalizing arbiter, I suggest that her engagement with the formal—and especially her pedagogical presentation of formal logic—is nonetheless political as it fits in a larger social and dialogic vision.

My answer to the questions raised above will revolve around Stebbing's portrayal of two divisions of labor: one among varieties of language or symbolism, and one among people. She conveys this vision for logic in human society in the *Modern Introduction* and makes its political stakes explicit in *Thinking to Some Purpose*. These divisions of labor indeed had a politics. Stebbing did not politicize mathematical logic in the straightforward strong

POLITICS OF SYMBOLIC LOGIC   195

sense of suggesting that the content of mathematical logic aligns with a partisan viewpoint or agenda. Rather, I suggest that she presented mathematical logic first as a form of expertise and second that she understood expertise as a political phenomenon insofar as it governs social arrangements of scientific authority. Mathematical logic was to be a *professional* science, its research necessarily distinct from, but continuous with, its contributions to the public sphere, which Stebbing considered an urgent priority. The development of advanced mathematical logic by a subset of society entailed differentiation between a professional sphere and the general public; logic would be a body of knowledge and skill that people would learn to different degrees and to different ends. This social gradient of citizens who engage with logic at varying levels, I argue, mirrored in Stebbing's presentation a practical gradient of linguistic systems that provide varying balances of flexibility and precision. The formal symbolism of the professional and the prose of the general reader existed on an analogous—and analogously political—spectrum from elite authority to democratic accessibility.

2 Logical Pedagogy: Two Divisions of Labor

Already in her *Modern Introduction to Logic*, Stebbing insisted on the unity of formal and informal reasoning. She wrote that "the principles of symbolic logic are not peculiar to a special kind of study but are principles exemplified in everyday reflective thinking no less than in mathematical deductions" (1942, xii). Against this backdrop, Stebbing had then to motivate a textbook that would present what was still a novel area of study, much of it sure to strike her undergraduate audience as far more mathematical than the stuff of everyday thinking. She pursued this motivation by depicting two divisions of labor: one among the linguistic systems appropriate to certain tasks, the other among people needing different things from logic.

The first division of labor, among varieties of symbolism, is quite explicit. Stebbing emphasized from the start that ordinary language is an imprecise instrument, and that this is not a fault; it must be flexible to the point of vagueness to serve its purpose well. She explained early on, "It is not a matter of regret that in ordinary language all words have some degree of vagueness. Were this not the case ordinary conversation would be impossible" (1942, 19). She returned to this theme at greater length when she arrived at a consideration of formal symbolism:

196   SUSAN STEBBING

> Since language [here a footnote clarifies that she means ordinary language in this chapter] is developed under the pressure of man's practical needs, and is primarily the means of expressing the emotional side of his nature, it is clear, first, that language must be employed to express an immense variety of different experiences; secondly, that the same language-forms must sometimes be used to express what is in fact different; thirdly, that language is ill-adapted to express what is relatively abstract and logically simple. (1942, 116)

By evoking development and adaptation, she points toward a historical understanding of language: it is something that has developed to meet specific needs: practical ones, and emotional ones too. Language has not evolved under any pressure from the esoteric needs of the logician. The result is an inverse relationship between logical and linguistic complexity: "It is the *logical simplicity* of the notions involved [in algebra] that makes their expression in language so cumbersome. For the purposes of logic, language is insufficiently analytic. Moreover, language only abstracts to the degree in which what is abstract interests the plain man" (1942, 117). Language is better suited to saying the sorts of things people ordinarily need to say rather than to speaking with the abstraction of algebra.

Unfortunately (if not surprisingly for a British philosopher in this period), Stebbing also uncritically invokes a framework of primitive versus civilized languages. Her use of these notions is muddled: she claims primitive languages lack abstraction, then immediately undermines that supposed criteria of civilization by acknowledging that so-called civilized languages employ widely varying degrees of abstraction—for example, Latin abstracts relatively little (1942, 118). This uncharacteristic logical lapse is a disappointing illustration of just how unexamined assumptions about so-called primitive and civilized cultures were in Stebbing's intellectual world.

Normative sorting aside, the overarching point is that *no* ordinary languages anywhere are sufficiently abstract for the needs of logic, nor should they be. For logic we need symbols. But this should not be seen as a rupture with all previously existing modes of expression. Stebbing stresses continuity: "The invention and development of the special symbolism found necessary for the purposes of logical technique is merely carrying to the utmost degree of analysis of thought and precision of expression that recognition of distinctions which is present to some extent in all language" (1942, 119). But continuity does not preclude specialized tasks: "Logical symbolism

POLITICS OF SYMBOLIC LOGIC   197

has, then, two important functions to perform. It economizes thought and thus makes possible the development of complicated inferences. Secondly, by means of appropriate symbols, form can be revealed; hence, generality can be attained" (1942, 121). So a clear division of labor obtains between logical symbolism and ordinary language. Language is powerful in all sorts of everyday situations because it is flexible; logical notation is powerful in a much narrower context due to its inferential economy and its formality.

This outlook is familiar from other mathematical logicians. Gottlob Frege, for instance, compared his Begriffsschrift notation to a microscope—far less versatile than a human eye, but far more powerful when applied to its own specific purposes (1964, v). Alfred North Whitehead and Bertrand Russell explained in *Principia Mathematica* that their symbolism was intended to meet a standard of rigor inappropriate even to ordinary academic mathematics, which could rely on ordinary mathematical notation (1910–1913, vol. I, 2–3). Stebbing's take is not new here; but, significantly, she foregrounds that picture of a division of expressive labor among linguistic systems *in a textbook*. She wanted British undergraduates to understand that the unfamiliar notations of modern logic serve an important purpose. They are not a rejection of ordinary language in its proper place but rather an effort to apply specialized tools to specialized problems.

This pedagogical context is what reveals the second division of labor, which governs what sorts of logic are needed by different sorts of people. Stebbing positions her textbook with respect to British university education in such a way as to characterize logic as a science, and hence a specialized expertise—one that every educated person should appreciate, while relatively few have any reason to attain it themselves.

Stebbing's *Modern Introduction to Logic* opens with a pedagogical dilemma. Since the 1840s, when the English mathematician George Boole proposed to write logical propositions with algebraic notation, the study of formal logic had undergone rapid changes. Stebbing, like many logicians in 1930, held up Whitehead and Russell's *Principia Mathematica* as the paragon of this movement and endorsed the view expressed in various ways by both of those authors that the late nineteenth-century's mathematical turn easily eclipsed the preceding millennia of logical study. "During the last half-century," she wrote, "greater advances have been made than in the whole of the preceding period from the time of Aristotle. But the introductory text-books now being used in British Universities show no trace of these developments" (1942, ix). So she brings a specifically pedagogical focus to

198 SUSAN STEBBING

the triumphant attitude common among mathematically inclined logicians at the time. Logic education had to be brought up to speed in light of mathematical logic.

Stebbing, however, was not a simplistic booster of novelty. She did endorse the impulse to distance mathematical logic from what came before, even taking as an epigraph Alfred North Whitehead's statement, "A Science which hesitates to forget its founders is lost. To this hesitation I ascribe the barrenness of logic." And yet, she promptly rejected such a forgetting! Instead, she characterized the relationship between traditional and mathematical logic as follows:

> It might be supposed that the science of logic thus conceived [i.e., mathematical logic] has nothing in common with Aristotle's conception of logic. But that would be a mistake. There are considerable grounds for supposing that, in recognizing that the ideal of logic is the exhibition of form, the mathematical logicians are carrying on the work which Aristotle himself initiated. . . . [T]hroughout the book emphasis is laid upon the continuity of some of Aristotle's doctrines with those of the mathematical logicians. (1942, xi)

Unlike Whitehead, Stebbing did not want to forget the figure long considered logic's founder. She resolutely affirmed the idea of progress in logic that the Whitehead quotation invoked. But for Stebbing, surpassing founders did not require losing them across imagined discontinuities.

Thus, she struck a delicate balance between traditional and mathematical logic. She defended that balance in two ways: it reflected, on the one hand, a principled commitment to the continuity she argued obtained between the logic of Aristotle and that of *Principia Mathematica*. But, on the other hand, she grounded her balancing act in the pragmatic needs of students, displaying constant awareness that what the average undergraduate needed from logic was different from what a philosopher or mathematician needed.

This difference was appropriate; its current configuration was not. While Stebbing approved of a foundation in traditional logic, she deemed the more technical details of syllogistic logic "nothing but elaborate trivialities" (1942, xii). If for the time being, however, universities required their students to master those trivialities, it would hardly serve learners well to write a textbook for a utopian logic course that did not yet exist. Stebbing wrote that

POLITICS OF SYMBOLIC LOGIC   199

she aimed "to reduce consideration of these technicalities to the minimum required to enable a student to pass elementary examinations in logic" (1942, xii). In this light her textbook became something of a stopgap:

> It is to be hoped that the time is not far distant when University examiners will no longer require proficiency in these technical dodges, but will seek to test the student's grasp of logical principles. But that time has not yet arrived. Its date must doubtless be postponed until there are sufficient textbooks written from a more modern point of view. It is difficult to break through the vicious circle constituted by the dependence of examiners upon the text-books, and by the dependence of the text-book upon the requirements of University examinations. (1942, xii)

In a sense, then, the perspective Stebbing adopted in the *Modern Introduction* was pragmatically and self-consciously only halfway modern—as modern as possible given the constraints of the exams her student readers would need to pass.[1] But alongside her continuous interpretation of the history of logic, the circle appears a degree less vicious. What traditional technicalities Stebbing felt obliged to include, she hoped future textbooks could dispense with. But the syllogism itself, along with a general approach informed by Aristotle and focused on ordinary reasoning, *deserved* sustained commitment. It would be refined rather than undermined by mathematical innovations. Those innovations did not, in most chapters, need to be an explicit concern: she wrote:

> It has not been my intention to take the student very far into mathematical logic, but only to enable him to realize that the principles of symbolic logic are not peculiar to a special kind of study but are principles exemplified in everyday reflective thinking no less than in mathematical deductions. I have not sought to write an *introduction to symbolic logic*; my purpose has been to emphasize the connexion between Aristotelian logic and symbolic logic, thus to write a text-book which will include as little as possible that the student has subsequently to unlearn, or for the teaching of which the modern logician feels it necessary to apologize. (1942, xii–xiii)

---

[1] On the conservatism of pedagogy as a general phenomenon in the history of science, see (Warwick 2003, e.g., 358).

200 SUSAN STEBBING

Rather than establishing mathematical methods as the new core of an introductory curriculum in the present, Stebbing endorsed a fairly traditional logic *provided it be understood as continuous with and informed by symbolic techniques.* Her view highlights the temporality of progress and displays comfort with the difference between introductory and expert views of the subject, provided that the introductory view doesn't undermine or contradict the cutting edge.

Stebbing's vision for a university course in logic was that it should be informed by mathematical logic, that it should convey to students that mathematical logic is the culminating and cutting edge of the Aristotelian foundation they learn in their introductory course. She heaped scorn on the degree of technicality demanded by current exams in their engagement with the syllogism but not on the orientation toward everyday reasoning conducted largely in prose. Mathematical symbolism, used sparingly, sheds additional light on such reasoning. If an introductory course based on Stebbing's book was to impart one thing, it was a respect for this illumination, not necessarily the formal literacy to engage with it in much detail. This vision of what it would mean to bring mathematical logic to university education came nowhere near suggesting that *Principia Mathematica* become required reading for all educated Britons. Rather, Stebbing offered an implicit model of hierarchical expertise: in this model, as with other disciplines, there is much more to formal logic than most people will learn, but the highest heights are continuous with the basics that belong to a general education.

3 Between Normativity and Expertise

If we expected to find in the *Modern Introduction* anticipations of Stebbing's later efforts to offer normative guidance to the general public, the book's conclusions might come as a surprise. In one of the closing chapters, she addresses the question of whether logic is a normative science. No, she insists. It is not.

Rather she paints a nuanced picture of logic's relationship to normativity. The first chapter had opened with a broad conception of logic, stating that "Logic, in the most usual and widest sense of the word, is concerned with reflective thinking" (1942, 1). And now she reinforces this, remarking, "The purpose of logical thinking is to reach conclusions" (1942, 465). But after considering the several ways people believe things—because they always

POLITICS OF SYMBOLIC LOGIC   201

have, because authority tells them to, because of self-evidence, persuasion, or conviction—she argues that "the art of thinking must not be confused with logic" (1942, 473). She elaborates:

> A normative science, as the name suggests, is concerned with norms, or standards. In so far as logic is concerned with the criticism of modes of thinking it has a normative aspect. . . . But this normative aspect is, as it were, a by-product. We do not study logic in order to establish norms by reference to which the validity of reasoning may be tested. The discovery of norms of thinking—when, indeed, they are discovered—results from the fact that valid thinking is formal and that logic is the science of possible forms. (1942, 474)

Logic, in this view, is not the science of deductions performed by a deducing subject but rather the forms of structural relationships between facts. Normativity, then, is not the essence of logic. But even so, an understanding of the formal structures that obtain between facts can come in handy when one is trying to deduce what conclusions might follow from known premises. And so Stebbing acknowledges, "Nevertheless, this is the aspect that is important from the point of view of reflective thinking, and which makes the study of logic useful even for journalists and politicians" (1942, 474). "Certainly we are less likely to be misled by erroneous reasoning," she writes, "if we have clear ideas with regard to the nature of proof and the forms of our arguments" (1942, 474). Logic is not intrinsically normative, but it has the capacity to play a regulatory role.

But here there does not appear to be anything particularly normative about logic compared with any other specialized expertise. Certainly expert knowledge of logic offers no automatic immunity to fallacies or other normative failings. "Knowledge of logical form," she quips, "no more suffices to make men good reasoners than knowledge of prosodical form suffices to make them good poets" (1942, 475). The analogy warns against overrating the value of a knowledge of forms, but it also points to the modest but real usefulness of such knowledge. A knowledge of prosodical form, while obviously insufficient on its own, is hardly irrelevant to an aspiring author of sonnets. Logic is the science of pure forms, not of individual reasoning. But it can and should inform an evaluation of specific forms of reasoning—perhaps as physics might inform the evaluation of a plan for a bridge. This does not mean physics is civil engineering.

202 SUSAN STEBBING

The political vision of logic here is subtle rather than immediate. The overriding theme is that logic is a science. But this designation has implications for the social organization of logical knowledge: all educated Britons should understand what mathematical logic is and why it's valuable, but not very many actually need to study it beyond a survey level. Just as different linguistic systems are appropriate to different kinds of expression and inquiry, different levels of engagement with logic are appropriate for different people. These divisions of labor may not be overtly politicized, but they do assume an arrangement of who does what, who knows what, and such arrangements are never apolitical. By asserting that mathematical logic belongs to its own domain of scientific expertise, Stebbing envisions a specific gradient of roles logic can play in people's lives.

4 Finding Politics, Finding *Purpose*

Nine years later the world looked rather different. The 1930s had pushed Stebbing toward much more direct engagement with the possible political implications of logic. As her reputation grew, the BBC asked her to deliver a series of twelve talks on the topic of thinking. She prepared to do so, but illness ultimately prevented her. Instead, she transformed her plans for the talks into a book published by Penguin in 1939, titled *Thinking to Some Purpose*.

In this work Stebbing explicitly embedded reason in the vicissitudes of human culture. In practice there simply was no such thing as idealized abstract thought, she insisted: "It is, we need to remember, persons who think, not purely rational spirits" (1939, 21). Faced with the alarming, growing precarity of democracy, she recognized the impurely rational thinking of real persons to be extremely consequential. Stebbing became committed to the idea that professional philosophy should speak to wider society, should help people confront the catastrophes of the age head-on.

Thinking to Some Purpose did not make an immediate splash with critics but rather grew into a strong seller. Other than a short, favorable notice that appeared in the *Times Literary Supplement*, the book received few reviews upon publication, falling through the cracks as a work too popular to be reviewed in academic journals but apparently too scholarly for many general periodicals. Despite this scantness of publicity, it became a commercial success both at home and in the United States. It quickly achieved considerable

POLITICS OF SYMBOLIC LOGIC   203

name recognition and it went through a handful of reprintings and reissues over the coming decades.[2]

Where the *Modern Introduction* straightforwardly occupied the genre of logic textbook, *Thinking to Some Purpose* approached logic from a different angle, opening with a prologue titled "Are the English Illogical?" The idea that the English are illogical, Stebbing remarked, is not only "prevalent among foreigners" but also, perversely, *celebrated* by English politicians (1939, 9). She quoted several examples, including one in which conservative statesman Stanley Baldwin explained that politicians must be "more interested in persuasion than in proof" for political audiences are "only imperfectly prepared to follow a close argument." Stebbing—with some irony, as she would go on to subject Baldwin to considerable incisive criticism—declared, "I am writing this book partly because I am in considerable agreement with this statement" (1939, 11). She acknowledged that any politician who hopes to accomplish something required an electoral victory, and "the victory of the party at the polls depends upon the votes of electors who are beset by hopes and fears and who have never been trained to think clearly" (1939, 11). The electorate was not equipped to apply logic to political choices.

But, of course, Stebbing could not condone Baldwin's complacent attitude toward this deficiency. She continued:

> This grim practical necessity is, however, no matter for congratulation. If the maintenance of democratic institutions is worth while, then the citizens of a democratic country must record their votes only after due deliberation. But "due deliberation" involves instruction with regard to the facts, ability to assess the evidence provided by such instruction and, further, the ability to discount, as far as may be, the effects of prejudice and to evade the distortion produced by unwarrantable fears and by unrealizable hopes. In other words, the citizens must be able to think relevantly, that is, to think to some purpose. Thus, to think is difficult. Accordingly, it is not surprising, however saddening it may be, that many of our statesmen do not trust the citizens to think, but rely instead upon the arts of persuasion. (1939, 11)

These practical concerns bring her to a new definition of thinking logically: "To think logically is to think relevantly to the purpose that initiated the thinking; all effective thinking is directed to an end" (1939, 11). Notice

---

[2] For a useful account of the book's reception, see (Chapman 2013, 138–140).

204   SUSAN STEBBING

the gap between this notion of what it is "to think logically" and "the ideal of logic" as "indistinguishable from pure mathematics" advocated in the Modern Introduction (1942, xi). Whereas logic was a theoretical science aiming to exhibit pure forms, thinking logically is defined in direct reference to an end—a specific human being's goal. If logic theorizes the formal relationships among propositions, to think logically is to use these formal relationships to evaluate the relevance of various propositions to one's current purpose.

5 What Logic Can and Cannot Do

Thinking to Some Purpose paints a fairly pessimistic picture of the status quo and Stebbing is far from sanguine about what is needed. She is under no illusion that all of Britain will just learn to think clearly and everything will be fine. "There are so many ways of being slipshod in our thinking," she writes in a chapter on fallacies, "that it would be impossible for us to attempt to examine them all" (1939, 122). The best she can do, as she sees it, is to shed light on as many of the largest obstacles to clear thinking as she can. Nor do these too numerous logical fallacies exhaust the list of ways we go astray. Other chapters treat prejudice and cherished beliefs, emotionally charged and question-begging language, or propaganda and convenient oversimplifications of complex situations.

Stebbing emphasizes that fallacies are not necessarily dishonest, nor are they limited to the context of disputes. People speaking in mutual agreement can fall into fallacies together, as can people thinking individually. "You and I, engaged in solitary meditation, have great need to be on our guard against drawing a conclusion that does not follow from our premises" (1939, 123). She stresses the distinction between the equally crucial matters of starting with true premises and drawing valid conclusions from them. "It is not enough to be honest; we need also to be intelligent; it is not even enough to be intelligent; we need also to be well informed" (1939, 123). Nobody ever said democracy was undemanding.

As discussed above, she sees logic as capable of offering moderate normative guidance, but Stebbing ridicules the idea that logic is the art of thinking—full stop. Logic does not enable us to distinguish truth from falsehood. "It is not from studying logic that we can find out ... whether there are any unicorns," she reminds the reader (1939, 124). Logic speaks only to the question of when conclusions follow from premises. Its role is thus tightly circumscribed, equipping one (at best) to more often catch flawed reasoning before it leads one too far astray:

> Some practice in detecting these fallacious modes of reasoning may enable us the more easily to notice them when we are not actively engaged in fallacy hunting. A knowledge of the formal conditions of valid arguments thus has its uses, but it would be a profound mistake to conclude that a knowledge of these conditions alone would suffice to guard us from error. (1939, 124–125).

But this is just another division of labor, clarifying precisely what cognitive role logic is to play alongside other aspects of inquiry. There's a modesty to such circumscription, which moderates the potential arrogance of the picture of logical expertise I have described. Stebbing does not advance an inflated view of the logician's importance. But she does insist it is important.

By 1939, Stebbing had shifted her attention toward the political urgency of purposeful thinking, but she did not fundamentally change her view of logic's place in society. Mathematical logic was always, in her account, a specialized expertise, conducted in a specialized symbolism—continuous with everyday thinking but differentiated by its scientific purpose. It is one piece of a complicated and communal picture of how thinking works: a society that can arrive at sound conclusions about the problems it faces will need a reliable apparatus for informing people; they will need to be trained in ordinary sound reasoning; they will need to be honest. And this training in sound reasoning is not a matter of bringing symbolic formalism to the masses but rather of symbolic formalism undergirding a properly scientific account of the valid forms of argument that, Stebbing believed, everyone could learn to appreciate.

6 Conclusion: Logic as a Condition of Freedom

Logic was coming to be powerfully illuminated by mathematical methods at the same time as it was needed more desperately than ever in the practice of modern democracy. On this account, the practice and pedagogy of mathematical logic would seem to be deeply political activities. As the cutting edge of research into possible forms, symbolic logic was the theoretical apex of

206   SUSAN STEBBING

the scientific expertise best equipped to offer a modest degree of normative guidance on the identification of facts relevant to a given purpose. Stebbing preserved the distance between, on the one hand, the specific inquiries of advanced mathematical logic and, on the other, the clear thinking ideally demanded of every citizen in a democracy. But they were two ends of a coherent spectrum, a spectrum of expertise in a specific scientific discipline. She hoped to convince British society to cultivate that full spectrum. She called on citizens to recognize what logic is and isn't. From such a recognition would hopefully follow societal support for the coterie of logicians plumbing new depths of abstraction. From their ongoing work would hopefully follow not only esoteric research but also increased engagement with a public in desperate need of education and empowerment in the art of clear thinking—an art distinct from logic but intimately related to it.

It was a tall order. Stebbing knew that. Surveying the political landscape with an eye for the unforgiving demands of rigorous, logical thinking, she arrived at nothing less than a definition of freedom. "If I want to make up my mind upon any problem of political action, I must be able to deliberate freely," she argued. "If it were in fact true that we were all politically and economically free, still it would not follow that we were possessed of the freedom of mind without which, in my opinion, no democratic institutions can be satisfactorily maintained" (1939, 183). Acknowledging that political and economic freedom also remained unattained by many in 1930s Britain, she insisted that even these unattained goals would fail to constitute full freedom on their own. Freedom required logic. In writing a book about "the obstacles that impede us in our attempts to think to some purpose"—which amounted to a book about "the difficulties created by our stupidity and by those who take advantage of that stupidity"—Stebbing politicized the science of pure form, rendering its rigor usable in a world where those who would take advantage of stupidity were legion (1939, 183).

The gradient of technicality evident across Stebbing's several books on logic clearly welcomed varying levels of interest among readers. It was okay that not every democratic citizen would wade through *Principia Mathematica*. The philosopher's task was to cultivate expertise in the science of logic, a science empowered by mathematical formalism, and then to use that expertise in the service of a British citizenry beset on all sides by illogical rhetoric. Stebbing defined freedom not just as an absence of coercion and immiseration but rather as a positive, logical capacity to overcome rhetorical manipulation. "To be thus free," she concluded, "is as difficult as it is rare" (1939, 187).

References

Beaney, Michael. 2013. "The Historiography of Analytic Philosophy." In Michael Beaney, ed., 30–60, *The Oxford Handbook of the History of Analytic Philosophy*. Oxford: Oxford University Press.

Chapman, Siobhan. 2013. *Susan Stebbing and the Language of Common Sense*. Basingstoke: Palgrave Macmillan.

Douglas, Alexander X., and Jonathan Nassim. 2021. "Susan Stebbing's Logical Interventionism." *History and Philosophy of Logic*, 42 (2):101–117.

Frege, Gottlob. 1964. *Begriffsschrift und andere Aufsätze*. Hildesheim: Georg Olms.

Stebbing, L. S. 1939. *Thinking to Some Purpose*. Harmondsworth, Middlesex: Penguin Books.

Stebbing, L. S. 1942. *A Modern Introduction to Logic*, 3rd ed. London: Methuen.

Warwick, Andrew. 2003. *Masters of Theory: Cambridge and the Rise of Mathematical Physics*. Chicago: Chicago University Press.

Whitehead, Alfred North, and Bertrand Russell. 1910–1913. *Principia Mathematica*. 3 vols. Cambridge: Cambridge University Press.

SECTION IV
NATURAL LANGUAGE, DEFINITIONS, AND VERBAL DISPUTES

Susan Stebbing

Philosophy, Pragmatics, and Critical Discourse Analysis

Siobhan Chapman

1 Introduction

Through her numerous publications and presentations, Stebbing established herself as a prominent voice in mainstream analytic philosophy in the early decades of the twentieth century. But she was atypical, even unorthodox, in her views on natural language. She worked in a discipline that, in general, regarded natural language and questions of actual usage as at best beside the point of philosophical study and at worst likely to mislead and confuse. Yet in some of her most celebrated and canonical analytic work, and increasingly in her later and more popular writings, she treated natural language, together with the ways in which it is used in everyday life, as an interesting and important focus of serious scrutiny in its own right.

This chapter offers an overview of Stebbing's ideas about natural language, emphasizing those aspects of her work that share common ground with later developments in the discipline of linguistics. Stebbing's concern for the relationship between meaning and context seems to foreshadow more detailed and theoretically developed work on the same topic in recent and present-day pragmatics. In her later writings, this concern developed into an interest in the practical analysis of actual examples of language use, showing how close attention to the linguistic choices made in newspaper reports, political speeches, and advertisements could reveal the ideology behind the production of such texts and the persuasive devices employed in them. In this, she has much in common with Critical Discourse Analysis, which is concerned with analyzing similar types of texts to reveal the often implicit ideological commitments that underpin them.

British analytic philosophy of the early twentieth century was concerned with the analysis of structure and its relationship to meaning. But for most

Siobhan Chapman, *Susan Stebbing* In: *Susan Stebbing*. Edited by: Annalisa Coliva and Louis Doulas, Oxford University Press. © Oxford University Press 2025. DOI: 10.1093/9780197682371.003.0010

212 SUSAN STEBBING

practitioners the correct focus of study was the logically sound structures of artificial languages. Natural language, in comparison, was messy and imperfect and had little to offer to serious analytic investigation. In *Principia Mathematica*, Russell and Whitehead proposed various formal mechanisms by which propositions could be combined, and according to which truth could be calculated within an autonomous system that was closed to the external world and to empirical evidence. The propositions of mathematics were to be explained within the same system; like the truths of symbolic logic mathematical statements were tautologies: true because of the rules of the closed system within which they existed. In relation to this ordered system, natural language would only prove a distraction: "Ordinary language yields no help [in logical philosophy]. Its grammatical structure does not represent uniquely the relations between the ideas involved" (Russell and Whitehead, 1910, 2). In his early work, Wittgenstein argued that natural language was not constrained by the rules of logic and should therefore not be included in philosophical discussion: "In order to avoid such errors [as are introduced by 'everyday language'] we must make use of a sign-language that excludes them ... that is to say, a sign-language that is governed by logical grammar— by logical syntax" (Wittgenstein, 1922, 3.325). A little later, Carnap explained explicitly why it was the syntax of formal or artificial language, rather than that of everyday language, that should interest the philosopher: "In consequence of the unsystematic and logically imperfect structure of the natural word-languages (such as German or Latin), the statement of their formal rules of formation and transformation would be so complicated that it would hardly be feasible in practice" (Carnap 1937, 2). Ayer also emphasized the potential pitfalls presented to the philosopher by natural language: "The metaphysician ... is misled by a superficial grammatical feature of his language" (Ayer, 1936, 57).

Moore is a possible, but by no means a clear-cut, exception to the generalization that analytic philosophers of the early twentieth century shunned natural language. For Moore, clarity of exposition was of paramount importance in philosophical discussion and this often meant, as he himself explained in a retrospective summary of his work, demanding of the philosophical statement "what does this mean?" (Moore, 1942, 18). Malcolm (1942) heralded Moore's attention to the language of philosophical discussion, and in particular the centrality of everyday language to his philosophical method, as perhaps his greatest contributions. Moore himself, however, wrote little explicitly about natural language.

PHILOSOPHY, PRAGMATICS 213

In contrast, Stebbing did write about natural language. She treated it as a topic worthy of serious philosophical study, and she described it in ways that were to recur, several decades later and independently of her work, in the linguistic fields of pragmatics and Critical Discourse Analysis. The emergence of these ways of considering language in different historical and social contexts and in relation to different disciplinary backgrounds offers compelling support for the importance of the contextual consideration of meaning and the critical analysis of language use.

2 Stebbing on Natural Language

Stebbing did not engage directly with philosophical views on natural language such as those quoted above. Moreover, in publishing works such as *A Modern Introduction to Logic* (*MIL*, 1930), she positioned herself as an advocate of the analytic approach in which such views were grounded. She identified *MIL* as belonging to the tradition founded by Russell and Whitehead: "The conception of logic as essentially formal, which results in the identity of pure logic and abstract mathematics . . . is the conception that underlies this book" (Stebbing, 1930, ix). She clearly saw no contradiction, however, between her allegiance to the latest developments in formal logic, and an interest in the way language is ordinarily used. In this pioneering textbook of mathematical logic, she drew attention to the ways in which the apparent counterparts of logical operators are actually used in natural language.

There are many near correspondences between logic and natural language, familiar nowadays to those working in formal semantics and theoretical pragmatics (see, for instance, McCawley, 1980). The conjunction "and," for instance, might seem to have much in common with truth-functional "$\land$"; "$p \land q$" is true only if both "p" and "q" are independently true. The ways in which natural language expressions are actually used and understood, however, often rule out complete convergence with logical expressions. In the case of "and," the order in which two events are presented is often extremely significant. "Judith fell ill and went to the hospital" just seems to describe a different situation from that conveyed by "Judith went to the hospital and fell ill." Formal logic is necessarily blind to ordering; "$p \land q$" is simply equivalent to "$q \land p$." In *MIL*, Stebbing picks up particularly on the superficial similarity but practical distinction between natural language "some" and its logical counterpart. She notes that in logic, "some" is a sign of quantity that

214   SUSAN STEBBING

means "some at least, it may be all." However, "In ordinary speech we usually, though not always use 'some' to mean 'some only', i.e. 'some but not all', e.g. 'Some men are fools'" (Stebbing, 1930, 48).

Philosophers had, of course, noted differences between the expressions of logic and those of natural language before. But in doing so they had generally explicitly endorsed the logical version as the "correct" one or had at least implicitly presented the natural language equivalent as less reliable or less philosophically significant. Mill, for instance, had drawn attention to various discrepancies between how certain terms are used in logic and in "common conversation in its most unprecise form" (Mill, 1868, 210; see Horn, 1989, for a discussion of Mill's work, and of other nineteenth- and twentieth-century logicians who made similar observations). In his seminal work on denoting phrases, Russell had drawn a distinction between how we "speak" and what (in accordance with logic) "it would be more correct to say" (Russell, 1905, 481). Stebbing, however, presents the two different uses of "some" as equally valid and potentially equally interesting. In later work, she was to indicate more strongly that she considered the natural language as well as the logical versions of such terms to be worthy of philosophical scrutiny.

Stebbing maintained her commitment to communicating the latest developments in logic. Right at the end of her life, in 1943, she published *A Modern Elementary Logic (MEL)*. Like *MIL*, this was explicitly aimed at introducing logical theory to students. As Stebbing explains in the Preface, it was motivated by her realization that there was no "simple, introductory textbook on formal logic, written from a modern point of view, that is both unencumbered with much dead traditional doctrine and yet meeting the needs of students preparing for an examination" (Stebbing, 1943, vii). This time, she was aware of the needs of those studying "without any guidance from a teacher," particularly those "in H.M. Forces," and the book is accordingly shorter, less technical, and more accessible than its 1930 equivalent. Even within these confines, however, Stebbing was still keen to alert her readers to differences between logic and natural language. On this occasion she focuses on the logical properties of negation; if "p" is true then "-p" (not p) is false and if "-p" is true then "p" is false. Since negation in effect toggles between truth-values, there is no logical bar to double or multiple negations; "--p" is simply equivalent to "p." The same is not the case in natural language, in which "not" and prefixes such as "un-" might both be seen as equivalents of logical negation. "Some cabinet ministers are intelligent" and "Some cabinet ministers are not unintelligent" are not interchangeable in ordinary usage. Expanding on the differences, Stebbing goes far beyond the usual constraints of logical discussion to comment on features of face to face interaction: "It must always be remembered that in ordinary discourse what we convey is in part dependent not only upon the context but also upon intonation, emphasis, and even subtle changes in facial expression" (Stebbing, 1943, 35). Stebbing did not believe that such interactive features ought to be incorporated into logic itself; she states categorically that "For the purposes of discussing logical relations we ignore these characteristics of speech." But what is significant is that for Stebbing the fact that such factors were outside of the system of logic did not mean that they were beyond the remit of serious, philosophical discussion. She adds a footnote to this effect: "To ignore them is justifiable in an elementary textbook, but this does not mean that they do not need investigation."

Stebbing also introduces her readers to the regularities of material implication; "p materially implies q" means "either p is false or q is true." (Stebbing, 1943, 136) To understand relationships of material implication, it can be easiest to express them using natural language "if . . . then." So, as Stebbing explains, if:

p = "A is the father of B"
and
q = "B is the child of A"

then a relationship of material implication between the two can be expressed as: "If A is the father of B, then B is the child of A." However, Stebbing is alert to the dangers of expecting too close an alignment between material implication and "if . . . then" expressions. Propositions that are true according to the laws of material implication can sound distinctly strange when expressed in natural language using "if . . . then," a strangeness that cannot straightforwardly be explained in relation to logical questions of truth and falsehood. Logic does not discriminate between propositions, meaning that any simple propositions could take the place of "p" and "q." Stebbing proposes the following:

p = "Italy is an island"
and
q = "The Pope is a woman"

216 SUSAN STEBBING

Logically, combining these two in the relation of material implication should yield a true complex proposition. In this case, "p" is false, fulfilling one of the sufficient conditions for the material implication as a whole to be true. Yet the natural language expression, "If Italy is an island then the Pope is a woman," is distinctly problematic. Most people would not respond to this as an obviously true statement, but as something that is at best a very odd thing to say. Stebbing identifies what is needed to make an "if . . . then" expression successful in natural language: the concept of relevance. She explains that in natural language, although not in logic, "The meaning of the premise must be relevantly connected with the meaning of the conclusion" (Stebbing, 1943, 145). As with the role of factors such as facial expression and intonation in communication, Stebbing does not see the fact that relevance is outside the scope of logic as a reason to dismiss it from serious inquiry. On the contrary, while acknowledging that the exact meaning of "relevantly connected" presents a problem, she argues that "to see that there is a problem to solve is to have taken the first steps essential to solving it."

Stebbing made it clear that *MEL* was aimed at students of philosophy, albeit with a wider understanding of what constituted this group than she had envisioned in 1930: an understanding which now included those outside of formal academia. But in other writings, most prominently in *Thinking to Some Purpose* (*TSP*, 1939; see also Stebbing, 1941), she had begun to address an even broader audience, committing herself to communicating the significance of logic and its relationship to principled thinking to the general reading public. Stebbing's choice of writing for a larger audience was driven by a strong sense of the urgency of the current political circumstances. The world was, clearly, on the brink of war, and Stebbing saw this situation as brought about at least in part by rhetoric, and by the ability of some in authority to manipulate opinions and to sway the electorate. Her explicit aim was to equip her readership with the cognitive tools necessary to respond to such tactics, particularly in relation to intentionally persuasive and potentially misleading uses of language: "Citizens must be able to think relevantly, that is, to think to some purpose. Thus to think is difficult. Accordingly, it is not surprising, however saddening it may be, that many of our statesmen do not trust the citizens to think, but rely instead upon the arts of persuasion" (Stebbing, 1939, 10; see Chapman, 2013, chapter 7 for an account of Stebbing's social and political motivations in the 1930s).

Stebbing collected, quoted, and examined a wide range of examples of persuasive language taken from recent, actual sources. This was an unusual procedure at the time. Even those of Stebbing's contemporaries with a similar intention of offering self-help guides to critical thinking for the general electorate tended to rely largely on the discussion of broad principles and of invented examples (Thouless, 1930 is a particular case in point). *TSP*, on the other hand, is packed with examples taken from a variety of everyday texts. Stebbing was interested in cases in which language could be used to reinforce and to promulgate implicit ideological commitments, particularly when this was done by those with some sort of institutional or social authority. She noted that an assumption of authority in itself was sometimes used as an apparently persuasive argument; failure to challenge such assumptions could result in an unquestioning acceptance of an unsupported claim. This was particularly the case in advertising. Stebbing offers a variety of examples of slogans from current newspaper advertisements and argues that in each case, "The advertiser reckons upon your not pausing to ask for evidence that 'they all' swear by the goods offered, nor for evidence of the credentials of 'the expert' who hides so modestly behind the description. The purpose of the whole lay-out of the advertisement is to persuade you that you have been offered reliable evidence, although, in fact, you have not" (Stebbing, 1939, 78).

Other examples of persuasive language use backed by real or assumed authority include political speeches, newspaper editorials, and sermons, and *TSP* contains examples taken from all these sources. Sometimes, Stebbing's analysis takes the form of general commentary on particular word choices, but she also identifies and labels various linguistic devices that, sometimes deliberately and sometimes unwittingly, are used with the effect of misleading. Just two of these devices will be discussed here: potted thinking and the argument from analogy.

The term "potted thinking" was coined in reference to "potted meats"; it "is easily accepted, is concentrated in form, and has lost the vitamins essential to mental nourishment" (Stebbing, 1939, 68). The motivation behind potted thinking is not inherently sinister. We often need to make sense of complicated matters, and it is convenient to be able to do so in ways that are easy to process and to remember. One means of doing this is by adopting and repeating concise statements and familiar word combinations. The danger of this, however, is that it can become easy to accept without question the assumptions that underlie these linguistic habits. We can be misled into thinking that the complicated matters we are confronting are in fact as simple as the concise statements make them appear, and we can become

218 SUSAN STEBBING

inflexible in our opinions, unable to revise them in response to new evidence. Examples of this include the tendency to identify simplistic oppositions between political systems that are "good" (e.g., democracy) and those that are "bad" (e.g., communism), and to inquire no further into the issues involved. Further examples are found in the currency of set phrases in which a type or group of people is routinely associated with a particular epithet, usually one that encodes either a negative or a positive judgment: examples such as "lily-livered pacifists," "bloated capitalists," and "our magnificent police force." Repeated use of such phrases may result in an inability to think about the group of people in question without also thinking about the evaluation conveyed by the modifying adjective; "Such emotional language compresses into a phrase a personal reaction and an implicit judgement about a class of persons" (Stebbing, 1939, 70).

The fixed mindset fostered by potted thinking is demonstrated for Stebbing in a letter recently published in *News Chronicle* (a British daily newspaper that was later absorbed into the *Daily Mail*). The correspondent takes exception to the use of the phrase "British cowardice" and writes to complain that "The combination of these two words, together, is unknown in the English language, or in the tongue of any country in the world. . . . "British Diplomacy" would be a more suitable alternative." The letter is signed "'A Britisher,' and Proud of it." Stebbing is struck by the fixed nature of the letter writer's ideas about which abstract nouns can be premodified by "British": ideas that apparently make him incapable of questioning his own beliefs. The letter "reveals very clearly the way in which our admiration (or, in other cases, our contempt) for a certain class makes us unable to contemplate the possibility that we might be mistaken" (Stebbing, 1939, 72).

Arguments from analogy, like instances of potted thinking, are not in themselves pernicious. They are based in sound logical reasoning, which takes the following form:

X has the properties $p_1, p_2, p_3 \ldots$ and f;
Y has the properties $p_1, p_2, p_3 \ldots$
Therefore, Y also has the property f.

Arguments from analogy can be used to suggest possible conclusions about one, unfamiliar entity (Y) on the basis of similarity to another, familiar entity (X). Problems arise, however, when people present arguments from analogy as if they afford conclusive proofs rather than tentative suggestions.

PHILOSOPHY, PRAGMATICS   219

This error is caused by unwitting or deliberate failure to consider the range of properties possessed by X and Y. It is not sufficient simply that X and Y must have some properties in common (p_1, p_2, p_3); it is also necessary that Y must have no other, independent property that is incompatible with the property f. If Y were to have any such property, "the argument that Y has f because X has and X and Y are alike in respect of the p's is fallacious, no matter how much we may extend the number of p's which both X and Y possess." (Stebbing, 1939, p. 113).

Political speeches provide Stebbing with numerous examples of fallacious arguments from analogy: arguments that fail to meet the criterion of no incompatible properties but are offered as apparent support for specific conclusions. She notes that politicians have been particularly keen on comparing government to a sea voyage and offers many examples of politicians straining the analogy implicit in the metaphor "the Ship of State." In a speech published in *Listener*, former prime minister Ramsay MacDonald said: "I began with a reference to the contrast between the state of the country in 1931 and its state to-day. The ship then near the rocks is again floating, and has been made seaworthy. There is rough and trying water ahead. How can it most wisely be encountered?" Ramsay MacDonald was here using the implied analogy between a ship in danger and a nation in a time of crisis to rally support for the National Government which had been in power since 1931. But the analogy was not sound because it was based on a few points of superficial similarity, while ignoring the many points of substantial difference between nation and ship. Analogies, even ones that were better than Ramsay MacDonald's, would eventually fail; "Our tendency to forget this is exploited by those who aim at persuading us to accept their views without offering us any grounds that would be acceptable to a reasonable thinker" (Stebbing, 1939, p. 126).

Stebbing's writings on the ways in which language can be used to communicate implicit, often unjustified, ideological commitments are undoubtedly among those elements of her work that "can now be seen to have been significantly ahead of their time and, more importantly, relevant to issues that are of pressing concern today" (Lee, 2020, 21). Their relevance and importance are increasingly recognized by present-day philosophers working at the interface between language and ideology. Stanley (2015) makes use of Stebbing's notion of "cherished beliefs" in his own account of the language of propaganda, and Duran argues that "Stebbing's work is an overlooked contribution to the project of conceptualization with respect to social justice"

220 SUSAN STEBBING

(Duran, 2019, 48). Cassam concludes his book on what he terms "epistemic vices": "in reality there is little prospect of our ever being able entirely to avoid unconscious bias or unrecognized ignorance, but Stebbing is right to insist that some of our failures in thinking can be overcome and that there is an urgent need to overcome them to the extent that this is possible" (Cassam, 2019, 187). The recent renewed interest in Stebbing's work in this area among philosophers has generally not been matched among linguists. But there are undoubted resonances between the different aspects of Stebbing's work on natural language and recent developments in linguistics. These are discussed in the next section.

3 Linguistic Approaches to Natural Language

There are some remarkable affinities between what Stebbing was writing about in the 1930s and '40s, and what has been said in separate fields of linguistics in recent decades. The similarities and differences between logic and language have been major themes in pragmatics; these are discussed in section 3.1 below. The ways in which linguistic choices introduce powerful but often implicit ideological assumptions to a variety of text types are central to Critical Discourse Analysis, the subject of section 3.2.

3.1 Pragmatics

Pragmatics, the subdiscipline of linguistics concerned with the relationship between meaning and context, can trace its origins to the style of ordinary language philosophy that flourished after World War II and was centered on Oxford. Proponents of this approach objected explicitly to many of the assumptions of early analytic philosophy. They argued that ordinary language should not be dismissed from philosophical investigation. On the contrary, it should be at the center of philosophical discussion and could help to elucidate and even to solve many philosophical problems. J. L. Austin was perhaps the most prominent member of this school of thought, and his work on speech acts, in particular, had a formative impact on pragmatics (Austin, 1962). But an arguably greater influence on the ways in which meaning has been discussed in pragmatics came from Grice. He was a colleague and near contemporary of Austin and, although far from being straightforwardly an

PHILOSOPHY, PRAGMATICS   221

orthodox philosopher of ordinary language, he did share some of Austin's commitments, particularly his belief that the way in which people ordinarily use language was a suitable subject for serious philosophical inquiry.

The ideas for which Grice is most celebrated, certainly in pragmatics, are those relating to the concept of "implicature." Grice coined this term to enable the systematic discussion of the use of language in context, and particularly the multifarious differences between what speakers are understood to "mean" and what they literally "say." "Logic and conversation," the published lecture in which these ideas were first publicly set out, begins not with a definition of implicature or indeed with a discussion of speaker meaning, but with a succinct summary of exactly the point about the relationship between logic and language that Stebbing had acknowledged in *MIL*:

> It is a commonplace of philosophical logic and there are, or appear to be, divergences in meaning between, on the one hand, at least some of what I shall call the formal devices ... and, on the other, what are taken to be their analogues or counterparts in natural language—such expressions as *not, and, or, if, all, some* (or *at least one*), *the*. (Grice, 1975, 22)

Grice goes much further than Stebbing. He does not just acknowledge the apparent differences in meaning; he is bold enough to attempt to explain them. In fact, his answer is to explain them away, arguing that to assume that such differences exist is a mistake, and that "the mistake arises from inadequate attention to the nature and importance of the conditions governing conversation" (Grice, 1975, 24). For Grice, logical devices fully determine the literal meaning of their natural language counterparts. The fact that people often understand words such as "and," "not," and "or" in ways that appear incompatible with these devices is to be explained not in relation to literal meaning at all but to various norms and expectations that accompany any communicative use of language between human beings.

Stebbing was certainly a long way from pre-empting Grice's theory of conversation. But she did recognize the relationship between logic and natural language, which was to underpin Grice's enterprise, as potentially philosophically significant, at a time when it was dismissed as a mere distraction by most analytic philosophers. Grice's theory, together with some of the later extensions and additions introduced in post-Gricean pragmatics, can explain all the phenomena that struck Stebbing some decades earlier. She noticed, for instance, that "some men are fools" is generally taken to mean "some but not all men are fools," although this is not licensed by its apparent logical equivalent. In the Gricean system this would be explained in relation to Quantity, particularly the first maxim of Quantity, which enjoined speakers to "Make your contribution as informative as is required (for the current purposes of the exchange)" (Grice, 1975, 26). On the assumption that the speaker of Stebbing's example is observing this maxim, the hearer is entitled to assume that if the more informative alternative "all men are fools" had been available—in other words, if the speaker had considered it to be true—she would have used it. Therefore, "some men are fools" routinely implicates "some but not all men are fools," even though it does not logically entail it. In *MEL*, Stebbing noted that "some cabinet ministers are intelligent" and "some cabinet ministers are not unintelligent" will not generally be taken to be equivalent in ordinary usage, although the logic of negation would seem to suggest that they should be. Here Grice's maxims of Manner are significant. A speaker who uses the form "some cabinet ministers are not unintelligent" has chosen it in preference to the simpler and more straightforward alternative "some cabinet ministers are intelligent." If she is assumed to be adhering to maxims such as "avoid obscurity of expression" and "be brief" (Grice, 1975, 27), then it is legitimate for the hearer to infer that the speaker has chosen the more cumbersome form of expression for a communicative reason. There is a conversational implicature that the cognitive capacity displayed by the ministers in question is not such that they could legitimately be described as "intelligent."

Subsequent theories developed in the Gricean tradition have differed from Grice's original theory, and from each other, in terms of the pragmatic principles and explanatory mechanisms called upon to explain meaning in context. Horn, for instance, developed Grice's notion of Quantity to posit the existence of "scalar implicatures," based on scales of semantic strength. His Q-Principle, "say enough" (e.g., Horn, 2007, 162), explains why the selection of a semantically weaker item on a scale will implicate, although it does not literally entail, the denial of stronger items on the same scale. Horn arranges his scales in descending order of semantic strength, from left to right. One of his scales is <all, most, many, some>, which accounts for Stebbing's observation of the association of meaning between "some" and "not all." Further, Horn's two pragmatic principles operate together to account for what he terms the "Division of Pragmatic Labor," an explanation as to why longer or more complex forms of expression will generally implicate the inapplicability of a shorter or simpler apparent equivalent. Horn suggests a comparison between (a) "it's not impossible that the Sox will win" and (b) "it's possible that the Sox will win." In the former case, he argues, "S is aware that H knows that S will be attempting to reduce her effort. Given this knowledge, H recognizes that S's choice of a relatively complex or marked utterance in (a) implicates that she was not in a position to use the simpler or less marked alternative in (b)" (Horn, 2007, 172). Stebbing's observations about the different statements concerning the intelligence of cabinet ministers can be explained in relation to Horn's Division of Pragmatic Labor.

In her discussion of the relationship of material implication, Stebbing noted that there was something distinctly problematic about the expression "if Italy is an island then the Pope is a woman," even though it should logically be straightforwardly true. She indicated that the differences between the logical operator and most everyday uses of "if . . . then" would need to be explained by means of a suitably elaborated notion of what it meant for propositions to be "relevantly connected." In recent post-Gricean pragmatics, the systematic significance of what might aptly be described as the relationship of being "relevantly connected" has been the focus of relevance theory. Here, relevance is central to an account of the mechanisms of both communication and cognition. For Sperber and Wilson, "relevance can be characterized in terms of contextual effects. . . . The sort of effect we are interested in is a result of interaction between new and old information" (Sperber and Wilson, 1995, 109). Working on this premise, they offer an explanation of precisely why relevance is at play in the interpretation of "if . . . then" expressions. In the context of a shared knowledge of the conditional "if Peter, Paul, and Mary came to the party, the party was a success," someone who processes the utterance "Peter, Paul, and Mary came to the party" can with confidence reach the conclusion that "the party was a success." This process relies on an expectation of relevance: "[the hearer] expects the information the speaker intended to convey, when processed in the context the speaker expected it to be contextualised in, to be relevant: that is, to have a substantial contextual effect, at a low processing cost" (Sperber and Wilson, 1995, 116). Stebbing claimed to have taken the "first steps" toward solving the problem posed by the interpretation of "if . . . then" expressions, in recognizing the importance of relevance. Some half-century later, Sperber and Wilson's much fuller and more sophisticated response to that problem drew on precisely that same notion.

224 SUSAN STEBBING

3.2 Critical Discourse Analysis

Critical Discourse Analysis (CDA) studies the relationships between language, power, and ideology. It developed during the later decades of the twentieth century, drawing on linguistic discourse analysis and on social theories of power. In introducing an awareness of the effects of power relations to the analysis of language in social contexts, it was undoubtedly pioneering new ground. But at the same time, this approach is in many ways reminiscent of what Stebbing was proposing to do in her study of language use and misuse in the 1930s. Like Stebbing, CDA draws on examples of spoken and written texts with a particular emphasis on those produced by people with some sort of official or assumed authority; its data are political speeches, advertisements, newspaper reports and so on. Also like Stebbing, it emphasizes the fact that if such uses of language are not carefully and critically scrutinized they can lead to the unquestioning adoption of underlying commitments; ideological representations can "come to be seen as non-ideological 'common sense'" (Fairclough, 2002, 322). Stebbing made clear that *TSP* had the specific, practical intention of strengthening the critical abilities of the electorate in their response to the use of language by those trying to manipulate them. A similar aim is explicit in CDA:

> CDA aims to make its users aware of, and able to describe and deconstruct, vectors and effects in texts and semiotic materials generally which might otherwise remain to wield power uncritiqued. In these respects CDA may be a kind of wake-up call, or consciousness-raising, about the coercive or anti-democratizing effects of the discourses we live by. (Toolan, 2002, xxii)

Published work in the framework of CDA extends over several decades and has necessarily had scope to cover far more ground than Stebbing was able to in a few years. It is also informed by descriptive frameworks for linguistic analysis that are much more sophisticated than anything that was available to Stebbing. Nevertheless, it is possible to spot analogies in CDA to what Stebbing was trying to do in her analysis of the language of political speeches, for instance, or of advertising. Stebbing identified the unnamed "expert" as a recurrent presence in newspaper advertisements, intended to convince the target audience that they have received reliable, informed advice when in fact they have been presented only with persuasive rhetoric. In his CDA-informed study of advertising, Guy Cook observes a very similar phenomenon, this time in relation to television advertisements. He notes the apparent "sober scientific authority" that advertisements routinely claim by including a report purporting to be from an expert. He continues: "sometimes the white-coated boffin even appears, like the good angel of medieval drama, in the kitchen or bathroom, either invisible to all the characters or conversing with only one of them while unseen by all the others!" (Cook, 2001, 187).

In *TSP* Stebbing concentrated particular attention on texts produced to persuade and influence in relation to significant current social and political issues; Ramsay MacDonald's electioneering speech for the National Government is a case in point. In a similar vein, recent CDA studies have considered, among other topical issues, the rhetoric of Donald Trump (e.g., Elnakkouzi, 2022), texts relating to the "Brexit" debate (e.g., Hansson and Page, 2022), and responses to the COVID-19 pandemic (e.g., Marko, 2022). Taylor (2020) considers the representation of the "Windrush Generation" in public discourse in the middle decades of the twentieth century. She compares this to the generally much more favorable representation of the same group in parliamentary debates in 2017, when it had become apparent that many of them were falling victim to current government policy on immigration. Further, she considers the contemporary representation of other groups of immigrants: those who have been constructed as "unwanted" or "undesirable." Here, she argues, there are some striking similarities to the ways in which the Windrush Generation were represented in parliamentary debates and in the national media in the 1940s and '50s, particularly in relation to metaphorical uses of language.

Taylor notes that the repeated use of adjectives such as "genuine" and "legal" in opposition to "bogus" and "illegal" to premodify the noun "immigrants," has successfully established a distinction between two groups of people that is in fact entirely without basis. She comments that "the creation of (false) binary opposites is a rhetorically efficient move" (Taylor, 2020, 4), in that it legitimizes the dismissal of a certain portion of a group of people as "undeserving." This is remarkably similar to Stebbing's discussion of "potted thinking," in which she argued that the repeated application of certain evaluative epithets to certain groups of people could lead to subjective appraisal and implicit judgment going unquestioned. Taylor focuses on a single noun, "immigrant," and on how epithets can divide this group of people into two categories, differently evaluated.

226 SUSAN STEBBING

In her study of how metaphor has been used to represent the negatively evaluated group of immigrants, Taylor draws attention to the fact that "when we liken one thing to another we do so on a partial basis" (Taylor, 2020, 3). That is, the use of a metaphor to describe one phenomenon in terms of another highlights some aspects of similarity between the two and backgrounds properties with respect to which they differ, or which are treated as irrelevant to the comparison.

Again, there is a similarity here to what Stebbing said about "arguments from analogy"; in effect, they are pernicious if points of dissimilarity are overlooked to the extent that illegitimate conclusions are presented as if they were evidenced. Taylor identifies particular metaphors that were used repeatedly in discourse surrounding the Windrush Generation in the 1940s and '50s, and also the subgroup of immigrants deemed "undesirable" in the twenty-first century, metaphors including those she labels "*immigrants are water*" and "*immigrants are invaders.*" As one example of the first she offers the following quotation from 1950s parliamentary proceedings:

> There are approximately 11,000–12,000 of these coloured colonial immigrants **pouring** into the country every year. . . . The cause of the **problem** is very obvious, and affects not only the West Indies, but Africa, Parkistan and other territories. I think however that the primary cause is the **influx** of Jamaicans. (Hansard, 1954, quoted in Taylor, 2020, 13, Taylor's emphases)

There are clear similarities between this type of language and that used in much more recent newspaper reports:

> In a corpus of newspapers from 2013, the strongest noun collocates that precede *illegal immigrants* are: *deportation, legalisation, apprehension, influx, child, flow, million, plight, category, population, status, percent, wave, issue, thousand.* Water is a feature in three of the collocates and in fact seems to be the only metaphorical element. (Taylor, 2020, 13–14, original emphases)

In relation to the metaphor "*immigrants are invaders,*" a newspaper report from the 1950s furnishes Taylor with this example: "Thousands of **Jamaicans, Barbadians, Trinidadians and West Africans** find jobs of one kind or another in public transport. Less conspicuous is their **invasion** of

PHILOSOPHY, PRAGMATICS   227

the catering, garment, and entertainment industries" (*Times*, 1958, quoted in Taylor, 2020, 14, Taylor's emphasis). Again, this is echoed in recent debate concerning the group of immigrants deemed undesirable, this time from parliamentary discussion:

> It is not unusual, however, for a country to have legislation that tries to **combat illegal migration** by saying that if someone wants to rent a flat, have a job or go to hospital, they need to show who they are. It is the right thing to do to **protect** people from too much **illegal migration**. (Hansard, 2018, Amber Rudd, Conservative, quoted in Taylor, 2020, 14, Taylor's emphasis)

Taylor uses the methods of corpus linguistics, enabling her to consider metaphor use quantitatively: "a particular strength of the corpus linguistic approach is that it offers a bird's eye view, looking at multiple occurrence simultaneously, which enables identification of patterns" (Taylor, 2020, 5). Such a methodology was, of course, simply not available to Stebbing, who had to rely on her general awareness that certain metaphorical comparisons, such as that implicit in the phrase "the ship of state," were used with high frequency. However, she too recognized the creation of apparent binary oppositions between "good" and "bad" systems or groups of people, and the subsequent use of partial analogies to reinforce these judgments, as examples of what Taylor describes as "rhetorical strategy intended to persuade" (Taylor, 2020, 19). The desire to identify and unmask such strategies underlies much present-day work in CDA. It was also a primary motivation for Stebbing in writing *TSP*, a task undertaken many decades earlier and with a comparative lack of linguistic and technological resources.

4 Conclusions

Stebbing stood out from her contemporaries in analytic philosophy in taking an interest in the properties and the use of natural language. More than that, she offered concrete examples of language in use to illustrate how it obscured arguments or deliberately misled uncritical readers or listeners. Some eight or nine decades later, philosophers are returning to Stebbing's work in this area with a new appreciation of what it might have to offer present-day discussions of language and ideology. But Stebbing's work has perhaps

228 SUSAN STEBBING

an even greater, though unacknowledged, affinity to work in the linguistic subdisciplines of pragmatics and Critical Discourse Analysis.

There is no apparent causal link between Stebbing's work and these developments in linguistics. This in itself might have striking implications for the importance of work now being undertaken in the two fields. These ways of considering language developed in different academic disciplines, and against different historical and social backgrounds. Biletzki has argued that the value of relatively recent theories of language, such as pragmatics, "can be, in part, checked by their philosophical roots" (Biletzki, 1996, 457). Stebbing's pioneering work foreshadowed the general approaches taken in pragmatics and CDA, and sometimes even dwelt on remarkably similar examples and explanations. In the study of natural language, the consideration of meaning in relation to context, and the critical analysis of usage, are both issues of central and continued importance.

References

Austin, J. L. 1962. *How to Do Things with Words*. Oxford: Clarendon Press.

Ayer, A. J. 1946. *Language, Truth and Logic*, 2nd ed. Harmondsworth: Pelican, 1971. [1st ed. London 1936].

Biletzki, Anat. 1996. "Is There a History of Pragmatics?" *Journal of Pragmatics* 25, 455–470.

Carnap, Rodolf. 1937. *The Logical Syntax of Language*. London: Routledge and Kegan Paul.

Cassam, Quassim. 2019. *Vices of the Mind: From the Intellectual to the Political*. Oxford: Oxford University Press.

Chapman, Siobhan. 2013. *Susan Stebbing and the Language of Common Sense*. Basingstoke: Palgrave Macmillan.

Cook, Guy. 2001. *The Discourse of Advertising*. London: Routledge.

Duran, Jane. 2019. "Stebbing on 'Thinking to Some Purpose,'" *Think* 18 (51), 47–61.

Rania Elnakkouzi. 2022. "The Argumentative Function of Rescue Narratives: Trump's National Security Rhetoric as a Case Study," *Critical Discourse Studies* 21 (1), 17–33.

Fairclough, Norman. 2002. "Critical and Descriptive Goals in Discourse Analysis." In Michael Toolan, ed., 321–345. *Critical Discourse Analysis*. London: Routledge.

Grice, Paul. 1975. "Logic and Conversation." In P. Cole and J. Morgan, eds., 22–40, *Syntax and Semantics*, vol. 3. New York: Academic Press. Reprinted in Paul Grice, 1989, *Studies in the Way of Words*. Cambridge, MA: Harvard University Press.

Hansson, Sten, and Ruth Page. 2022. "Legitimation in Government Social Media Communication: The Case of the Brexit Department." *Critical Discourse Studies* 20 (4), 361–378.

Horn, Laurence. 1989. *A Natural History of Negation*. Chicago: University of Chicago Press.

Horn, Laurence. 2007. "Neo-Gricean Pragmatics: A Manichaean Manifesto" In Noel Burton-Roberts, ed., 158–183, *Pragmatics*. Basingstoke: Palgrave Macmillan.

Lee, Barry. 2020. "Introduction," in Barry Lee, ed., 1–37, *Philosophy of Language: The Key Thinkers*, 2nd vol. London: Bloomsbury.

Malcolm, Norman. 1942. "Moore and Ordinary Language." In Paul Arthur Schilpp, ed., 345–368, *The Philosophy of G. E. Moore*. La Salle, IL: Open Court.

PHILOSOPHY, PRAGMATICS 229

Marko, Karoline. 2022. "Extremist Language in Anti-COVID-19 Conspiracy Discourse on Facebook." *Critical Discourse Studies* 21 (1), 92–111.

McCawley, James. 1980. *Everything That Linguists Have Always Wanted to Know About Logic but Were Ashamed to Ask.* Chicago: University of Chicago Press.

Mill, John Stuart. 1868. *An Examination of Sir William Hamilton's Philosophy*, vol 2. Boston: William V. Spencer.

Moore, G. E. 1942. "An Autobiography." In Paul Arthur Schilpp, ed., 3–39, *The Philosophy of G. E. Moore.* La Salle, IL: Open Court.

Russell, Bertrand. 1905. "On Denoting," *Mind*, 479–493.

Russell, Bertrand, and Alfred North Whitehead. 1910. *Principia Mathematica.* Cambridge: Cambridge University Press.

Sperber, Dan, and Deidre Wilson. 1995. *Relevance.* Oxford: Blackwell.

Stanley, Jason. 2015. *How Propaganda Works.* Princeton: Princeton University Press.

Stebbing, L. Susan. 1930. *A Modern Introduction to Logic.* London: Methuen.

Stebbing, L. Susan. 1939. *Thinking to Some Purpose.* London: Penguin.

Stebbing, L. Susan. 1941. *Ideals and Illusions.* London: Watts.

Stebbing, L. Susan. 1943. *A Modern Elementary Logic.* London: Methuen [University Paperbacks, 1966].

Taylor, Charlotte. 2020. "Representing the Windrush Generation: Metaphor in Discourse Then and Now." *Critical Discourse Studies* 17 (1), 1–21.

Thouless, Robert. 1930. *Straight and Crooked* Thinking, 2nd ed. London: Hodder and Stoughton; London: English Universities Press, 1936.

Toolan, Michael. 2002. "General Introduction." In Michael Toolan, ed., xxi–xxvi, *Critical Discourse Analysis.* London: Routledge.

Wittgenstein, Ludwig. 1922. *Tractatus Logico-Philosophicus.* Kegan Paul, Trench and Trübner, trans. D. F. Pears and B. F. McGuinness. Routledge and Kegan Paul, 1961.

Stebbing on Linguistic Convention

Understanding, Definition, and Verbal Disputes

Bryan Pickel

In *Philosophy and the Physicists* (1937/1944, 209–210), Susan Stebbing suggests that "the most pressing need in the philosophy of science is the determination of the scope of convention in science" and that this project would require a book-length treatment. Had she lived long enough, Stebbing hoped to write such a book (Chapman 2013, 143). The details of this envisaged book obviously cannot be reconstructed in full. Yet, there is ample material to piece together some of Stebbing's views of convention. Indeed, Stebbing's writings on convention span her entire career, from her first book *Pragmatism and French Voluntarism* through her final book *A Modern Elementary Logic*.[1]

This chapter explores one particular thread in Stebbing's treatment of convention: the claim that language is conventional. It is common and now almost trivial to say that language is conventional. Yet philosophers have derived radical conclusions about ordinary, scientific, and philosophical inquiry from the conventionality of language. The conventionality of language purportedly explains the status of definitions, the nature of necessity, and the special status of logic. Stebbing readily allows that language is conventional. But she investigates this conventionality against the background of a broader theory of signification. This investigation reveals that the conventionality of language lacks the radical implications many have supposed. Understanding Stebbing's view of linguistic convention sheds light on her philosophy of language. It also helps situate her views in the philosophy of science. More generally, the nature and importance of linguistic convention has never been settled in philosophy. Stebbing made a significant contribution to this topic

---

[1] For instance, as early as (Stebbing 1914/2018, 69–83), Stebbing discusses the view that the truth of a hypothesis is a matter of convention in connection with the views of M. Le Roy and Poincaré.

Bryan Pickel, *Stebbing on Linguistic Convention* In: *Susan Stebbing*. Edited by: Annalisa Coliva and Louis Doulas, Oxford University Press. © Oxford University Press 2025. DOI: 10.1093/9780197682371.003.0011

STEBBING ON LINGUISTIC CONVENTION 231

that has implications for even contemporary debates about ordinary inquiry and about philosophical methodology.

1 Convention in Language

According to Stebbing, the most "important function" of language is to communicate *information* (Stebbing 1930/1948, 16; cf. 1934, 159–160). The speaker knows some piece of information—a proposition or fact—and wants to share this information with an audience. The speaker may know *that Smoodger, the dog, has died.* The speaker finds a sentence appropriate to communicate this to the audience such as "Smoodger has died." The speaker utters this sentence. The audience comes to know the proposition it expresses. Language also performs functions beyond mere communication of information. It may also be used "to arouse in the hearer a certain response, to create in him a certain state of mind" (Stebbing 1930/1948, 17) or to communicate "thoughts, feelings, and desires to others" (Stebbing 1930/ 1948, 10).

Language can be used to communicate information and induce states of mind because it functions as a system of signs. Stebbing has a general theory of signs of which linguistic signs form a special case. According to Stebbing, a sign signifies something relative to an interpreter. For one thing to be the sign of another, there must be an interpreter who "has learnt from past experience to associate the one occurrence with the other" (Stebbing 1930/1948, 10). Thus, signification requires an interpreter who possesses background knowledge relating the sign to the thing signified.

1.1 Natural and Conventional Signs

Stebbing (1930/1948, 11, cf. 1943/1961, 12) distinguishes *natural* signs from *symbols* which are "consciously designed to signify." As an example of a natural sign, Stebbing considers *the fact that the sun is setting into a bank of clouds* as a sign of *the fact that it will rain tomorrow* (1930/1948, 10). This is a sign *to an observer* who knows of the relation between the clouds in the sunset and the subsequent weather. Stebbing (1943–1961, 12) later gives the example of "[a] symptom, in the medical sense, is a sign of a disease." The symptom is a sign to the observer who knows that it is associated

232 SUSAN STEBBING

with the disease. Thus, in a situation in which one thing is a sign of another, Stebbing requires that there be a sign, the thing signified, and an interpreter.

Symbols are a subclass of signs. Symbols are "consciously designed to signify." They can be used as instruments in thinking by a single interpreter or as instruments of communication by multiple interpreters, a speaker and their audience. For successful communication, the sign must signify the same things, or have the same referent, for both speaker and audience.[2]

Even at the level of symbols, Stebbing identifies a class of natural signs. That is, Stebbing believes that some signs are both consciously designed and natural. One type of natural symbol is a demonstrative gesture. A demonstrative gesture literally points at its referent. Another type of natural symbol is an imitation or copy. Stebbing (1930/1948, 11) considers a speaker who imitates drinking to convey that he is thirsty, or cases of onomatopoeia such as the word "cuckoo" to imitate the bird's call, or the sound "ping-pong" to designate the game.

> Such signs are called "natural [symbols]" owing to the fact that since they resemble the thing or action signified, they are the most natural means of indicating what we want to indicate. (1930/1948, 11).[3]

A natural symbol has "an inherent fitness to represent what it signifies" (Stebbing 1930/1948, 12).

In contrast, conventional symbols are conventional because "there is no essential connection between a word and what it expresses" (Stebbing 1930/1948, 426). Conventional signs are not demonstrations of or imitations of their referents. Conventional symbols have meanings in virtue of how they are used rather than in virtue of standing in some natural relation to their referents. For instance, speakers use the word "Smoodger" to refer to a particular dog. Speakers use the word "red" to refer to a particular shade of color. In a linguistic community, a speaker and their audience may use these signs because they know that this is how they have been used in the past either

---

[2] Stebbing uses "referend" because "referent" already had a use in her time to designate a relatum of a relation.

[3] Stebbing distinguishes mere natural signs from symbols most clearly in (Stebbing 1930/1948, 10–12). But it is only later, in (1943/1961, 12), that Stebbing calls the mere signs such as a symptom of a disease "natural signs." She refers to natural symbols as "natural signs" in (Stebbing 1930/1948, 10–12). Despite alternating labels, Stebbing is consistently clear about the threefold division between natural signs, natural symbols, and conventional symbols.

STEBBING ON LINGUISTIC CONVENTION   233

by themselves or by other speakers. A speaker who does not know these conventions will not understand the symbol.

Because the meaning of a conventional symbol depends on how it is used by an individual or community, knowledge of conventional signs "does not form part of the common experience of the human race" (Stebbing 1930/1948, 12). Speakers in different communities lack a common stock of conventional signs. Stebbing considers the word "moon". The word has a certain meaning and so is able to *refer* to a certain object in the world, the *moon*. The word "moon"—or a word with its sound and shape—could have been used to refer to something else. And the thing, *the moon*, can be and is referred to using another word such as "luna" (Stebbing 1930/1948, 426). To know the reference of "moon" or "luna," one must look beyond the speaker's immediate situation and investigate how the sign is used by members of the community.

In contrast, natural symbols do not depend on culturally specific information. Human beings in a wide variety of cultures understand the significance of pointing to an object. To know that the demonstrative gesture signifies the object pointed, one does not need specific cultural knowledge of the pointer and that which is pointed at. Similarly, the general notion of imitation is common across cultures, even if the speaker may need knowledge of the broader situation to know *what is imitated*.

The contrast here is not that conventional symbols require prior experience to understand but natural symbols do not. Both natural symbols and conventional symbols require relevant experience. Natural signs—for instance, the symptoms of a medical disease—require experience to understand. Even in the case of natural symbols, relevant knowledge is required. Stebbing (1930/1948, 10) gives the example of a man standing on a beach. People on a cliff above him shout, point to the incoming tide, and then point to a rock on the beach. The man understands the final demonstration to be a sign that the rock is safe from the incoming tide. This understanding of the demonstration goes beyond what is perceptually available to the man at the time and relies on his background knowledge of tides.

The difference is that one must have specific cultural knowledge in order to understand a conventional symbol. One must know what the symbol signifies when used by the agent or in the community. In the case of the natural symbol demonstrating the rock as safe from the tides, general knowledge of how people demonstrate combined with subject-specific knowledge about the tides sufficed for understanding the sign. In the case of a word such

234   SUSAN STEBBING

as "red" or "Smoodger," one must also know how the sign is used by agents in a specific cultural context.

Stebbing sometimes describes a conventional symbol as "deliberately devised to stand for something and [having] thus acquired a relatively fixed significance" (Stebbing 1930/1948, 11). This does not mean that a speaker *explicitly* decided that, for instance, "red" would refer to a particular shade. Stebbing (1935, 7) outright denies that there is always "an explicit convention arising out of a definite agreement." She compares the convention to the hypothetical contract of social contract theories.[4] The convention to use a word with a certain meaning grew out of its history. It is the present conventions of use that matter to meaning. Stebbing (1930/1948, 426) argues, "However a particular word (or sound) may have originally come to be associated with what it expresses, its meaning now depends upon its use." Thus, Stebbing sharply separates questions about how a word came to be used by a given community from questions of what it is now used to signify. Only the latter are relevant to conventional meaning. There is often an explanation of why a given word is used with a certain meaning by a given community. To explain how an expression acquires its conventional meaning "would be to write a history of the growth of languages" (Stebbing 1930/1948, 13). The fact that "red" is a sign for the color red is due to the fact that the speaker or the community uses "red" to refer to the color because of their mutual knowledge of how the sign "red" is used by other speakers in their community. The fact that "Smoodger" is a sign for the dog Smoodger is due to the fact that the speakers or the community uses "Smoodger" to refer to the dog because of mutual knowledge of how the sign "Smoodger" is used.[5]

Stebbing's distinction between natural signs and symbols corresponds to Grice's (1948/1989) distinction between natural and non-natural meaning. The distinctions are illustrated by many of the same examples. Stebbing uses the symptoms of a disease as an example of a natural sign. Grice too uses the symptoms of a disease as an example of natural meaning: the spots mean measles. Stebbing says that imitations—such as the imitations of a chicken clucking or flapping its wings—are symbols, consciously designed to signify. Similarly, Grice uses resemblances— paintings—as examples of non-natural

[4] Ayer (1936, 18) later appeals to this same analogy.
[5] According to David Lewis (1969), a convention is a certain type of solution to a decision problem that is arbitrary insofar as there are other solutions. Lewis straightforwardly acknowledges that—on his account—whether a word is conventional will depend on how the decision problem is characterized. This is related to Stebbing's position that even though a convention is in some sense arbitrary, its adoption may have a causal explanation.

meanings. Finally, both Stebbing and Grice use this dichotomy to understand human language. There are two salient differences. One difference—as we have seen—is that Stebbing further divides the natural and the conventional at the level of symbols. Another difference is that Grice's choice of the term "meaning" makes it difficult to see how there could be natural misrepresentation. It is odd to affirm "those spots mean measles" unless the patient actually has measles. Stebbing would say instead, "those spots are a sign of measles," which seems compatible with the patient suffering from a different disease.

1.2 Conventional Use

The meaning of an expression is determined by how it is used. However, there may also be specific conventions governing the use of an expression that are independent of its meaning. Stebbing considers the uses of the expressions "dear" and "sincerely" in addressing and signing letters.

> Words and phrases have a conventional use. For example, "Dear Mr. Brown" and "yours sincerely" may be used in a conventional sense by a letter-writer to whom Mr. Brown is in no ordinary sense "dear" and to whom he does not feel "sincerely." (Stebbing 1939, 81)

The use of these particular expressions is conventional in something like the senses described above: it is not essentially connected to the practice of letter writing, it is not part of the universal experience of human beings, and it requires culturally specific knowledge. Yet, the conventions governing the use of these expressions are independent of their meaning. "Dear" refers to something for which one has affection, and "sincerely" is an adverb referring to actions done honestly. It is conventional to use these words in letters even if the use is known to be insincere, as when addressing a stranger as "dear."

1.3 Sentence Meaning

The discussion so far has centered on the conventions that determine the use and meaning of individual expressions, but communication normally works by the assertion of sentences. According to Stebbing, the meaning of a sentence is only derivatively conventional. The conventions governing

236 SUSAN STEBBING

sentences just are the conventions governing the words that make them up together with the conventions governing how the words are put together.

> We do not first construct [a sentence] "S" and then attach a meaning to "S." The meaning of "S" is determined by the meanings of the constituent words and by the rules of syntax of the language in which "S" is constructible. (Stebbing 1939, 82)

Stebbing must be referring here to the conventions of language having to do with meaning. Presumably, she would allow that there can be separate and additional conventions governing the use of sentences, such as the convention in some places to use "how are you?" as a greeting rather than a genuine question.

This leads to our first application of Stebbing's analysis of linguistic convention. Stebbing (1939, 81–82) uses this picture of sentence meaning to pose problems for Wisdom's claim that philosophical statements are purely verbal.

> A philosophical answer is really a verbal recommendation in response to a request which is really a request with regard to a sentence which lacks a conventional use whether there occur situations which could conventionally be described by it. (Wisdom 1937, 71)

According to Wisdom, statements that philosophers are liable to make—he mentions "I know what is going on in Smith's mind"—are neither ungrammatical nonsense nor are they "in conflict with conventional usage" as would be a contradictory statement. Yet, Wisdom suggests that these sentences lack a conventional use. Stebbing's complaint is that the conventions governing the meanings of words together with the conventions governing the significance of the syntactic formation rules determine the conventional meanings of sentences. Once the words in Wisdom's sentences have conventional meanings and their syntactic formation rules determine the significance of the sentence in terms of the significance of its parts, there is nothing left for convention to do to determine the meaning of the sentence. Perhaps, there might be a one-off convention as is the case with "how are you?" above. But Wisdom is not suggesting that philosophy contributes one-off uses for sentences such as "I know what is going on in Smith's mind." Stebbing similarly argues that in judging a use of sentence in a situation not to "conflict with

STEBBING ON LINGUISTIC CONVENTION 237

conventional usage," Wisdom is presupposing that there are conventions governing the sentence's conventional use in the case at hand. Thus, Wisdom is wrong to think that philosophical statements give an existing sentence a new signification.

2 Definition

Given that language is conventional, what a word is used to signify is in some sense arbitrary. The word could have been used to signify something else. A different word might have been used to signify the referent. This might lead one to think that definitions—which are used to state more precisely what a word signifies—are arbitrary as well. If it is a matter of convention what the word refers to, it is a matter of convention how the word is defined. Those who hold that definitions are arbitrary may also assign them a special metaphysical or epistemic status. What follows from definition is contributed by the mind or is *a priori*.

Yet, Stebbing rejects these consequences. Definitions are not arbitrary. Their content is not contributed by the mind. And definitions may be discovered empirically.[6] To demonstrate this, Stebbing investigates various notions of definition. According to Stebbing, the best way to investigate the notion of a definition is by "asking under what circumstances in ordinary discourse we should need to ask for a definition" (Stebbing 1930/1948, 241). Stebbing argues that we seek definitions when "we are confronted with a problem" and "we find that we are thoroughly muddled" Stebbing (1933, 80). Thus, one seeks a definition for a term that one already understands and uses but which has led to difficulties in thinking through some problem. The definition is meant to help the inquirer think more clearly about the problem. In these cases, one may need a more precise understanding of how an expression is

---

[6] The account of definition developed in this chapter may usefully be compared with discussion of the analytic clarification of a concept developed in Schliesser (this volume). Schliesser ascribes characteristics to analytic clarification that are similar to those I have ascribed to definition. This should be expected. According to Stebbing (1933, 80), analytic clarification "consists in the elimination of elements supposed to be referred to whenever we use a symbol 'S', but which are not such that these elements *must* be referred to whenever we so use a sentence 'S' that the sentence says what is true." In other words, a speaker had previously believed in a certain *necessary condition* on the use of a symbol in a true sentence. In analytic clarification, the speaker revises their view: the expression can be used in a true sentence even in cases where the condition fails. It seems likely, then, that revision of an offered definition would be one means to effect an analytic clarification.

238 SUSAN STEBBING

used. Stebbing gives the example of a speaker who tries to understand how "appeasement" is used by Chamberlain and his supporters.

> We seek definitions as a means of thinking more clearly about something; we want to think more precisely, to know exactly what it is that we are saying. For instance, "What is the policy of appeasement, as understood by Neville Chamberlain and his supporters between, say, 1936 and 1939?" (Stebbing 1943/61, 117)

The need for definition of a problem arises in specific contexts and in response to specific difficulties. Presumably, in this case, the problem is to determine what sorts of concessions Chamberlain proposed to make to Hitler.[7]

2.1 What Is a Definition?

Stebbing (1930/1948, 421; 1943/1961, 120) suggests several conditions on definitions, which she extracts from reflection on the occasions on which a speaker asks for a definition. A first constraint is that in giving a definition one uses two expressions: "the defining expression and the expression to be defined" (1930/1948, 423). A definition, for instance, might take the form "appeasement is a policy whereby...," where "a policy whereby..." is the defining expression and "appeasement" is the expression to be defined.

A minimum condition is that the defined expression and the defining expressions are *equivalent* or apply to the same objects (1930/1948, 423). That is, the defining expression and the defined expression must be true of the same objects (or, if sentences, they must be true in the same situations). Stebbing (1930/1948, 424) gives the example of defining "first cousin" using terms for sibling relationships.

First cousins are people whose parents are siblings.

In this definition, "first cousins" is the defined expression, and "people whose parents are siblings" is the defining expression.

These examples bring out another constraint on definition. The definition must have more symbols than the original (1930/1948, 423). Thus, "people whose parents are siblings" is not only equivalent to "first cousins" but it also includes symbols not present in the original. A definition of an

---

[7] Cf. (Stebbing 1934b, 78).

STEBBING ON LINGUISTIC CONVENTION   239

expression E must assert an equivalence between E and some other expression E^* where E^* is longer. This characterization is what Stebbing calls an *analytic definition* (1930/1948, 424; 1933, 79–82; 1934a, 34–35).[8] One additional constraint on definition is that it cannot be circular, otherwise the point of giving the definition—to clarify the original word—would be defeated (1930/1948, 425).

Stebbing later contrasts analytic definition—which she says gives an analysis of the expression "at the same level" (Stebbing 1934a, 34)—with directional analysis, which gives an analysis at a new level. The contrast is that an analytic definition of an expression gives a precise but longer equivalent to the expression. A directional analysis gives a recipe for *contextually eliminating* an expression from sentences that contain it. That is, a directional analysis will begin with a sentence such as "the committee adjourned" and give a replacement of the sentence as a whole that lacks any constituent corresponding to one of the constituents such as "the committee." Thus, "the committee adjourned" might be replaced with a complicated statement about its members such as "the chair hit the gavel and everyone who had been deputized left." In the latter sentence there is no constituent corresponding to "the committee."

In what follows, I will focus on analytic definitions. The constraints on definitions that we have discussed will help evaluate the claims about the epistemic and logical status of definitions. The arguments in this section can be viewed as supplementing the arguments in Coliva (this volume) that Stebbing "comes close to the rejection of the analytic/synthetic distinction," at least insofar as definitions are often paradigm instances of analytic truths (cf. Coliva and Doulas, this volume).

2.2 Definition Versus Introduction

Stebbing sharply distinguishes understanding an expression from being able to define it. Comprehension does not require definability.

> [W]e may understand a word although we cannot describe the referen[t] in other words, still less be able to *define* the word. The reader would probably

---

[8] The phrase "analytic definition" likely derives from Moore, as reflected in his posthumously published lectures from 1925–26 (Moore 1966, 116–118).

240 SUSAN STEBBING

hesitate were he asked, "what does the word 'table' mean?" (Stebbing 1930/1948, 14).

Most speakers can correctly apply the word "table" in the majority of cases. They can provide more or less adequate descriptions of tables. But they may not know a precise equivalent of the word "table." This level of understanding is adequate for the purposes of ordinary life.

Stebbing, therefore, must develop an account of how the conventions governing the use of a symbol are established and transmitted to novices that does not require the novices to be able to define the expression. How does a conventional symbol come to be a sign for a novice? Stebbing considers two ways of transmitting the conventions governing the use of a word. I will call these *Ostensive Introduction* and *Verbal Introduction*.

> *Ostensive Introduction*: The novice is shown the individual or some individuals to which the word refers.

> *Verbal Introduction*: The novice is given a verbal description of the individual or the individuals to which the word refers.

I will briefly consider what Stebbing says about each type of introduction and then draw some general lessons.

2.2.1 Ostensive Introduction

Imagine introducing a new speaker to the name "Smoodger" by pointing to a dog and uttering, "he is called 'Smoodger.'" The new speaker would then be able to use "Smoodger" as a sign for the dog on subsequent occasions. This is an *Ostensive Introduction*. In her own writing, Stebbing (1930/1948, 13) imagines teaching a new speaker the word "triforium" by pointing to the open gallery above the arches in Notre Dame in Paris and saying "that is a triforium." Finally, Stebbing (1930/1948, 422) considers a speaker who is taught the meaning of "sonnet" by being given examples of poems that are sonnets. In these cases, the new user would understand what the word stood for if she could go on to correctly apply "Smoodger," "triforium," and "sonnet."

While this process can initiate a speaker into the practice of using a word, Stebbing rejects the claim that *Ostensive Introduction* is a kind of *definition*. According to Stebbing (1930/1948, 423), a definition always gives an "equivalence between words" (1930/1948, 422). Learning a word by associating it with a thing given in experience is a radically different process from learning a word through a linguistic description. One core difference is that speakers cannot understand a language by being given only verbal explanations since "verbal expressions must, at certain points, link up with other things than words unless definition is to remain merely a set of verbal manipulations. Such linking up can be given by *pointing*" (1943/61, 118).

Because the processes are different, Stebbing rejects the claim that teaching by *Ostensive Introduction* gives the definition of words. Thus, Stebbing rejects Johnson's (1884/1906, 94) characterization of teaching a speaker to use a name such as "Smoodger" by pointing at its referent as an *ostensive definition*. Similarly, she rejects the claim of J. N. Keynes (1921, §22) according to which one can *define* a general term such as "triforium" by pointing to instances of it. Stebbing (1930/1948, 423) argues that both logicians "confuse *understanding* a symbol with *defining* it." The practice of *Ostensive Introduction* enables the speaker to use the word as a sign for its referent. It does not teach the novice speaker a verbal equivalent that gives insight into the word's usage.

Moreover, *Ostensive Introduction* does not satisfy the purposes for which we engage in the practice of asking for and giving definitions. As we saw, one seeks a definition for an expression to clear up a difficulty. In this purpose, we are not satisfied with being shown an instance of it. Demonstrating Chamberlain's actions would not clarify his use of "appeasement" to one who was puzzled. Thus, *Ostensive Introduction* is not definition.

2.2.2 Verbal Introduction

Stebbing gives several examples of what I have called *Verbal Introduction*, whereby a speaker is brought to understand a new word through a verbal description of its referent. Stebbing considers the following examples in which I have italicized the word being introduced.

- "A *saxophone* is something like a U-shaped trumpet" (1930/1948, 13)
- "A *bass viol* is an instrument very much like a 'cello but much larger"
- "A *sonnet* is a short poem of fixed length, expressing a single experience"
- "A *sonnet* is a verse form consisting of fourteen iambic pentameters, having a fixed rime scheme of one or other of two forms" (1930/1948, 421–422)

242 SUSAN STEBBING

Although some *Verbal Introductions* above may have the syntactic form of a definition, they are not all definitions. Only the final *Verbal Introduction* of "sonnet" above is a definition, while the other three *Verbal Introductions* are not definitions. In particular, only the final sentence states an equivalence between the defined expression and another expression.

In each case, Stebbing says that these statements may enable the speaker to understand the term being defined. In the case of the introduction of "bass viol," Stebbing says that the audience would probably be able to "apply 'bass viol' correctly" on the basis of this *Verbal Introduction*. Similarly, if the description above enables the speaker to apply the word "saxophone" correctly, Stebbing suggests that this is evidence that the audience has understood the word (1930/1948, 14). But a speaker who comes to understand a word by this sort of *Verbal Introduction* need not be able to define the word.

3 Consequences

Stebbing's discussion of definition has important consequences for ordinary inquiry and for philosophical methodology. In ordinary inquiry, definition is useful when one's loose understanding of a word causes one to think unclearly. Yet, Stebbing suggests that the solution is not to "jump to a definition" since a good definition can be neither wider nor narrower in extension than the expression being defined, "but the difficulty is just to know *what* would be too wide, or too narrow" (Stebbing 1934b, 78). In philosophy too, definition requires investigation into the world. Stebbing agrees with the logical positivists that philosophy involves logical clarification of language, the substitution of clear expressions for equivalent unclear expressions. But the investigation to find a clear equivalent expression requires investigation into the subject matter rather than investigations that focus exclusively on words or concepts (Stebbing 1933, 86).

3.1 Are Definitions Arbitrary?

Stebbing argues that the conventionality of language does not entail that definition is arbitrary.[9] Words are meaningful as a result of linguistic convention.

---

[9] See, for instance, C. I. Lewis (1923, 171).

A definition does not typically initiate that convention. Rather, definitions are important equivalences selected out of a body of sentences that already have conventional uses. For Stebbing, definitions must be true and "[a] definition is true if the defining expression is equivalent to the correct uses of the *definiendum*" (1930/1948, 426). The correct use of an expression "is not always easy to determine" (1930/1948, 426). As we saw above, speakers can use and understand expressions without being able to clearly articulate what they apply to. Thus, even though language is conventional, the process of definition requires substantive investigation the referents of the expressions. Indeed, Stebbing (1930/1948, 427) says, "It is because definitions are not arbitrary that they are useful."

Along these lines, Stebbing criticizes Whitehead and Russell's (1910/1957, 11) view that "a definition is a declaration of a newly-introduced symbol . . . [and] is to mean the same as a certain other combination of symbols." Stebbing's complaint is that Whitehead and Russell (1910/1957, 12) add that a definition will be useful when "what is defined is (as often occurs) something already familiar." Stebbing rightly argues that a symbol cannot be both newly introduced and already familiar. Insofar as a familiar use is informing the equivalence being asserted, the purportedly defined expression is not newly introduced.

Yet, Stebbing does allow that there are cases in which an arbitrary definition may be given. Stebbing imagines an utterance of the form (*) "I am going to use "X" to mean so-and-so" to introduce an expression "X" (Stebbing 1930/1948, 427, 440). This stipulation *may* both introduce and define a symbol. Stebbing gives the example of speaker who introduces the term "safeguarding duties" and clarifies that they mean "what are usually called 'protective duties'" (Stebbing 1930/1948, 427, 440).

This type of stipulation may introduce a new term. Moreover, it may take the form of a definition. However, Stebbing argues that there is no guarantee that these purported definitions are *true*, and thus no guarantee that the defining and defined expressions are equivalent. That is, a speaker can utter (*) to introduce expression "X", and yet (*) is false. The stipulative introduction (*) will be true only if the speaker goes on to use X as they have proposed (Stebbing 1930/1948, 427, 440). Whether (*) turns out to be a satisfactory definition of the newly introduced as opposed to a mere *Verbal Introduction* will depend on whether it achieves the goals for which it was introduced.

Stebbing here anticipates Quine's (1960, 361–362) later discussion of legislative definition. A legislative definition such as (*) establishes the use

244 SUSAN STEBBING

of an expression such as "X." In contrast, a discursive definition clarifies the meaning of an existing expression. Quine allows that only legislative definitions are conventional. But the conventional status of a legislative definition is wholly confined to its role in establishing the convention of using the expression "X" with a certain meaning. As Quine suggests, after the term is introduced a later user might prefer a definition (or postulation) from "elsewhere in the corpus" (1960, 362). A bit further on, Quine suggests that he would also agree with Stebbing that legislative definitions can turn out to be false. In a famous passage, Quine (1960, 373) imagines a scientist legislatively defining an expression for a force. Subsequent developments in the science may lead the scientist to reject the claim stating the legislative definition as false. These legislative definitions, then, are corrigible for both Quine and Stebbing.

3.2 Verbal Disputes

Stebbing links her view of definition to the topic of *purely verbal disputes*, which has been of interest in recent philosophy.[10] A verbal dispute is a factual dispute about correct usage (Stebbing 1930/1948, 426–427). It is agreed that there is some correct usage of a term, but the two parties disagree about what that is.

Stebbing (1930/1948, 427) doubts that "any serious disputes are purely verbal." She does not mean to say merely that serious disputes are not verbal. That claim threatens to be a tautology. She presumably means that certain apparently serious disputes have been wrongly classified as verbal disputes. Stebbing (1930/1948, 427) says that "what appear to be verbal disputes may arise" about topics such as art and religion. She uses as an example a dispute about whether a certain sculpture (Epstein's *Night*) is a work of art. This was a live controversy at Stebbing's time with some characterizing the work as obscene.[11] Presumably, there must have been some question about whether this dispute was verbal at the time.

Stebbing argues, however, that these are not usually verbal disputes. The disputes are not resolved by the two parties deciding that they mean different things by the word "art."

[10] See Chalmers (2011).
[11] See Cohen (1939).

STEBBING ON LINGUISTIC CONVENTION 245

If it were purely verbal it could be properly terminated by the agreement "Oh! well, what you call a work of art is not what I call 'a work of art.'" Such disputes do not usually end thus. (Stebbing 1930/1948, 427)

Instead, Stebbing says that the two parties have different "conceptions of the nature of art." That is, there is some underlying factual disagreement about the purpose or function of art that gives rise to the dispute. The underlying disagreement leads the two parties to disagree about whether a certain piece is a work of art. But this is not because they disagree about how the word "art" is used in the community. Stebbing's view of this case is interesting, in part, because similar disputes arise in contemporary literature on verbal disputes and conceptual engineering.[12]

Based on this case, I find it doubtful that Stebbing would think serious disputes in philosophy—about moral responsibility, the nature of persons, or the reality of physical objects—are purely verbal. This connects to Stebbing's remark in "The Method of Analysis in Metaphysics" that "we cannot hope to solve metaphysical problems by assigning out-of-the-way meanings to ordinary expression" (Stebbing 1932–1933, 86). Insofar as the significance of the expression arises from its continuance of its ordinary use, attempting to assign an out of the way meaning to it will not solve the problem that prompted the search for the definition. As Coliva (2021, 13, footnote 22) notes, this passage prefigures the contemporary "subject change objection" to the project of conceptual engineering and to Carnapian explication.

Yet, Stebbing fully acknowledges that the use of language can be an obstacle to clear thinking. For Stebbing, thinking is a response to a problem. Thinking is intelligent when it draws connections that are relevant to solving the problem. An obstacle to clear thinking either prevents the speaker from drawing a relevant connection or causes them to draw irrelevant connections (Pickel 2022, 16–17). A thinker, for instance, might be trying to solve the problem of understanding why Chamberlain adopted such a disastrous policy as *appeasement* toward Hitler, perhaps with an eye toward avoiding a repetition of the policy in the future. In this context, the word "appeasement" refers specifically to Chamberlain's policy. However, the word can also be used in other more mundane contexts, with different shades of meaning and different connotations. A failure to distinguish how the word was used in Chamberlain's specific context might lead a thinker to

---

[12] See debates discussed in (Liao et al. 2020) and (Cantalamessa 2020).

246 SUSAN STEBBING

overgeneralize: to draw irrelevant connections. For instance, any concession to an opponent might be viewed as a form of appeasement. A thinker who is not careful to distinguish the specific use of the word in the context might then wrongly take the concession to be as objectionable as Chamberlain's policy. In this volume, Kouri Kissel discusses the propensity of words in context to have different meanings and its consequences for Stebbing's view of verbal disputes and her account of how the choice of words can lead to ineffective thinking.

4 Analyticity and Logic

The fact that language is conventional has been taken to have deep implications extending outside of the topic of definition. In this section, I will discuss Stebbing's view of two such implications endorsed by philosophers such as A. J. Ayer and C. I. Lewis. One implication is that the conventionality of language can explain why certain propositions are necessary or certain. The other implication is that the principles of logic themselves are conventional. Stebbing rejects these arguments on the grounds that they misrepresent the role of convention in language.

I will take Ayer's remarks in *Language, Truth and Logic* as paradigmatic of the view that necessity and certainty can be explained by convention. Ayer thought that certain propositions—such as the propositions of pure geometry—were necessary and certain. They would never be contradicted by experience. Ayer's explanation is that these propositions make no statements about the world but rather they record our conventions.

> [Analytic propositions] simply *record our determination to use words in a certain fashion*. We cannot deny them without infringing on the conventions which are presupposed by our very denial, and so falling into self-contradiction. And this is the sole ground of their necessity. (Ayer 1936/1952, 84)

In her review, Stebbing puzzles over Ayer's statement. She asks what it means to say that a statement "records" a convention or a determination to use words in a certain way, especially in light of Ayer's previous statement that experiential propositions record actual or possible experiences (Ayer 1936/1952, 38).

STEBBING ON LINGUISTIC CONVENTION 247

I find a difficulty in understanding Mr. Ayer's usage of the word "record." Analytic propositions are said to record our determination to use words in certain fashions; an experiential proposition is said to be one which records an actual or possible observation. I do not see how the word "record" can be used in the same sense in both these contexts, and I do not find it possible to determine how exactly it is being used in either. (Stebbing 1936, 364)

Without some further explanation of what it means to say that a truth "records" conventions, Stebbing thinks that Ayer's theory does not give any further explanation into why the relevant propositions would be necessary or certain. The conventionality of language does not, for Stebbing, lead to any obvious conclusions about the modal or epistemic status of particular sentences.

I will take C. I. Lewis as a representative of the view that logic is conventional. Like many others, Lewis was led to this view in part by his analysis of the fact that there are different consistent systems of pure geometry. As Stebbing would describe the situation, Euclidean geometry can be formulated as a deductive system. It is a body of statements divided into axioms and theorems, which are entailed by the axioms. In the nineteenth century, it was shown that alternative deductive systems are consistent. Specifically, mathematicians investigated deductive systems based on axioms that are inconsistent with the claim that for every point p and line l, there is exactly one line through p that is parallel to l. They showed that deductive systems never lead to contradiction. This was shown by giving alternative interpretations of "point" and "line" in standard geometry. In this respect, these different geometries were "pure" deductive systems, meaning that the basic vocabulary ("point," "line," and so on) was not given an interpretation.[13]

Lewis observed that logic itself constitutes a deductive system. The system has its own primitive vocabulary such as 'V,' '¬,' and '⊃.' Just as in geometry, many alternative deductive systems using the same symbols can be developed, where these alternative deductive systems yield different theorems.

The fact is that there are several logics, markedly different, each self-consistent in its own terms and such that whoever, using it, avoids false premises, will never reach a false conclusion. (Lewis 1923, 170)

---

[13] (Stebbing 1930/1948, 458).

248   SUSAN STEBBING

Lewis gives the example of the logic of *Principia Mathematica* where '⊃' is interpreted as material implication. In this logic, for any two sentences p and q, the sentence $\ulcorner(p \supset q) \vee (q \supset p)\urcorner$ is a theorem. Lewis takes this to mean that for any two sentences one sentence implies the other in this logic. In Lewis's preferred logic, '⊃' corresponds to a strict conditional so this theorem does not follow.

Lewis concludes that the laws of logic are conventional: they are "the parliamentary rules of intelligent thought and speech" (Lewis 1923, 170). For example, Lewis says that the inclusion of the law of the excluded middle ($\ulcorner p \vee \neg p \urcorner$) in a logic is a mere convention.

> Similarly the law of the excluded middle formulates our decision that whatever is not designated by a certain term shall be designated by its negative. It declares our purpose to make, for every term, a complete dichotomy of experience, instead—as we might choose—of classifying on the basis of a tripartite division into opposites (as black and white) and the middle ground between the two. (Lewis 1923, 170)

So on Lewis's view, there are many alternative logics, and the selection of a logic is a matter of convention. The conventionality of logic explains why it is necessary and certain.

Stebbing gives a sophisticated two-part response to Lewis. First, she responds that there are not in fact multiple logics but rather multiple formalisms. Second, Stebbing responds that logical principles play a different role in deductive systems from the axioms of a geometry.

Stebbing argues that Lewis has not shown that there are multiple logics as there are multiple geometries. For Stebbing, logic is the study of formal implications. Logic articulates logical forms and determines which sentences imply which other sentences in terms of these logical forms. The examples of different logical systems that Lewis articulates are merely uninterpreted deductive systems. They are not theories of *implication* (Stebbing 1933, 195). Lewis's example of the deductive system of *Principia Mathematica* is surprising only because Russell proposed to read '⊃' as "implies." Stebbing agrees with Lewis that there can be pairs of sentences that do not imply each other. Yet, there is nothing problematic about the uninterpreted deductive system that Russell offered. Indeed, the deductive system has true interpretations, as when one reads $\ulcorner p \supset q \urcorner$ as $\ulcorner$either q or it is not the case that $p\urcorner$. But in so interpreting '⊃,' we are not giving a theory of implication.

The second part of Stebbing's argument is that principles of logic play a different role in constructing a deductive system from the role played by axioms of geometry. The axioms of a geometry (such as "for any two points, there is a straight line connecting them") are connected to the theorems of geometry by the relation of *implication*. That is, the axioms *imply* the theorems. In this sense, the principles of logic are not further axioms in the deductive system of geometry. They are the principles that validate the move from the axioms of the system to the theorems. On Stebbing's view, logic is the theory that describes the implication relations. As such, it is assumed by any deductive system that divides a body of statements into axioms and theorems related by the relation of implication. This point generalizes. For Stebbing, any deductive system is just a body of statements divided into axioms and theorems connected by implication. The principles of logic that connect the axioms to the theorems just are the formal rules governing the notion of implication. They are thus presupposed by any deductive system. A system that appears to articulate different laws of logic is actually just a theory of something other than the implication relation.

Although there are some important differences, Stebbing's argument against the conventionality of argument bears more than a passing resemblance to Quine's (1936) later argument to the same conclusion in "Truth by Convention." Both arguments focus on the need for logical principles to connect the premises of a deductive system to their consequences.

5 Conclusion

Stebbing allows that language is conventional. Words bear no inherent relations to their referents. A word could have referred to something else. And other human languages use different words to signify the same referent. Yet, Stebbing argues that this conventionality does not have radical consequences for science and philosophy that some have drawn. Definitions are not arbitrary but require one to find an equivalent expression to a word in one's vocabulary. Thus, ordinary and philosophical disputes are not to be resolved by "jumping to a definition." Nor does the conventionality of language straightforwardly explain the apparent interesting modal or epistemic status of definitions, geometrical statements, or logic.

I have focused on the role of convention in language. I have examined how this conventionality bears on the nature of ordinary, scientific, and

250 SUSAN STEBBING

philosophical inquiry. However, Stebbing sees a wider role for convention in the practice of inquiry itself. Her view of the interaction between convention and hypothesis plays a central role in her philosophy of science. More work is needed to understand the implications of the interplay between convention and hypothesis for Stebbing's philosophy of science.[14]

References

Ayer, A. J., C. H. Whiteley, and M. Black. 1936. "Truth by Convention." *Analysis* 4: 17–32.

Ayer, Alfred Jules. 1936/1952. *Language, Truth and Logic.* New York: Dover.

Cantalamessa, Elizabeth. 2020. "Appropriation Art, Fair Use, and Metalinguistic Negotiation." *British Journal of Aesthetics* 60: 115–129.

Chalmers, David J. 2011. "Verbal Disputes." *Philosophical Review* 120: 515–566.

Chapman, Siobhan. 2013. *Susan Stebbing and the Language of Common Sense.* London: Palgrave Macmillan.

Cohen, David L. 1939. "Jacob Epstein." *Atlantic Monthly* (December Issue): 751–758. https://www.theatlantic.com/magazine/archive/1939/12/jacob-epstein/654124/.

Coliva, Annalisa. 2021. "Stebbing, Moore (and Wittgenstein) on Common Sense and Metaphysical Analysis." *British Journal for the History of Philosophy* 29: 914–934.

Grice, Paul. 1948/1989. "Meaning." In Grice. 1989. *Studies in the Way of Words.* Cambridge, MA: Harvard University Press, 213–223.

Grice, Paul. 1989. *Studies in the Way of Words.* Cambridge, MA: Harvard University Press.

Hallett, H. F., L. S. Stebbing, and J. H. Muirhead. 1933. "Symposium: The 'a priori.'" *Proceedings of the Aristotelian Society, Supplementary Volumes,* 12, 150–219.

Johnson, W. E. 1884/1906. *Logic: Part 1.* London: Macmillan.

Keynes, John Neville. 1921. *Formal Logic.* Cambridge: Cambridge University Press.

Lewis, Clarence Irving. 1923. "A Pragmatic Conception of the A Priori." *Journal of Philosophy* 20: 169–177.

Lewis, David Kellogg. 1969. *Convention: A Philosophical Study.* Cambridge, MA: Wiley-Blackwell.

Liao, Shen-yi, Aaron Meskin, and Joshua Knobe. 2020. "Dual Character Art Concepts." *Pacific Philosophical Quarterly* 101: 102–128.

Moore, G. E. 1966. *Lectures on Philosophy.* London: Routledge.

Pickel, Bryan. 2022. "Susan Stebbing's Intellectualism." *Journal for the History of Analytical Philosophy* 10 (4).

Quine, W. V. 1936. "Truth by Convention." In *Philosophical Essays for Alfred North Whitehead.* London: Longmans, Green, 90–124.

Quine, Willard van Orman. 1960. "Carnap and Logical Truth." *Synthese* 12: 350–374.

Stebbing, L. S. 1932–1933. "The Method of Analysis in Metaphysics." *Proceedings of the Aristotelean Society* 33: 64–94.

Stebbing, L. S. 1933. "Logical Positivism and Analysis." *Annual Philosophical Lecture, Henriette Hertz Trust,* 53–87.

Stebbing, L. S. 1935. "Sounds, Shapes, and Words." *Aristotelian Society Supplementary Volume,* 14, 1–21.

Stebbing, L. S., L. J. Russell, and A. E. Heath. 1934. "Communication and Verification." *Aristotelian Society Supplementary Volume* 13, 159–202.

---

[14] Thanks to Louis Doulas and Annalisa Coliva for comments.

Stebbing, L. Susan. 1914/2018. *Pragmatism and French Voluntarism: with Especial Reference to the Notion of Truth in the Development of French Philosophy from Maine de Biran to Professor Berson*. ilo glifo ebooks.

Stebbing, L. Susan. 1930/1948. *A Modern Introduction to Logic*. London: Methuen.

Stebbing, L. Susan. 1934a. "Directional Analysis and Basic Facts." *Analysis* 2: 33–36.

Stebbing, L. Susan. 1934b. *Logic in Practice*. London: Methuen.

Stebbing, L. Susan. 1936. "Review of *Language, Truth and Logic* by A. J. Ayer." *Mind* 45: 355–364.

Stebbing, L. Susan. 1937/1944. *Philosophy and the Physicists*. Middlesex: Penguin Books.

Stebbing, L. Susan. 1939. "IV.–Some Puzzles About Analysis." *Proceedings of the Aristotelian Society* 39: 69–84.

Stebbing, Susan. 1943/1961. *A Modern Elementary Logic*. London: Methuen.

Whitehead, Alfred North, and Bertrand Russell. 1910/1957. *Principia Mathematica*. London: Cambridge University Press.

Wisdom, John. 1937. "V.–Philosophical Perplexity." *Proceedings of the Aristotelian Society* 37: 71–88.

Stebbing, Translations, and Verbal Disputes

Teresa Kouri Kissel

1 Overview

Merely verbal disputes can be problematic. They have the potential to derail conversations and prevent progress. The purpose of this chapter is twofold. First, I will provide evidence that Susan Stebbing, in *Ideals and Illusions* (1941), provided a test that foreshadowed some of the more modern work on verbal disputes. This test, I will argue, has a potentially fatal flaw that can be fixed by making use of some of Stebbing's previous work. Second, I will show how some of the problems, identified by Vermeulen (2018) for a test provided by Chalmers (2011), could have been avoided if Stebbing's work had been readily available. One major upshot of this is that Stebbing is an integral member of the tradition that gives rise to the idea of merely verbal disputes and should be treated as such.

2 Introduction

Merely verbal disputes can be problematic. They have the potential to derail conversations and prevent progress.[1] The purpose of this chapter is twofold. First, I will provide evidence that Susan Stebbing, in her 1941 *Ideals and Illusions*, provided a test that foreshadowed some of the more modern work on verbal disputes. This test, I will argue, has a potentially fatal flaw that can be fixed by making use of some of Stebbing's previous work. Second, I will show how some of the problems with a similar, more modern test, provided

---

[1] Recent works suggests that some verbal disputes may not be problematic in this way. See, for example, Balcerak Jackson (2014), Belleri (2020), and Mankowitz (2021). Since some verbal disputes will still be problematic, we do not investigate these issues here.

Teresa Kouri Kissel, *Stebbing, Translations, and Verbal Disputes* In: *Susan Stebbing*. Edited by: Annalisa Coliva and Louis Doulas, Oxford University Press. © Oxford University Press 2025. DOI: 10.1093/9780197682371.003.0012

TRANSLATION AND VERBAL DISPUTES   253

by Chalmers (2011), could have been avoided if Stebbing's work had been readily available. In effect, the fix I propose for her test could be just as easily applied to the problems suggested by Vermeulen (2018) for Chalmers. One major upshot of this is that Stebbing is an integral member of the tradition that gives rise to the idea of merely verbal disputes and should be treated as such.

In section 3, I will provide a short synopsis of Stebbing's *Ideals and Illusions* and give the details of the translation test she provides there. Then, in section 4, I will provide some of the details about the system Stebbing called directional analysis and show how we can make use of that system to resolve a potential problem with Stebbing's translation test. In section 5, I will show how the modified version of Stebbing's translation test is similar to Chalmers's test for merely verbal disputes. Finally, I will show that Stebbing's modified translation test can solve a problem for Chalmers's test, as proposed by Vermeulen in section 6.

Before we begin, it is helpful to have an example of a merely verbal dispute. Suppose two teachers discussing whether Mila, who usually gets A-minus grades, is an A-student. One says she is, while the other says she is not. Unbeknown to them, one thinks A- students are students who get A's or A plusses, and the other thinks A-students are students who get A minuses or above. Once they realize this, the debate about whether Mila is an A-student disappears. They can both agree about the grades Mila actually gets. The original dispute, about whether Mila was an A-student, was merely verbal.

3 The Translation Test in *Ideals and Illusions*

Ideals and Illusions is Stebbing's attempt to explain how ideas help to "determine social change" (p 203). She holds that the book shows how ideas can be just as important as economic structure and political power. In certain respects, it is an extension of her work in *Thinking to Some Purpose* (Stebbing, 1939), where she discusses the necessity of clear and precise thinking in everyday activities. In *Thinking to Some Purpose*, she argues that clear thinking, being definite, and reflecting on our ideals are essential to living a life and to making those lives we lead better.[2] *Ideals and Illusions* expands on that work

---

[2] Being definite amounts to, as far as I can tell, being specific, using clear understandable terms, and not using language to mislead people. Interestingly, one of the things Stebbing criticizes herself most for is not being definite enough.

254 SUSAN STEBBING

by using the current political situation (the book was written during World War II) as an example and by suggesting that not only can we not lead a good life if we are not definite, clear thinkers, but, even further, that a good life without definite, clear thinking easily devolves into evil.

Ideals and Illusions is divided into several sections, somewhat by theme. Stebbing starts by explaining why ideals and ideas are important. Stebbing argues for the conclusion that we must examine our moral principles, reflect on them, and make them explicit. We need to do this to make sure we are living the lives we think we are living and that those lives are good. The question is, then, what would our principles look like to make the world better? Stebbing's requirement of being definite means that "building a better world" needs to transition from a catchphrase to something precise and clear.

Stebbing demonstrates one way we can help make abstract things like catchphrases more precise and clear. In particular, she focuses on how abstract words can sometimes be misleading. She proposes an interesting test for when the use of abstraction can mislead. The test requires replacing an abstract word with less abstract words that mean the same thing. She states

> If a sentence in which a main word is translated into an equivalent sentence in which the word is replaced by corresponding, less abstract words, and if the new sentence thus obtained would be dissented from (or assented to) by someone who had formerly assented to (or dissented from) the original sentence, then the use of abstract words was harmful. (p 154)

She gives an example in which "war" is used in a harmful way. Someone might assent to the sentence "War alone brings up to their highest tension all human energies and puts the stamp of nobility upon the peoples who have the courage to meet it" (p. 155) while they would assuredly dissent from

> Human beings who are engaged in an **organized effort to kill, wound, starve or otherwise injure other human beings organized in the same way for the same purpose** will have all their specifically human energies raised to the highest tension, and this **organized effort to kill, wound, starve or otherwise injure other sets of human beings, similarly engaged,** is admittedly noble if these human beings thus **organized to kill, wound, starve or otherwise injure other sets of human beings, similarly organized,** meet with courage the organized efforts of the second set of human beings to **kill, wound, starve or otherwise injure them.** (p. 155)

TRANSLATION AND VERBAL DISPUTES   255

Since "organized effort to kill, wound, starve or otherwise injure other human beings organized in the same way for the same purpose" is just (claims Stebbing) a less abstract way to say "war," this means that, according to our test, "war" is a harmful abstract term. Those who originally assented find that they now dissent, and that they should have dissented from the original sentence as well. These abstractions, then, are harmful because they confuse people and make the truth of the matter less clear.

Stebbing focuses mostly on the failings of people and morality throughout *Ideals and Illusions*, but in the epilogue, she takes a hopeful tone. She suggests that if people are willing to appropriately reflect on their principles and their actions, and think clearly and be definite, the world will slowly improve. She says:

> Amidst the ruins [of the current state of the world] it is still possible to preach the ideal of freedom, truth, happiness and love. The choice offered us is evil, but it is not necessary to choose the worse. The way before us is hard, but it is not impossible to make it lead towards a world where men can be free and happy because they are not afraid of the truth, however uncomforting, and have learnt that love casts out fear and brings peace. (p 205–206)

4 Translations and Analyses

There is a major problem here: it is not clear what counts as a translation. Stebbing does not give adequacy conditions for acceptable translations. She only makes one quick remark in *Ideals and Illusions* about what counts as a good translation. It immediately follows her discussion of the translation test itself. She states:

> For my present purpose it is enough to say that two sentences composed of different words and syntactically different are equivalent if they both state the same fact, in the sense that, if the first is true, the second is true; and, if the first is false, the second is false. Equivalent sentences may be said to be translations of each other. (Stebbing, 1941, p. 154)

Stebbing has thus proposed the following criteria for a good translation of one sentence into another: they are truth-valuationally equivalent. This, of

256 SUSAN STEBBING

course, will not be enough for us here, because though many sentences share truth values, they do not seem to be translations of each other. For example, "2+2=4" and "A cup of coffee is a cup of coffee" are both always true, but do not in any intuitive sense mean the same thing. Sharing truth-values, though, can be a necessary condition of a good translation.

Further, it cannot be that some term is a translation of another just in case substitution of one for the other preserves assent and dissent conditions. Unfortunately for Stebbing, a typical characteristic of a good translation just is that it preserves assent and dissent conditions in context. So, whether we translate "café" as "coffee" or "coffee shop," there will be a right choice of translation for a particular context, and in that context, assent and dissent conditions will not shift when we use the term "café." This is fine for now, since it does not seem that "café" is a typically problematic abstraction. However, we have a more robust issue when we look at our "A-student" example. If we use the shift of assent and dissent conditions both to identify when something is a good translation *and* when something is a problematic term, we will find that for any potentially problematic term, we really just did not have an adequate translation to begin with. Using our example, suppose we offer two translations of "A-student." The first is something like "good student" and the second specifies a GPA. Now, if we find that the interlocutors shift their assent and dissent to the original sentence, "Mila is an A-student," then we will find we have evidence for one of two things: either "A-student" is a problematic abstract term, or our translation was inadequate to begin with. This second option, of the translation being inadequate, would essentially take the teeth out of Stebbing's translation test. Any time we happened upon something that might be a problematic abstract term, we would find that, in reality, we did not have an adequate translation.

So, if we relied only on assent and dissent conditions to ascertain when a translation was adequate, then we would never find problematic abstract terms. Each time someone's assent or dissent to the sentences in questions switched, we would instead have an inadequate translation rather than a problematic abstract term. This would defeat the purpose of the translation test. We need something to identify as a translation that is subtler.

To solve this problem, we need adequacy conditions for translations that do not rely on assent and dissent conditions. We need translations to preserve something that isn't assent and dissent conditions. Ultimately, I will suggest translations as we normally conceive of them won't do at all and that we need to turn to something like an analysis instead. In fact, I think directional analysis, as characterized by Stebbing herself, will do nicely as a starting point to make the translation test she proposes more precise. This section is devoted to arguing for that claim. I suggest that we should look for an "analysis test," which replaces the potentially problematic term in a sentence with something like a directional analysis of it. Directional analyses won't preserve meaning, as our intuitions about translations might suggest, but they will preserve something close to it: truth-makers.[3]

Meaning and truth-makers are also going to be tied closely enough here to preserve the original spirit of Stebbing's translation test, if not simply to make it more precise. For our purposes, when two sentences have the same meaning, they also have the same truth-makers. Though this relationship probably does not go the other way (sentences might have the same truth-makers, but not share a meaning), this is enough to suggest a strong connection between meaning and truth-makers and so preserve the original spirit of Stebbing's proposal. Stebbing's earlier work, particularly Stebbing (1932) and Stebbing (1933), focuses on the role of analysis in philosophy, and we will modify it to provide us with a more refined notion that we can substitute for "translation."

For Stebbing, analysis is the goal of philosophy. In doing an analysis, we "reveal the structure of that to which reference is made in true statements" (Stebbing, 1932, p. 65). I take this to mean that when we analyze something, we come to know better what the world must be like for that thing to be true. Roughly, an analysis is directional if it moves from more high level to more basic, simpler, concepts. So, "organized effort to kill, wound, starve or otherwise injure other human beings organized in the same way for the same purpose" can be thought of as a "directional analysis" of "war" since it breaks up the concept "war" into simpler, or more basic, concepts in context (like "kill" and "wound"). Further, Stebbing claims that we get a better understanding of concepts the further we take their analysis.[4] So in performing this "directional analysis" of "war," we come to understand it better. This improvement

---

[3] See Janssen-Lauret (2017), Coliva (2021), and Egerton (2021) for more information about the relationship between directional analysis and truth-makers.

[4] There are two roles that Stebbing requires understanding to fulfill to make her view coherent. We need an immediate level of understanding, which we gain when we know the immediate reference of a proposition, and which is required in order to analyze a proposition. In addition, we need a scalar notion of understanding, so that we can get a deeper and deeper understanding of a proposition the further we take its analysis. I am not sure whether, on her view, there is one notion of understanding, a scalar notion which starts with some fixed point, an immediate understanding, or there are two notions of understanding, a binary one and a scalar one. Either way, it does not directly affect the picture I draw here, so I will not discuss this issue further.

258   SUSAN STEBBING

in understanding is what can be taken to account for the changing assent and dissent conditions. Directional analyses preserve truth-makers and are context-sensitive.[5]

In a bit more detail, directional analysis is a method of analysis that Stebbing opposes to the type of analysis the logical positivists were engaged in. Logical positivism, claims Stebbing, starts with the basic building blocks of the world and attempts to construct the world from those. Directional analysis, on the other hand, starts with what we take to be commonsense truths, and "aims at making precise the reference of all true belief" (Stebbing, 1932, p. 70). We proceed in our analysis by starting with our commonsense truths and replacing the terms and concepts involved in that truth with more basic terms and concepts. In so doing, we learn more about what our commonsense truth means and implies, and we come to understand it better.

An example will be of use here. The statement we will provide an analysis for is "Everyone on the committee is a professor" (see Stebbing (1930)). A candidate for the directional analysis of the statement "Everyone on the committee is a professor" is

Person 1 is a professor, and Person 2 is a professor, and . . .

where "Person n" is the *name* of the *nth* committee member. In this way, we reduce the complexity of the original statement, by eliminating one concept from it; we have eliminated the concept "committee." This, then, may serve as the first step in a directional analysis. Of course, to reduce this analysis to basic facts, we would need to know the directional analysis of "professor" and of each person. We can go further here, too. The next step in this analysis might be something like

> The atoms arranged Person 1-wise works in research and teaching at a university, the atoms arranged Person 2-wise works in research and teaching at a university . . .

Anachronistically, we can think of directional analysis as seeking to uncover precise truth-makers for any proposition, and to simplify it.[6] All three of our propositions ought to have the same truth-makers, but each of them

---

[5] It is not clear how Stebbing actually felt about directional analysis. In Stebbing (1932), she seems to be supporting it as a viable philosophical position, but later (in, for example, Stebbing (1934a)), she claims she never issued such support. For more details on her actual position, see Chapman (2013) and Coliva (2021).

[6] See Egerton (2021) for why this may in fact not be so anachronistic.

TRANSLATION AND VERBAL DISPUTES 259

gets more and more precise about the exact details of those truth-makers. In Stebbing's own terms, we analyze something in order "to enable us to understand something more clearly" (Stebbing, 1933, p. 29). For a more detailed explanation of directional analysis, see chapter 4 of Chapman (2013).

This is ultimately the solution to our problem of "what counts as a good translation?" Directional analysis preserves the truth-makers of a proposition (or potential truth-makers, if the analysand is false), and simplifies it. This means that we have what we were missing. With the original translation test, as characterized by Stebbing, we lost sight of what was preserved in the substitution of terms. But now we know: if we use the modified "analysis test" instead and replace sentences that contain potentially problematic terms with their directional analyses, then we know what is preserved: the truth-makers of the two sentences will be the same, and the result will be simpler than the original.

This, in fact, matches the remark that Stebbing makes after introducing her translation test about which features are preserved in translations. We saw above that Stebbing suggested that what we need to preserve in translations are the truth-values of sentences, rather than meanings. Two sentences being equivalent in truth-value, though, is still too broad for our purposes, as all necessary sentences will then be translations of each other. But we can certainly refine this notion to consider truth-makers instead. If two sentences share truth-makers, they will certainly share truth-values, and so Stebbing's criterion is still a necessary condition of our more refined test.

We have a second good-making feature here, too. Stebbing also thinks analyses are dependent on context. Stebbing (1934b, pp. 53–54) says "the importance of taking note of the context in which a word occurs is very great." Additionally, Stebbing (1939, p. 214) claims that "we may easily misunderstand the import of an assertion and may do an injustice to the speaker, if we forget to take note of the context within which the assertion is made." These two passages show us that for Stebbing, context is essential to understanding. This helps us see that analyses can only be good or bad in contexts. Since analyzing a term helps us understand it better, and context is essential to understanding, we can only really be said to analyze things in a given context. This squares with the simplicity requirement: things can only be ranked by simplicity within the confines of a context (though even then it can be challenging). Without the information provided by a context, and the information provided by what we are trying to do within that context, we cannot tell which of two terms is simpler.

260   SUSAN STEBBING

This squares with an analysis preserving truth-makers, too: until you know how to properly interpret a sentence in a given context (say, "John is tall"), you cannot know what its truth-makers are. So, we cannot know what makes (or would make) "John is tall" true until we know what height you have to be to be tall, and that will depend on context.

Now, directional analysis full stop is going to be too strong a requirement here. It only applies to whole sentences. Instead, we will call something a "directional translation" of a word when it translates that word in a sentence into something more basic—this is something like a partial directional analysis of a sentence, focusing only on one term in it. This type of care is needed here, since analysis is a technical term. Though these "directional translations" will be akin to analyses, they may not themselves be analyses. Stebbing had very specific requirements for what types of terms and concepts in sentences could be analyzed, and it may be that not all terms that are candidates for directional translations fit the bill. I do not know whether Stebbing would hold that all directional translations can be analyses, but for our purposes it does not matter; all we need is a similarity between the two.[7] Since whether an analysis is good can be relative to a context, we will assume that our new directional translations are also relevant to a context.

So, then, a directional translation of a term or concept in a sentence replaces that term or concept with simpler terms or concepts, the uses of which have the same truth-makers as the original sentences in the context of concern.

We can use this to test whether a "directional translation" of an abstract term is adequate in a way that does not rely on preserving assent and dissent conditions, or equivalent truth-values. To check whether a directional translation is adequate, one checks whether it

1. Replaces complex concepts and words with simpler ones,
2. is appropriate to the context, and
3. has the same truth-makers when used in the original sentence.

With this in hand, we can propose a modified translation test: the directional translation test. The directional translation test works as follows:

An abstract term is harmful when it is used in a sentence in a context where, upon the replacement of the sentence in which it occurs with an adequate

---

[7] Thanks to Siobhan Chapman for suggesting this here.

TRANSLATION AND VERBAL DISPUTES   261

directional translation, the assent and dissent conditions for the sentence switch.

If we chose to replace the term "A-student" with a directional translation, like a particular GPA, we would find at least one of our participants would switch their assent/dissent from the original sentence, "Mila is an A-student." So, "A-student" above, then, would be such a term in some contexts.

Treating Stebbing's translation test as an extension of her work on directional analysis also accords with how Stebbing herself saw her work on this topic. Stebbing saw her publications on critical thinking not as "a distraction from or an adjunct to her more serious work as a philosopher; they were how she saw her professional responsibilities as being now best carried out" (Chapman, 2013, p. 140). So, if Stebbing herself saw this work as stemming from her old work, then there is no surprise in finding that her older work should still be applicable and useful.

Here's one interesting aspect of this test: directional translations cannot be applied to words alone, but only to the whole sentence in which those words occur. In our anachronistic terms, this means that we cannot find truth-makers for a word, but only for sentences. This fact will ultimately solve a problem presented by Vermeulen (2018) for Chalmers (2011).

5 Verbal Disputes

From our (anachronistic) perspective, Stebbing's harmful uses of abstractions are what we would think of as words that can cause merely verbal disputes.[8] Merely verbal disputes are arguments that are caused by divergent word use and don't "go anywhere." The people involved are merely talking past each other, because (usually), even though they are using words that sound the same, the speakers mean something different by them. If we applied our version of Stebbing's original, un-directional, translation test to such disputes, the result would be that the words causing the misunderstanding are harmful uses of abstractions.

---

[8] Stebbing does discuss what she calls "verbal disputes" in *A Modern Introduction to Logic*. These are disputes "about a matter of fact, namely, as to how a word is used by those who use it correctly" (Stebbing, 1930, p. 427). Bryan Pickel's contribution to the present volume discusses this issue more explicitly, but Stebbing's usage is slightly different from the modern usage, where it is not always assumed that there is some fact of the matter.

262   SUSAN STEBBING

As we saw, when we interpreted Stebbing's directional translation test as a test for merely verbal disputes, the A-student example above came out merely verbal. The directional translation test thus accurately predicts that our token example of a verbal dispute is indeed verbal. Further, there is good reason to think that the directional translation test will usually make good predictions. This is because, on a certain characterization of verbal disputes, the meanings of the terms involved are where the problem lies. And our version of Stebbing's test can identify just those terms in sentences that are problematic. So, the directional translation test will in fact make good predictions about when disputes are merely verbal.

The thought that translation plays an important role in merely verbal disputes has been taken up more recently by Chalmers (2011),[9] who has developed a more precise and formal test for merely verbal disputes based on translations of terms. The test is like Stebbing's in that it relies on a notion of translation, but it is more precise.

Chalmers holds that "a [merely] verbal dispute is one that can be resolved by at- tending to language and resolving metalinguistic differences over meaning" (Chalmers, 2011, p. 526). To check whether a dispute is merely verbal, "one eliminates use of the key term, and one attempts to determine whether any substantive dispute remains" (Chalmers, 2011, p. 526). On Chalmers's view, as long as there is no dispute once the language is appropriately adapted, then the dispute was merely verbal. In this sense, the dispute resolves itself once the language issues are appropriately dealt with. In the Mila case, what we would have to do is eliminate the use of the term "A-student." But once we do that, we must replace it with something. Presumably, we replace it with the list of grades Mila actually gets. Since the teachers in our examples agree about this, the dispute is diffused, and Chalmers's test predicts it was merely verbal, as expected.

There is a strong argument to be made that the directional translation test, and so Stebbing's original test, foreshadowed Chalmers's test for merely verbal disputes. Stebbing's test for harmful abstractions requires us to identify terms causing confusion in the discourse and replace them with simpler analyses. Chalmers's test also requires us to eliminate problematic terms. In Chalmers's test, we identify problematic terms and remove them. So, too, with Stebbing's. Chalmers attributes the problematic nature of the dispute at hand to these problematic terms. So, too, does Stebbing. And finally, both

---

[9] Among others. See, for example, Hirsch (2005), Jenkins (2014), and Belleri (2018).

TRANSLATION AND VERBAL DISPUTES   263

Chalmers and Stebbing suggest the solution is to remove these terms from the dispute and replace them with something non-problematic.

This is (anachronistic) evidence that Stebbing's test for harmful abstract terms and Chalmers's test for verbal disputes actually identify the same problematic feature of language: some terms can be misleading, or mean different things in different speakers' mouths, or can be unclear, etc. Further, both Stebbing and Chalmers claim that these problematic terms cause what we would today call verbal disputes, but what Stebbing took to be problematic exchanges more generally. Of course, Stebbing did not have the language at the time to discuss merely verbal disputes in the way we do today, but the similarities between the directional translation test and Chalmers's test for merely verbal disputes cannot be overlooked. It seems clear that Stebbing's test foreshadowed Chalmers's.

6 Stebbing's Solution to Vermeulen's Problem

Vermeulen (2018) argues that Chalmers's account of merely verbal disputes is not without its problems. She claims that cases of merely verbal disputes where "the linguistic confusion happens on the sentential rather than the subsentential level" (Vermeulen, 2018, p. 338) cannot be captured by Chalmers's account.[10]

Chalmers's account, Vermeulen (2018) claims, cannot account for cases like the following (p. 338):

Muriel, "I've seen a thief with our telescope." (I've seen a thief through my telescope)
John "No you haven't. The telescope is upstairs, right where it belongs." (You have not seen a thief carrying our telescope)

Here, both Muriel and John can agree on all the meanings of the words involved. So, eliminating any particular term (per Chalmers's guide) or replacing a particular term with a translation (per Stebbing's original proposal) would result in the claim that this dispute is not merely verbal. But it seems to be a clear case of a merely verbal dispute. So, claims Vermeulen,

---

[10] Since Chalmers proposes to only be giving an indicator of merely verbal disputes, and not necessary and sufficient conditions, he may not be bothered by this failure.

264 SUSAN STEBBING

the Chalmers (and thereby the Stebbing) account has a problem. Here is the interesting thing: if we use Stebbing's *directional* translation test, which also takes into account the directional translation of a word *in the sentence*, we would have a solution for both Chalmers and Stebbing to this problem pointed to by Vermeulen. So, if we directionally translate the sentence "I've seen a thief with our telescope" as uttered by Muriel, we may replace "telescope" with "'through the lens of our telescope" and wind up at something like "Muriel saw a thief through the lens of the telescope." Replacing her utterance with this sentence would resolve the dispute, since both Muriel and John would clearly understand the precise meaning/truth-makers of what each had said. Further, Chalmers could adapt something like this for his test. Rather than eliminating the use of a key term, per his original test, he might eliminate the use of a key phrase, like "saw a thief with our telescope." Using Stebbing's insight about directional translations always needing to be about sentences, rather than just terms, Chalmers can address Vermeulen's worries.[11]

7 Conclusion

Stebbing produced what she called the translation test in Stebbing (1941). This test, she proposed, showed people how to eliminate problematic terms from debates, allowing them to process with more clarity than they would otherwise have. This test foreshadowed work on merely verbal disputes. Once the test is augmented with Stebbing's notion of directional analysis (which we called the directional translation test), we can see how it both predicts merely verbal disputes and gives us a method for resolving them. Additionally, some of Stebbing's insights can be used to resolve certain contemporary issues in the literature.

---

[11] This advantage of Stebbing's assumes that the problem Vermeulen presents is actually a problem for Chalmers. One possible solution to the worries is to consider the example a verbal dispute about the word "with" rather than about the whole sentence. This would avoid Vermeulen's original worries, and Chalmers certainly has the machinery to replace "with" with either "'together with" or "by means of," as seems to be called for in each interpretation. Thanks to the editors of this volume for pointing out this issue. If the original issue with Vermeulen's problem was in fact with a particular term in a sentence, rather than the sentence as a whole, then it is not the case that it would be problematic for Chalmers, and so not the case that Stebbing's solution would have an advantage over Chalmers's. This does not affect the status of Stebbing's test as foreshadowing Chalmers's work on merely verbal disputes, but even if it did, there may be other examples that her test would predict more accurately than Chalmers's. See, for example, Balcerak Jackson (2014), Belleri (2020), and Thomasson (2016).

One major upshot of this is that Stebbing is an integral member of the tradition that gives rise to the idea of merely verbal disputes and should be treated as such.[12]

References

Balcerak Jackson, B. 2014. Verbal Disputes and Substantiveness. *Erkenntnis 79* (1): 31–54.

Belleri, D. 2018. Two Species of Merely Verbal Disputes. *Metaphilosophy 49* (5): 691–710.

Belleri, D. 2020. Ontological Disputes and the Phenomenon of Metalinguistic Negotiation: Charting the Territory. *Philosophy Compass 15* (7): 1–11.

Chalmers, D. J. 2011. Verbal Disputes. *Philosophical Review 120* (4): 515–566.

Chapman, S. 2013. *Susan Stebbing and the Language of Common Sense*. New York: Palgrave Macmillan.

Coliva, A. 2021. Stebbing, Moore (and Wittgenstein) on Common Sense and Metaphysical Analysis. *British Journal for the History of Philosophy 29* (5): 914–934.

Egerton, K. 2021. Susan Stebbing on the Truthmaker Approach to Metaphysics. *Logique et Analyse 256*: 403–423.

Hirsch, E. 2005. Physical-Object Ontology, Verbal Disputes, and Common Sense. *Philosophy and Phenomenological Research 70* (1): 67–97.

Janssen-Lauret, F. 2017. Susan Stebbing, Incomplete Symbols and Foundherentist Meta-Ontology. *Journal for the History of Analytical Philosophy 5* (2): 7–17.

Jenkins, C. S. I. 2014. Merely Verbal Disputes. *Erkenntnis 79* (S1): 11–30.

Mankowitz, P. 2021. How to Have a Metalinguistic Dispute. *Synthese 199* (3–4): 5603–5622.

Stebbing, L. 1932. The Method of Analysis in Metaphisics. *Proceedings of the Aristotelian Society 33*: 65–94.

Stebbing, L. S. 1930. *A Modern Introduction to Logic*. London: Methuen.

Stebbing, L. S. 1933. *Logical Positivism and Analysis*. Annual Philosophical Lecture Henriette Hertz Trust.

Stebbing, L. S. 1934a. Directional Analysis and Basic Facts. *Analysis 2* (3): 33–36.

Stebbing, L. S. 1934b. *Logic in Practice*. London: Methuen.

Stebbing, L. S. 1939. *Thinking to Some Purpose*. London: Penguin Books.

Stebbing, L. S. 1941. *Ideals and Illusions*. London: Watts.

Thomasson, A. L. 2016. Metaphysical disputes and Metalinguistic Negotiation. *Analytic Philosophy 58* (1): 1–28.

Vermeulen, I. 2018. Verbal Disputes and the Varieties of Verbalness. *Erkenntnis 83* (2): 331–348.

---

[12] Acknowledgments: Work on this project has been generously funded by a National Endowment for the Humanities Fellowship, number FEL-281-677-22. I would like to thank Annalisa Coliva and Louis Doulas, the editors of this volume, for helpful feedback on an earlier draft. I am grateful for feedback from helpful audiences at Society for the Study of Analytic Philosophy and the Pacific APA, both in 2018. Additionally, I owe a debt of gratitude to colleagues who read earlier versions of this chapter and provided feedback, including Mike Beaney, Siobhan Chapman, Nathan Kellen, Andrew Kissel, Matt LaVine, Graham Leach-Krouse, Shay Allen Logan, Eileen Nutting, and Justin Remhoff.

Name Index

For the benefit of digital users, indexed terms that span two pages (e.g., 52–53) may, on occasion, appear on only one of those pages.

Tables are indicated by an italic *t* following the page number.

Analysis, 2, 55, 151, 193
Aristotle, 198, 199
Austin, J. L., 123n.37, 188, 220–21
Ayer, A. J., 58, 60, 211–12, 246–47

Baldwin, Stanley, 203
Beaney, Michael, 84
Bedford College, University of London, 5, 7n.24, 151, 193
Bergson, Henri, 4, 4n.14, 165–66, 174–75
Boole, George, 197–98
Bradley, Francis Herbert, 32–33, 174–75
Broad, C. D., 159–60

Carnap, Rudolf, 65, 176. *See also* Carnapian
Cassam, Quassim, 22–23, 219–20
Chalmers, David, 262–64, 263nn.10–11
Chapman, Siobhan, 84, 194
Cook, Guy, 224–25
Constance Jones, Emily Elizabeth, 3n.11, 175n.1

Dummett, Michael, 9
Duncan-Jones, A.E., 2n.4
Descartes, René, 32–33, 37, 119, 129

Eddington, Arthur, 15–16, 94–97, 122, 132, 134–38, 155–56
Einstein, Albert, 60–61. *See also* relativity theory

Flew, Antony, 188
Frege, Gottlob, 42–43, 56–57, 197

Genzen, Gerhard, 183
Girton College, University of Cambridge, 3, 4–5, 87–88, 174
Glock, Hans-Johann, 9, 183, 184–85, 184n.8
Grice, Paul, 220–23, 234–35

Hume, David, 157–58

James, William, 175
Jeans, James, 131–32, 133, 139, 140
Joad, C. E. M., 140
Johnson, William Ernest, 241

Kant, Immanuel, 86. *See also* Kantian
Keynes, John Maynard, 182–83
King's College, University of London, 4, 174
Kuhn, Thomas, 60–61, 66, 159n.7

Leibniz, Gottfried Wilhelm, 53–54
Lewis, C. I., 247–48
Lewis, David, 115n.27, 130, 234n.5
Lippmann, Walter, 74n.27, 75n.31
Lotze, Hermann, 175n.1

MacDonald, Ramsay, 219, 225
McTaggart, John M. E., 32
Mill, J. S., 214
Moore, G. E., 4, 4n.15, 8n.29, 16–18, 34–37, 39–40, 55, 81–94, 101–20, 175–76, 182–83, 212. *See also* Moorean

Nagel, Ernest, 59, 64–67
Neurath, Otto, 7n.24
Newton, Isaac, 60, 63, 140

Peirce, C. S., 53–54

Quine, Willard van Orman, 62–63, 64, 124n.41, 243–44

Ramsey, Frank, 54
Russell, Bertrand, 42–43, 137–38, 141, 163–64, 176–77, 185–87, 197, 211–12, 243
Ryle, Gilbert, 7n.25, 8n.29, 188

268 NAME INDEX

Schlick, Moritz, 7n.24
Schwartz, Stephen P., 9
Soames, Scott, 9, 173–74, 189
Socrates, 165–66
Sperber, Dan, 223
Strawson, Galen, 94
Strawson, Peter, 44n.21, 189n.14
Stroll, Avrum, 9

Taylor, Charlotte, 225–27

Urmson, J. O., 9

Vermeulen, Inga, 263–64

Warnock, G. J., 9
Weinstein, Jack, 166–67
Whitehead, Alfred North, 5–6, 5n.18, 84–85, 175, 197, 198, 211–12, 243
Wilson, Deirdre, 223
Wisdom, John, 1, 39–40, 236–37
Wittgenstein, Ludwig, 34, 36–37, 38, 39–40, 44–45, 48–49, 56, 57, 183–84, 211–12
Woolf, Leonard, 182
Woolf, Virginia, 182
Williamson, Timothy, 166–67

Subject Index

For the benefit of digital users, indexed terms that span two pages (e.g., 52–53) may, on occasion, appear on only one of those pages.

Tables are indicated by an italic *t* following the page number.

a priori, 12–13, 21, 32, 39, 46–47, 49, 180, 181, 237
a posteriori, 90–91
analysis
  Cambridge, 6, 39–40
  directional (or metaphysical, or new-level), 6–8, 7n.23, 12–13, 32–34, 39–40, 40n.12, 42–43, 44–49, 58, 81–82, 83–84, 88, 90–92, 93, 98–99, 108–9, 108n.13, 114, 176–77
  same-level (or conceptual, or linguistic, or logical, or postulational), 6–8, 12, 16–17, 39–40, 58, 81–82, 88, 90–91, 92–93, 160, 176, 224–25
  Vienna, 39
analogy, argument from, 218–19, 226
analytic clarification, 13–15, 45, 58–64, 124, 237n.6
analytic/synthetic, distinction, rejection of, 11–12, 13, 45, 49, 239
  synthetic, 129

basic facts, 13, 40n.12, 43, 45, 46n.23, 47, 48–49, 82, 88–89, 91–93, 98, 258

Carnapian, 52–53, 63n.24, 65, 245
construction
  logical, 86–87, 89
  symbolic (or mathematical), 122, 123, 134, 176
corpus linguistics, 227
Critical Discourse Analysis, 22–23, 211, 213, 220, 224–27

democracy, deliberative, 52–53, 68n.26, 69
descriptions, definite, 12–13, 108n.15, 176–77

elucidation, 56, 176, 183–84
ethics, differences from science, 123n.39, 180

freedom, 21, 70–73, 74, 141–42, 152–53, 157, 160, 162–63, 164–65, 179, 181, 206, 255

ideals, 21, 180–81, 190, 253–54
idealism (or British idealism, or Absolute idealism), 16–17, 32, 35, 48–49, 55, 82–84, 86, 87, 88, 89, 93–94, 109–10, 116, 132, 154, 173–74, 175. *See also* panpsychism
ideology, critique of, 20–21, 22–23, 180, 188, 211, 219–20
implicature, 221–23
incomplete symbols, 176–77
intellectualist (or intellectualism), 7n.25, 174–75

Kantian (or neo-Kantian), 65–66, 129

linguistic convention, 23–24, 230–51
logical fictions, 42n.15, 176–77
Logical Positivism (or logical empiricism), 10n.31, 10, 41n.14, 57, 64, 65–66, 67, 176, 183, 258

material implication, 22–23, 176–77, 215, 216, 223, 248
materialism, 5–6, 16, 88, 116
method
  philosophical, 93, 185–86, 212
  scientific, 87–88, 121, 147–48
Moorean, 4n.15, 16–17, 37, 81, 83, 84n.2, 84–86, 102, 103, 112n.21

naturalism, 128, 129–30, 131, 146
negation, logical, 214–15, 221–22

Ordinary Language Philosophy, 10, 22, 123n.37, 188–89, 189n.14, 220–21

270 SUBJECT INDEX

panpsychism, 16–17, 94, 96–98
perception (theory of, account of, object of), 17, 41n.14, 83–84, 85–86, 113, 140, 188
politics, 21, 71–72, 161, 162, 178, 180–81, 185, 187, 190, 193, 194–95
popular science, criticisms of, 7–8, 128–30, 159–60, 161
pragmatics, 211, 213–14, 220–23, 227–28
pragmatism, 4, 54, 175
probable knowledge, 17–18, 118–20

quantum theory (or quantum mechanics), 15, 116, 129, 133, 141–42, 152

realism (or new realism, or robust realism), 5–6, 17, 83, 109, 116, 143, 143n.8, 167n.15, 176, 180–81, 182
relativity theory, 13, 15, 61, 83n.1, 95, 116, 129, 132, 152

sense-data, 47, 85–87, 88–89, 92–93, 188
skepticism: responses to, 17, 35–36, 37n.6, 38, 49, 109–10
solidity (philosophical problem of), 12–13, 15–16, 82, 85, 90, 124, 137. *See also* two tables

thinking
critical thinking, 1, 20, 24, 68–69, 148–49, 167–68, 169, 187, 216–17, 261
potted thinking, 7–8, 8n.26, 20, 22–23, 145–46, 157, 158, 217–18, 225
thinking clearly, 73, 74–75, 161–63, 164–65, 169
thinking to some purpose, 19–20, 164, 169
truth-makers, 12–13, 39, 42–43, 49, 256–57, 258–59, 260
two tables (philosophical problem of), 15, 91–92, 137, 138, 140. *See also* solidity

verbal dispute, 22–24, 244–46, 261–63